# ONCE UPON A STRANGER

# ONCE UPON A STRANGER

The Science of How "Small" Talk
Can Add Up to a Big Life

## DR. GILLIAN SANDSTROM

HarperOne
*An Imprint of HarperCollinsPublishers*

Without limiting the exclusive rights of any author, contributor or the publisher of this publication, any unauthorized use of this publication to train generative artificial intelligence (AI) technologies is expressly prohibited. HarperCollins also exercise their rights under Article 4(3) of the Digital Single Market Directive 2019/790 and expressly reserve this publication from the text and data mining exception.

ONCE UPON A STRANGER. Copyright © 2026 by Gillian Sandstrom. All rights reserved. No part of this book may be used or reproduced in any manner whatsoever without written permission except in the case of brief quotations embodied in critical articles and reviews. For information, address HarperCollins Publishers, 195 Broadway, New York, NY 10007. In Europe, HarperCollins Publishers, Macken House, 39/40 Mayor Street Upper, Dublin 1, D01 C9W8, Ireland.

HarperCollins books may be purchased for educational, business, or sales promotional use. For information, please email the Special Markets Department at SPsales@harpercollins.com.

harpercollins.com

FIRST EDITION

*Designed by Jason Kayser*

Library of Congress Cataloging-in-Publication Data has been applied for.

ISBN 978-0-06-338541-2

Printed in the United States of America

26 27 28 29 30  LBC  5 4 3 2 1

For my parents

And for all the hot dog ladies (literal and otherwise)

# Contents

| | | |
|---|---|---|
| | Introduction | 1 |
| 1 | Why Talking to Strangers Is Hard | 11 |
| 2 | No Strings Attached | 45 |
| 3 | Puzzle Pieces | 71 |
| 4 | Sowing Seeds | 103 |
| 5 | Feeling Seen and Seeing Together | 125 |
| 6 | Skeleton Key | 151 |
| 7 | The Kindness of Strangers | 179 |
| | Conclusion | 205 |
| | | |
| | Acknowledgments | 227 |
| | Appendix: How to Talk to Strangers | 235 |
| | Notes | 269 |
| | Resources | 291 |

# Introduction

When I was a kid, I thought my dad was embarrassing—not because he told groan-inducing jokes or teased me about boys (though he did those things too) but because he was constantly talking to strangers. It was almost like he was compelled to do it, couldn't help himself. I'd blush with embarrassment as he told the checkout clerk at the supermarket about which university I was heading off to in the fall ("Dad—she doesn't care!"). I grew up in a small city in Canada, close to the American border, and we did lots of day trips and camping holidays in the US. I'd quiver with impatience when, instead of simply answering the border crossing agent's standard questions, Dad would sincerely ask the agent how they were doing and strike up a friendly conversation ("Dad—we're holding up the line—there are dozens of cars waiting!").

I could always see it coming. My dad is extremely observant—he always spots the deer on the edge of a field at twilight—and I'd catch him eyeing his next target. He would spot someone wearing a

T-shirt from a triathlon they had participated in or a hat from somewhere they had visited. He would casually sidle up to them with his slightly bowlegged saunter and ask them about the triathlon or the place on the hat or whatever other detail he glommed onto as a spark for conversation. Over the years, he has developed endless ways to turn an observation or an overheard snippet of dialogue into a conversation starter.

Dad especially loves talking to kids. He still laughs about a conversation he had at a grocery store one December about a decade ago, when he asked a young boy whether he had been well-behaved all year and was expecting a visit from Santa. The boy thought for a few seconds, presumably considering a few of his transgressions, before cannily responding that he'd been *pretty* good that year. Dad has a few finely honed openers that all involve saying something so outlandish that kids feel compelled to respond, to tell him how silly he is. He'll ask a kid whether they have a pet crocodile. ("Noooo!" they say with a giggle.) He'll ask a kid with an ice cream cone if they need any help finishing it. (Still no takers on that "kind" offer.)

As I got older, the way I thought about my dad's unusual habit shifted. I'd been worried that he was bothering people, that people wouldn't want to talk to him, but I eventually realized that he (almost) never gets rejected. Instead, somehow he (almost) always gets people laughing, usually through self-deprecating humor. (I've heard him tell approximately fifty-seven different people about how he's on a waiting list for a brain transplant.)

I also eventually realized that Dad's willingness to talk to strangers is often useful. Whenever we needed information or directions, we'd just send Dad over to ask someone for help. Whenever we needed an extra chair at a restaurant, we'd send Dad over to ask someone for a spare. Of course, it would take ages for him to return because he'd start chatting. . . . He'd always come back with a story as well as the chair.

I grew to admire my dad's lack of inhibition and the ease with which he could connect with strangers and make people feel comfortable. I thought he had a rare skill—one that seemed completely unattainable to me because I was nothing like him. I was shy.

In my mid-twenties, I was flying on my own for work for the first time. I had just boarded and settled in my seat when I heard an announcement: "Will passenger Sandstrom please identify themselves to a member of the flight crew?" My heart started racing. I wondered what was wrong and why they wanted to talk to me. Then I grasped at the world's tiniest straw: They couldn't possibly be looking for me because I was traveling under my married name, not Sandstrom (my maiden name). Although I desperately wanted to believe that they weren't looking for me, in my heart I knew they were. It would have taken so little effort to find out.

All I had to do was reach up and press the flight attendant call button. But I really, really didn't want to. Pressing the call button would mean drawing attention to myself. It would mean talking to a flight attendant. Although the now-Gillian writing this book recognizes that flight attendants are mere humans, past-Gillian saw them as worldly and glamorous, intimidating. Past-Gillian wouldn't dare ask a flight attendant for a bottle of water, extra pretzels, or even help. In fact, she couldn't conceive of a single reason that would compel her to push that button—even when she was being asked to do exactly that over a public announcement system. So she/I didn't.

When I arrived at my destination, I waited patiently as the baggage carousel grew emptier and emptier and finally stopped moving. Even before it stopped, I knew what my shyness had cost me. When I arrived at the convention center for my work event the next morning, it was in a souvenir T-shirt that I'd bought at the airport gift shop.

Fast-forward twenty-five years, and it's obvious that I'm my father's daughter because I'm now in the habit of talking to strangers. (An artsy acquaintance once referred to it as a "practice" that I have developed, which I find to be a pleasing description.) The first conversation I remember deliberately starting was on the subway in Toronto, and that stranger taught me that people can ride ostriches (see chapter 3). I was hooked. That conversation made me want to have others. To help me remember these small moments of connection—and hopefully inspire others to reach out too—I started sharing my #Talking2Strangers stories on social media. I've now shared hundreds of them—and those are just the tip of the iceberg.

One conversation that I had while working as a computer programmer put me on the path to a new career. Now, not only do I regularly talk to strangers, I also study talking to strangers for a living, as a professor of psychology. (I'm a researcher, not a therapist or clinical psychologist—no couches in sight.) I've made it my scientific mission to understand the reasons that we feel anxious about talking to strangers and all the ways that we benefit if we're able to push past our fears. In this book, I'll share what I (and other researchers) have learned.

Through trial and error and lots of practice (not to mention watching my dad), I've learned how to confidently approach someone I don't know, have a brief chat, and then walk away, never to see them again. (It's a bit different when you might see the person again and potentially develop a relationship with them—for example, with a neighbor or colleague; the focus of this book is mostly on one-off interactions.) I've learned that my dad's skills are *not* unattainable but rather skills that we can all develop. Being a confident stranger-talker doesn't mean that I never get rejected (though it's extremely rare—see chapter 1), but I've learned not to take rejection personally. Being a confident stranger-talker doesn't mean that I'm now a paragon of social skill, perfectly at ease in any social situation. But talking to strangers *has* helped me develop a range of skills that have been valuable in ways that I wouldn't have expected (see chapter 6). Being a confident stranger-talker doesn't mean that I've banished all my fears, but I've learned that I can reach out and connect with my fellow humans in spite of my fears—and that it's worth doing.

## What about stranger danger?

It's hard to shake the idea of "stranger danger," which many of us were taught as children, but the vast majority of strangers aren't dangerous.[1] You're a stranger to most people, and you're not dangerous, right? A more nuanced message is being taught to children these days, recognizing that, yes, a vanishingly small number of strangers are dangerous, but if you're ever in danger, there are also kind strangers that you can turn to for help. I'm not suggesting that you strike up a conversation the next time you're walking down a proverbial dark alley. Choose a situation that feels safe, such as a public place in broad daylight with plenty of people around. (And, it goes without saying, but I'll say it anyway: Please don't be a dangerous stranger to others. When you talk to a stranger, be mindful of their feelings and reaction—you wouldn't want anyone to feel that you're harassing them or being creepy.)

In my life, instead of being a danger, strangers have been game changers. I'll tell you stories of conversations with strangers that literally changed my life. By having lots of conversations with strangers, you increase the odds of having one of these exceptional interactions. But mostly, my stories are about everyday moments. For me, talking to strangers has been transformative not just because of a few standout conversations, but also—and, I believe, especially—because of the accumulation of small, ordinary moments, which add up to me seeing the world differently: with a pervasive sense of trust, safety, and connection.

## What you will (and won't) find in this book

Over the course of this book, I'll share my personal journey with you. You'll hear the unlikely story of how a young woman who had her suitcase removed from a plane because she was too shy to press the flight attendant call button turned into a habitual, confident stranger-talker. Talking to strangers didn't come naturally to me. I could never have imagined that one day I'd find so much joy and meaning in it. If I've been able to confront my fears and learn how to talk to strangers, you can too. As the proverb goes: Wise men learn from others' mistakes, fools from their own. I've played the fool, and I wrote this book so that you can benefit from what I've learned.

But this book isn't just about stories, because I'm also a scientist who has studied thousands of conversations between strangers. I'll share the latest research about talking to strangers, conducted by me and my colleagues, to help you understand the psychological barriers that make it so hard to reach out (so that you can learn to overcome them) and the benefits of talking to strangers (so that you know why it's worthwhile). You'll feel reassured to know that you're not alone in feeling nervous about talking to strangers—most people have doubts about their social skills. You're probably already more competent than you think. And be prepared to get sick of me telling you: You worry far too much. My research studies consistently find that conversations with strangers go better than you expect, and people like you more than you think.

This is *not* a book about how to make friends, how to find love, or how to network your way to success. However, to do any of these things, you'll need to talk to strangers. It's not unreasonable, therefore, to expect that feeling more comfortable talking to strangers will make it a little easier to achieve these goals (see chapter 6). But I hope that you'll talk to strangers for no particular reason and with no expectations, just for the joy and humanity of it.

If there's a foolproof formula that we can follow to guarantee that a conversation will be successful, I haven't found it yet. However, there are tips and tricks that can help, and you'll be able to glean some ideas from the stories that I'll share about my conversations with strangers. I've also compiled a how-to appendix (page 235) with some ideas for you to try. (I even asked my dad for his best advice because to me he'll always be *the* expert.) My goal is to give you enough ideas to start experimenting, so you can find out what works for you. After all, each of us is a scientist, experimenting with our own life.

## Is this book for you?

Over the next seven chapters, by sharing my personal stories and the latest scientific research, I'll highlight some of the many benefits of talking to strangers, some of which you might not have considered. You'll learn how strangers sometimes carry the pieces to your life's puzzle, how talking to strangers adds spontaneity and novelty to your everyday, and how this makes you more creative (see chapter 3). You'll learn just how important it is to see and be seen by others, and how we see the world differently when we see it together—even with someone we don't know (see chapter 5). You'll even learn how talking to strangers will enable you to tap into your inherent kindness and make the world a little better (see chapter 7).

Wherever you're currently at, in terms of talking to strangers, this book has something for you. If you want to talk to strangers but something has been holding you back, this book will help you find the confidence that you need—and give you the permission that you might not even know you've been seeking. If you're already a regular stranger-talker, this book will help you reflect on and celebrate the many benefits of talking to strangers—especially if you have people in your life who don't understand it. (I wish past-Gillian could have read this book to better understand her irrepressible stranger-talker dad.) And if you hadn't really thought about talking to strangers before now, this book will inspire you to give it a try.

Every day, we have opportunities to create moments of connection with our fellow humans. Often we don't even notice them, and when we do, we fail to appreciate just how powerful and meaningful these moments can be. After reading this book, when you walk into a shop, wait in a line, or sit next to someone you don't know, you'll understand that it is an opportunity for a laugh, for learning, for connection. I believe our world would be better if more people talked to strangers. We can all make a difference by confronting our fears and reaching out. I hope you'll join me—and my dad. To get started, all you have to do is say, "Hello."

# 1

## Why Talking to Strangers Is Hard

My friend and frequent research collaborator Erica Boothby sat at a table in her neighborhood café, drinking an iced latte and carefully rereading her notes for the third time. She was meeting a potential new collaborator (let's call her Kristyna\*), someone whose work Erica admired, and she wanted to make a good impression. Kristyna arrived, and after some small talk, the two got down to business, throwing research ideas back and forth to see if they could identify a project to work on together.

After the meeting, Erica collected her things and joined her husband, Gus Cooney, who had been sitting at a nearby table, working away on his laptop during her meeting. When Gus asked Erica how the meeting had gone, she told him that she had enjoyed the

---

\* Most names throughout this book are pseudonyms for reasons of privacy (and because I seldom learn the names of the strangers I talk to). As a sign of acknowledgment for all the help they've provided over the years, I've used the names of some of my research assistants for the pseudonyms.

conversation but doubted that Kristyna would want to collaborate with her. The conversation had gone in a different direction than she had expected, and she had felt less prepared than she would have liked.

"I think I kind of blew it," she said.

"Are you serious?" Gus asked.

Gus had a completely different take on things. Sitting within earshot, he had overheard some of Erica's meeting. From his perspective, the two had hit it off, and Erica's thoughtfulness and competence had shone through in her insightful comments.

After discussing their contrasting perceptions, Erica and Gus wondered: Who was better able to judge what Kristyna had really felt? Was it Erica, who had the firsthand experience of the conversation? Or was it Gus, who had the objectivity that comes from being an observer? (Objective about the conversation, that is—less objective about Erica's positive qualities and ability to make a good impression.) Gus is also a psychology researcher, so instead of simply engaging in idle speculation, he and Erica decided to run some studies to find out. If Gus was right, people might be worrying too much about their social skills and missing out on a chance to laugh, learn, and connect.

I didn't know yet that Erica and Gus were asking this question in their research, but I already had some data that hinted at the answer. In 2015, I'd developed a How to Talk to Strangers workshop, to help people think about why they were reluctant to start a friendly conversation with a stranger and help them cultivate the skills they needed to do so. I ran the workshop one Saturday afternoon in a bright, open space, upstairs at a London pub. People arrived, usually one at a time, often with a glass of liquid courage—we were at a pub, after all—and looked around the room nervously before taking a seat and invariably pulling out their phones. The room was quiet, and the tension was palpable. After introducing myself and describing the plan for the workshop, I threw people straight into the deep end, asking them to talk to a stranger at their table.

I've run this workshop many times now, so I'm no longer surprised by the immediate change that happens in the room *every* time: the beautiful buzz of people talking to each other. It's thrilling. Without fail, once people start talking, it's getting them to *stop* that's the challenge.

Partly to help workshop attendees reflect on their experience but mostly to collect research data, I asked workshop attendees some questions immediately following their first conversation. All but one of ninety-one attendees (drawn from multiple workshops) thought that they found their conversation partner more interesting than their partner found them to be.[1] In other words, all but one felt like Erica had with Kristyna. But they were wrong. I know this because their partner had also answered my questions, meaning that I knew what their partner said about them. The data was undeniable: Their conversation partners liked them more than they realized.

By good fortune, I found out that Erica and Gus were doing this research (with Margaret Clark), sparked by their debate about what Kristyna had thought about Erica. I'd never met Erica, but I reached out to her, and we arranged a meeting. She and Gus were much further ahead on this work than I was, but they generously offered to collaborate, and we pooled our results. My How to Talk to Strangers workshops provided one source of data that revealed what we named the "liking gap": a measurable asymmetry between (1) how positively people had judged their conversation partner and (2) how positively they thought their partner had judged them. Erica and Gus had run multiple studies and found the same social asymmetry in every one.

What causes the liking gap? Erica and Gus had that covered. After pairs of strangers had conversations in the lab, they were asked to list the moments in the conversation that had most influenced the impression they had formed of their conversation partner. They also listed the moments that had most influenced the impression their partner had formed of them. Then, they rated the positivity/negativity of each of these pivotal moments. People thought that their partner's impression of them was influenced by more negative moments, whereas their own impression of their partner was influenced by more positive moments. When they thought the moments that formed their partner's impression of them were more negative, they reported a larger liking gap. We seem to be our own worst critic: We see the best in our partner but the worst in ourselves.

The liking gap is all in our heads. Erica and Gus recorded pairs of strangers, like Zamena and Silje, having conversations. Observers watched the video, focusing on Zamena and estimating how much Zamena had liked Silje. They watched the same video a second time, focusing on Silje and estimating how much Silje had liked Zamena. Meanwhile, Zamena and Silje each reported how much they liked their partner and how much they thought their partner had liked them. The observers *couldn't* see how much Zamena thought Silje liked her (and vice versa), but they *could* see how much Zamena actually liked Silje (and vice versa). In other words, the cause of the liking gap is *not* that we can't tell what our conversation partner thinks of us. Our partners *are* sending signs, through eye contact and smiles and tone of voice that the objective observers were able to pick up on. However, when we're the one having the conversation, we don't notice these signs because we're distracted by the negative voice in our head that is telling us that we're failing as a conversation partner.

This negative voice is, unfortunately, a main character in our lives and in this book, so I think it needs a name. Given its in*sid*ious nature, I'm going to call this devious character Sid. I'm hoping that, by giving this voice a name, we'll be able to think about it in a more objective way and learn to question and challenge it. (I encourage you to give yours a silly name too.)

How strong is the negative voice in our head? Surely Sid pipes down after people get to know each other, and then the liking gap disappears? The size of the gap does shrink over time but more slowly than you'd expect. In another study, Erica and Gus found that even after college students shared a suite for five months, they *still* thought their roommate didn't like them as much as they liked their roommate. It took six months of living together, day in and day out, before the gap finally disappeared. But there's nothing magical about six months, and the liking gap can last even longer. In a workplace study that Erica and Gus carried out with Adam Mastroianni and Andrew Reece, the gap was intact even after colleagues had worked together for more than six months.[2] The sweet spot, where our insecurities diminish and our perceptions start to align with reality, probably relates more to our feelings of closeness than to any particular amount of time.

People are surprised to learn about the liking gap, and I think that's because it's hard to learn about it firsthand. One kid might ask another "Do you want to be friends?" or be told by another

"You're weird." Adults, however, don't solicit or receive social feedback in the same way that children do. It would be inconceivable for Erica to have asked Kristyna after their meeting: "Did you like me?" Instead, we try to read our conversation partner's body language and nonverbal behavior, and we listen to Sid, the unforgiving critic who's constantly putting us down. (Kids exhibit the liking gap too, but only when they start to think about the impression they make on others, which happens around their fifth birthday.)[3] My research with Erica and Gus sneakily sidestepped the taboo about asking for social feedback, and people have been surprised to learn what their conversation partners really think of them.

You might be thinking *But people really* don't *like me—I'm an exception.* For this to be true, there would need to be something unusual about the hundreds and hundreds of people who have now participated in various studies that find evidence of the liking gap, including young children, university students, and adults; people in the US and in the UK; people having conversations in a research lab, at work with their colleagues, or at a workshop held at a pub. It's possible that you're an exception, but it's far more likely that other people like *you*—yes, even you!—more than you think.

On *Today* in 2018, Sheinelle Jones told viewers about our research on the liking gap.[4] The idea of not knowing how much someone really likes you hit home with cohost Dylan Dreyer, who commented: "I'm always saying: Does Al (Roker) really like me? I'm not sure. . . ."

News anchor Craig Melvin agreed: "Funny you should say that because I wonder the same thing."

Al Roker appeared dumbfounded. "Are you serious?"

And so, a news report about the liking gap resulted in a perfect example of the liking gap in action, even between colleagues who have worked together for years.

## It's natural to worry about talking to strangers

There are people who absolutely love talking to strangers and seem devoid of fear. My dad is one of these people. You might be another one. Chances are, though, that you're a bit (or a lot) apprehensive about talking to strangers, and that's the reason that you bought this book. (Thanks, by the way!) I want you to know that it's completely normal to be nervous about talking to strangers.

Imagine that you're in the waiting room at the doctor's office, and you notice a friendly-looking stranger who's knitting what appears to be a purple octopus. Obviously, you might want to know: What's up with the purple octopus? There's only one way to find out. . . . How will this stranger react if you decide to strike up a conversation? Will they be happy to chat or annoyed that you interrupted their knitting? If you end up getting into a conversation, how will they act and what will they say? Will you have anything in common (besides your shared octophilia), or will their beliefs and values be fundamentally different from yours? What if they're a member of some weird octopus cult and they try to indoctrinate you? There's no way to know in advance. We humans generally like to feel that we have some control over what happens to us. When we talk to a stranger, it can feel like we're giving up that control. No wonder it makes us nervous.

Adding to our trepidation is the fact that the stakes feel high. Researchers in psychology have long believed that social connection is critically important for our well-being. In 1943, Abraham Maslow proposed, in his now-famous pyramid of needs, that once we have food, shelter, and financial security, our strongest need is to find acceptance, belonging, and love.[5] Half a century later, researchers scoured the academic literature and concluded that the empirical evidence collected through hundreds of research studies supported Maslow's theory: Belonging is a *need* (not just a desire), and humans are motivated to fill that need because we can only thrive when it is filled.[6]

We can't help but care deeply about what people think about us. We care precisely because it's fundamentally important for us to feel that we are included and valued by others. We may not *want* to care what others think, but we can't dismiss our need to belong any more than we can dismiss our need for food and shelter. It makes sense that we care what a new colleague thinks of us, when we'll be working with them for years. It makes sense that we care that a potential romantic partner thinks we're funny and charming. It makes no sense at all, however, that we care what a complete stranger, who we'll never see again, thinks when we ask them about their purple octopus. But we humans are sense-makers and pattern-detectors, and sometimes this leads us to overgeneralize.

The unpredictability of talking to strangers means that it's natural to worry. But what, exactly, do people worry about? When I started running How to Talk to Strangers workshops, I asked attendees to tell me about their biggest concerns. I'll admit, I thought I'd be able to identify a handful of fears that were common to most people, figure out a way to assuage these concerns, and voilà: I'd be able to help people feel more comfortable talking to strangers. I was wrong on several counts.

For one thing, there doesn't seem to be a small number of especially potent fears that are shared by most people. Instead, over the years, people have shared with me a seemingly endless list of concerns (see the following list for some examples). Different people are worried about different, sometimes conflicting, things. More introverted people, like me, might worry about talking too little; when I get nervous, my mind goes blank, and I can't figure out anything at all to say. In contrast, more extroverted people, like my friend Mayce, might worry about talking too much; when Mayce gets nervous, she feels compelled to fill the empty space with words, and afterward, she often regrets oversharing.

A nonexhaustive list of things that people worry about:

| | |
|---|---|
| I might talk too much. | They might talk too much. |
| I might talk too little. | They might talk too little. |
| I might overshare/disclose too much. | They might overshare/disclose too much. |
| I might not enjoy the conversation. | They might not enjoy the conversation. |
| I might feel uncomfortable. | They might feel uncomfortable. |
| I might not like them. | They might not like me. |
| I might not understand them. | They might not understand me. |
| I might say something insensitive or offend them. | They might take what I say the wrong way or be offended. |
| I might not trust them. | They might not trust me. |
| I might not have anything in common with them. | They might not want to talk to me. |
| I might feel that I can't speak openly or honestly. | I might not know how to start the conversation. |
| I might feel awkward. | I might not know how to keep the conversation going. |
| I might say the wrong thing. | I might not know how to end the conversation. |
| I might ask too many questions. | |

On a positive note, although people confess a wide variety of fears, most of us are moderately, rather than extremely, worried. And even people who worry more than average about others' evaluations (i.e., people who are shy) tend to enjoy talking to strangers, when they do it.[7] It's easy to think that you're more worried than other people are, but it's important to remember that none of us are mind readers. Even people who *seem* as if they wouldn't be worried about talking to strangers might actually be just as worried as the rest of us. I was walking with my friend Lena, who's super talkative, who relishes social gatherings, and who I think of as extremely confident. Midway through our walk, we stopped at a pub for a drink. (Pub walks are one of my favorite things about living in the UK.) It was a warm, blue-sky day, so it was no surprise that all the picnic tables in the pub garden were occupied.

"I guess we should just find a seat inside," Lena sighed.

But who wants to sit inside on a beautiful summer day? Instead, I turned to a couple, who were sitting at a huge table with lots of space: "There are no tables free. Would you mind if we shared yours?"

The couple politely invited us to take a seat.

Maybe it didn't occur to Lena to ask, but I suspect that she just wouldn't have felt comfortable doing so. I think the realization that there are Lenas hiding in plain sight is one of the most impactful things people learn in my workshop. You're not alone. Others share your worries, even though it's sometimes hard to tell.

Of course, some people do worry more than others and in a problematic way. According to the National Institute of Mental Health in the US, approximately 12 percent of people experience social anxiety disorder (SAD) at some point during their life.[8] How can you tell whether you experience a "normal" amount of worry about talking to strangers or whether you might have SAD? I'm not a clinician, but what I do know from trusted resources is that if your fear of rejection is one of your biggest fears, if it has troubled you for at least six months, and if it prevents you from doing things that you'd like to do (e.g., you'd like to go to the cinema, but you don't because you're anxious about sitting next to a stranger in the theater), then you might have SAD. It's very treatable with professional help, and, with sustained effort, you may even be able to work through it yourself. I've included some resources in the endnotes,[9] and much of the advice in this book draws on the same principles that these resources describe (e.g., suggesting that you look at your thoughts more objectively and learn to challenge them, and desensitize yourself by gradually building up to a feared activity).

Let's take a closer look at some of the things that you might be worried about:

- Talking to strangers will be boring.
- You won't know what to say . . .
- . . . because you're an introvert, and introverts can't talk to strangers.
- People won't want to talk to you.
- People will misinterpret your intentions.
- You'll be judged for breaking "the rules" of social interaction.

These are all completely understandable worries. I've felt every single one of them. But are these fears rational? How likely is it that these fears will come true? And if they did, how bad would it be? Is there anything you can do to mitigate the fallout?

## What if it's boring?

According to Wikipedia, small talk is "polite and standard conversation about unimportant things." It is, almost by definition, boring. Communications researcher Jeffrey Hall at the University of Kansas has found that the more time we spend in small talk with people we know—discussing current events or generic topics like pets, sports, and entertainment—the *less* close we feel to them.[10] That resonates with me—I crave deeper conversations with my friends and family, and I feel frustrated when I get stuck in small talk with them.

I don't expect a deep conversation with a stranger, so I don't feel the same frustration about engaging in small talk. Instead, I can enjoy a conversation with a stranger even when it's a bit shallow. A quick exchange to marvel at the sunshine and mild temperature on a January day may not be a riveting conversation, but it still provides a moment of human connection and might even help me savor the lovely weather a bit more. Hall's definition of small talk includes talking about pets, but I love hearing stories about strangers' pets. One late afternoon while walking in the park, I met a dog named Koko, who was waiting attentively for his human "sister" after school. I offered this good boy a treat but was told that he's not food oriented. Unless that food is cheese. He can hear a package of cheese being opened from across the house. Small talk, maybe, but it made me laugh.

Conversations with strangers are often short—maybe too short to be boring. I know I'd get bored talking about the January warm spell for too long, and after a while even funny stories about Koko would lose their charm. Sometimes small talk stays small, but ideally it's just a starting point that builds a bridge to more meaningful and interesting conversations. Longer conversations with strangers needn't be boring if we can figure out a way to cross that bridge.

I asked people who attended my workshops to think about what good might come from talking to a stranger. They came up with a long list of possible benefits (many of which we'll consider throughout this book) that includes:

- exchanging ideas,
- learning something new,
- gaining a new perspective,
- making a new friend or business contact, and
- having fun.

A conversation involving any of these outcomes sounds far from boring to me. And if that's not enough, throughout this book I'll be sharing stories of conversations that I've had with strangers that have literally changed my life. It doesn't get more (personally) meaningful than that.

Earlier I mentioned research by Jeffrey Hall, who found that the more time we spend in small talk with someone we know, the *less* close we feel to that person. Hall has spent time thinking about what it takes to move a conversation beyond small talk. He proposes things like catching up with someone (e.g., recapping the day), joking around, and showing care. When Hall and his colleagues instructed people to engage in these behaviors, they reported greater well-being afterward (e.g., more connection and less stress, anxiety, and loneliness).[11] There's no reason that you can't do these things in a conversation with a stranger:

- Catch up: I've asked many people about what they are currently doing, plan to do, or have done that day. One of my favorite and most effective conversation starters is "Whatcha doin'?" One time, I asked this question of a group of university students who were fiddling with a strange piece of equipment in a public park. Their answer: Measuring gravity. Actually, tiny variations in gravity, in the hopes of being able to predict seismic activity.
- Joke around: I asked two Freemasons (who, incidentally, have the best job titles: One was a Right Illustrious Intendant-General, and the other was a Most Worthy Grand Master) who were in matching formal wear—striped trousers and a black tuxedo jacket with tails—whether they had called each other in the morning to decide what to wear to the annual gathering.
- Show care: I've asked plenty of people who looked lost or upset whether they were OK.

Strangers are surprisingly good to talk to when we're struggling. At first glance, this seems counterintuitive. After all, we expose our vulnerability when we disclose our personal challenges, so it makes sense that we would only trust our close others to see our soft, inner self. However, in practice, when we're looking for advice or support, we often turn to whoever's available in the moment.[12] And there are even some advantages to drawing on strangers, rather than close others, for support (see chapter 2).

Clearly it's possible to have a deep, nonboring conversation with a stranger. Maybe we just don't think we should—maybe we don't think our conversation partner would be receptive to it. Luckily, researchers have studied this very question. They find that when we meet someone new, most of us (presumably including the strangers that we initiate conversations with) prefer to have meaningful interactions over superficial chatter, and we feel happier and more connected when we have a deeper conversation.[13] That suggests to me that it's Sid's negative voice in our heads, more than anything else, that's holding us back. You can go deeper than you think, if you can find a way to be brave and give it a try (and a way to quiet or ignore Sid).

What if you strike up a conversation with a stranger (and I hope you do!) and you get stuck in small talk? Yep—that's going to happen sometimes. I've had hundreds of conversations with strangers. Sometimes, they're literally life-changing. Those conversations are rare. Mostly my conversations with strangers are interesting or informative or fun, in an everyday sort of way, especially since I've gotten better, with practice, at crossing the bridge from small talk to more meaningful conversations. But sometimes my conversations with strangers are forgettable, lackluster, or boring.

First, it's important to know that getting stuck in a boring conversation probably happens less frequently than you think. Often, we start conversations with strangers in circumstances that allow us to just walk away—circumstances where the conversation is unlikely to drag on long enough to be boring.

Second, it might be worth asking: Why would we expect every conversation to be scintillating? We don't give a 5-star rating to every movie that we watch. When we watch an average movie, we don't think: *Well, that wasn't life-changing. I guess there's no point in watching another movie ever again.* We keep watching, knowing that there will be more good movies in the future, new favorites waiting to be discovered. Similarly, there's no need to be disheartened by average or even boring conversations with strangers. There will be more enjoyable conversations in your future.

Finally, I'd like to think that even boring conversations have value. On the train home after a night out, I started a conversation with a man sitting opposite me. He started complaining about his job and his boss, droning on and on—ugh. I won't lie: This conversation (if you can even call it that, when he did all the talking and I did all the listening) was boring. But it was also a good reminder that I should be careful about complaining too much. Confucius said something along the lines of:

"If I am walking with two other men, each of them will serve as my teacher. I will pick out the good points of the one and imitate them, and the bad points of the other and correct them in myself."

Also, I'd like to think that I did this disgruntled worker a favor by giving him a chance to vent his frustration. I made him feel seen and heard, and we all need that. I think of boredom as the occasional price that I have to pay in order to have so many enjoyable conversations.

## What if I can't figure out what to say?

We've all been there. One minute the conversation's flowing smoothly, and then, suddenly: silence. We stare awkwardly at each other. Each second that ticks past feels like a minute. If you're like me, you panic, and your thoughts get stuck in a loop: *What do I say? What do I say? What do I say?*

Emma Templeton, a psychologist at Dartmouth College, and her colleagues have been studying awkward silences. They look at how much time there is between one person finishing what they're saying and the other person responding. On average, these gaps are tiny: only about a quarter of a second. When people are really interested in a conversation and are paying attention to each other, the gaps tend to be shorter. That explains why, when the gaps are shorter, people tend to enjoy their conversations more and feel more connected to their conversation partner.[14] These gaps are noticeable to outside observers too. When people watch videos of conversations where the length of the gaps has been edited, they think that the conversation partners enjoyed the conversation more and felt more connected because the gaps are shorter.

Our fear of awkward silences might make us read too much into these gaps. There's nothing intrinsically good or bad about the length of these gaps. For one thing, a study of ten languages from around the world found that the average size of the gaps depends on the language: Japanese had the smallest gaps, and Danish had the largest.[15] Surely this doesn't mean that Japanese speakers have more enjoyable conversations than Danish speakers. For another thing, people interpret gaps differently depending on context. Templeton and her colleagues found that our interpretation depends on who we're talking to.[16, 17] When we're talking to a stranger, a longer gap can feel awkward and uncomfortable because we interpret it to mean that our conversation partner is bored, confused, or not paying attention. It is a harbinger of a dreaded awkward silence, when neither of us knows what to say next. When we're talking to a friend, however, a longer gap might show us that they're really listening and reflecting on what we've said, or simply signal that they're enjoying companionable time with us.

Besides, awkward silences probably happen less often than we fear. Psychologists Michael Kardas, Juliana Schroeder, and Ed O'Brien have studied whether strangers run out of things to say by pairing up people to have a chat over Zoom.[18] After talking for five minutes, both people reported how much they had enjoyed the conversation so far and how much they'd had to talk about. Then they learned that they would be talking for twenty more minutes. They were asked to predict how much they would be enjoying the conversation after ten minutes, fifteen minutes, twenty minutes, and twenty-five minutes. They were also asked to predict how much they would have to talk about at each of these time points. After making all their predictions, the strangers picked up the conversation where they had left off and talked for twenty more minutes, stopping every five minutes to report on how things were going.

People thought they would enjoy the conversation less and less and would have fewer and fewer things to say to each other. (There's Sid, making another appearance, illogically telling you that despite all the successful conversations you've had in your lifetime, *this time* you won't find anything to say.) In reality, people continued to enjoy the conversation and continued to find new things to talk about for the entire time. Some of the gaps between their conversation turns were surely longer than others, and there may have been some moments that felt a bit awkward, but think about what the results of this study mean: Complete strangers talked for twenty-five minutes without running out of things to say. I'm not surprised by this because I've found similar results. In a study I ran with Erica and Gus during the early days of Covid, we matched up pairs of strangers to meet online.[19] On average, they expected to talk for fourteen minutes, but they ended up talking for forty minutes!

Of course, not everyone in these studies had long, flowing conversations. Inevitably, some conversations are going to be more awkward than others. You might be convinced that *your* conversations are going to be the ones that suffer this fate, but you're not alone in believing this. A recent study by Erica and her colleagues found that people think they're worse than average at having a casual conversation "at a cocktail party, dinner party, or similar social event."[20] In fact, it was one of only two activities, out of almost fifty different ones, where people rated themselves as worse than average (the other exception was playing a new sport).

The fact that people are so pessimistic about their social skills is puzzling to psychologists because people tend to think they're better than average in pretty much every way, even when they have no grounds for it.[21] We think we're better than average in terms of abilities (e.g., driving skill, leadership), attributes (physical attractiveness), and traits (intelligence, honesty). A recent market research poll even found that 20 percent of women and 46 percent of men felt somewhat or very confident that they could land a plane if the pilot was incapacitated[22]—a feat that, according to experts, would be nearly impossible for someone with no experience.[23] In other words, many of us think we'd have almost as good a chance of landing a plane as we do of successfully navigating a conversation with a stranger at a party. This is not only ridiculous but untrue.

## But I'm an introvert, and introverts can't talk to strangers

Statistically speaking, the majority of people are at least average conversationalists, but there are, of course, a minority who are worse than average. You might feel like *you're* more likely to fall into this minority because *you're* an introvert. You'd be mistaken. It's not simply a matter of introverts being worse than average and extroverts being better than average.* It *is* true that introverts are more worried before talking to a stranger, according to the data from 750 of my research participants.[24] However, there's little evidence to suggest that introverts have worse social skills than extroverts.[25] Introverts are less motivated to socialize, and they prefer to socialize in different ways. (I'd much rather have a one-on-one chat in my living room than hang out with a group of people in a noisy pub.) However, when they do socialize, introverts tend to enjoy it just as much as extroverts. In many ways, introverts and extroverts are more alike than you might expect.

For a long time, I thought that I could spot an introvert a mile away. Then I met Harvard psychology professor Brian Little. His energy, warmth, and humor are surely part of the reason that he's so beloved by his students and has received numerous teaching awards. The first time I met him, he bounded across the room, telling me in a booming voice how much he'd been looking forward to meeting a fellow Canadian. (It was very kind of him, since I was a junior researcher at the time, and he had little reason to know who I was.) If you had asked me, I would have been 100 percent sure that this force of nature was an extrovert. I would have been wrong. If you watch his wonderful TED talk, you'll hear him admit that he's *so* introverted that, after giving a talk or teaching one of his award-winning classes, he will retreat to a bathroom stall to recover from the overstimulation.[26]

Although extroverts aren't any more socially skilled than introverts, research consistently finds that extroverts are, on average, happier.[27] If you're an introvert, like me, you might be

---

\* I use the words "introvert" and "extrovert" for conciseness, though of course there's a continuum, and "person who is more/less extroverted" would be more accurate.

thinking: *Nonsense! I'm perfectly happy, thank you very much.* It's important to note that psychological studies tend to look at averages across lots of people. This particular finding means that, on average, people who are more extroverted are a bit happier, but, of course, there will be plenty of people who are highly extroverted yet unhappy, and plenty who are highly introverted yet happy.

If you're an introvert and want to increase the odds in your favor, you might want to consider a "fake it until you make it" approach. Researchers have asked people to act in a more extroverted way (talkative, assertive, and spontaneous) or a more introverted way (deliberate, quiet, and reserved). Consistently, both introverts and extroverts are happier when they act in a more extroverted way, and they're less happy when they act in a more introverted way.[28-30] And acting like an extrovert doesn't seem to have any negative side effects for us introverts: It doesn't take more effort, feel inauthentic, or lead to negative emotions that cancel out the positive ones.[31]

Maybe that's what I'm doing when I talk to strangers: I'm an introvert acting like an extrovert. You might think that it would feel unnatural, but I think talking to strangers actually suits introverts. It feels safe because I can choose who to approach and when to end the conversation and walk away. I often talk to strangers on the Tube in London, which is considered a huge faux pas. As an introvert, I find being on the Tube overwhelming: It's always noisy, often crowded, and usually uncomfortably overheated (somehow both in the summer *and* the winter?). If I turn to the person next to me and have a little chat, I can focus on the conversation and ignore, or at least be less overwhelmed by, the sensory overload. It's a way of coping, a way to make the time pass more quickly, until I can return to a more comfortable environment.

You probably already have better social skills than you give yourself credit for—even if you're an introvert. But what if you start a conversation with a stranger and it stalls, leaving you stuck in a moment of awkward silence? Yep—that's going to happen sometimes. (To be fair, though, I sometimes experience awkward silences even with my nearest and dearest.) Don't panic! Your conversation partner doesn't like awkward silences any more than you do, and they will be doing their best to get the conversation going again (and to avoid the silences in the first place). You're partly responsible for the success of a conversation, and with practice, you'll strengthen your skills, which will increase your success rate. However, your conversation partner is also partly responsible. So, if a conversation languishes, remember that it isn't entirely your fault. When a conversation goes well, we tend to give the credit to (or at least share the credit with) our conversation partner, but when a conversation goes badly, we usually blame ourselves.[32] (Does Sid never take a break?)

I once read some advice designed to help actors deal with the rejection that inevitably comes with auditioning for roles. The actors were told: Maybe the casting director was looking for an apple. You are an exquisite peach, but none of your perfect peach qualities matter if they're looking for an apple. I try to remember all the wonderful conversations I've had in the past (I found some apples—yay!) and not worry too much when a conversation doesn't work out (I found a gorgeous peach that someone else will enjoy). I know that there are plenty of apples, and the next conversation is likely to go better.

## What if nobody wants to talk to me?

A conversation can't be boring or full of awkward silences if it doesn't happen in the first place. What if you try to start a conversation with a stranger and they shut you down?

Rejection is rare when talking to strangers. Much rarer than you probably fear. In a study by Nicholas "Nick" Epley at the University of Chicago and Juliana Schroeder, now at Berkeley, commuters in Chicago believed that fewer than half of the people on the same train would be willing to talk to them.[33] In reality, not a single commuter reported being rebuffed when they tried to initiate a conversation. Of course, maybe only the commuters who had successful conversations filled in the survey and mailed it back to the researchers.

Recognizing that this is a major worry that people have, I've also estimated how often rejection occurs, in my own studies. In a study that I ran with Erica and Gus (that you'll read about in chapter 6), nearly two hundred American and British university students talked to strangers repeatedly over the course of a week.[34] Before they attempted their first conversation, we asked them whether they thought that the first person they approached would be willing to talk. Only 40 percent of participants thought their first attempt would be successful. The actual success rate for their first conversation was 90 percent. Over the course of the study, participants had 1,336 conversations, and 87 percent of the time, those conversations occurred with the first person they approached. That's a mere 13 percent rejection rate. A stunning *lack* of rejection.

If you find that hard to believe, think about how often you reject other people. You try your best to adhere to the golden rule, right? If someone smiles at you, I'd bet that you usually smile back, even if you have had a rotten day and are feeling grumpy. If someone talks to you, I'd bet that you usually say something back because it would be rude to just ignore someone. In the same way, strangers are unlikely to outright ignore you if you strike up a conversation with them—they're far more likely to smile and say at least a few words.

So, what do we mean by rejection, anyway? Is it when we make an overture to a stranger but it ends after a polite acknowledgment, rather than leading to a conversation? Maybe, but it depends on how we explain our (wannabe) conversation partner's behavior. Humans are meaning-makers. We try to make sense of things by telling ourselves a story—and we can choose which story to tell.

When I start chatting with a stranger, I imagine they have two major questions. The first is: "Who are you?" Sometimes people have resolved this question by concluding that they must know me—I've been mistaken for a neighbor on multiple occasions. If someone seems confused about who I am (e.g., their brows are crinkled, or their tone of voice seems hesitant or questioning), I will sometimes try to reassure them by saying: "We don't know each other. I'm just being friendly."

People also seem to need to know "Why are you talking to me?" (That's why conversation starters that provide a "why" can make things go more smoothly; see the appendix on page 235 for some ideas.) If they can't understand the "why," they may feel confused or concerned. Maybe they're socially anxious, and their automatic response is to worry. Maybe they've become mistrustful because of negative experiences in the past. (Bad experiences stick with us for longer than good ones, so even if someone has had countless good experiences, they're sure to remember the rare bad ones.)[35] If someone seems confused or concerned about why I'm talking to them, I might persist for a bit, trying gently to help them understand that I'm just being friendly. Other times, I'll just completely back off. I don't want to make people feel uncomfortable.

I've learned from experience that if I'm patient, most people will get past the "who" and "why" questions, and we'll have a nice chat. But if they don't, I can understand why. Confusion and concern can be conversation killers. Because I can come up with an explanation, it might not seem like a rejection at all, or at least if it does, it doesn't hurt as much.

But sometimes, a person's reason for not talking isn't as obvious. Sometimes, even after they no longer seem confused or concerned, they'll pick up their phone, plug in their headphones, or signal with their nonverbal behavior or body language that they don't want to talk. Ouch. We want to know why. We need an explanation. Luckily (*eye roll*) Sid is happy to provide one: "They don't like you." But we could choose to tell ourselves a different story: "They had a rough day and are preoccupied." Or "They have a book club meeting next week, and they're behind on their reading." Or "They can't understand/hear me properly." There are so many other reasons that might explain why someone doesn't want to talk.

Let's say you're still learning how to tell yourself a more positive story, and, for now, you still believe that scoundrel, Sid. You will be comforted to know that rejection from a stranger probably doesn't sting as badly as you expect. Humans aren't very accurate in predicting how intensely and for how long we'll feel bad when bad things happen. Researchers asked people to imagine how they would feel three months after breaking up with their romantic partner.[36] To test the accuracy of the predictions, the researchers compared participants' predictions to the reports of people who had recently broken up with their romantic partner ("experiencers"). People imagined they would feel a lot worse three months after a breakup than the experiencers actually did. If breaking up with a romantic partner hurts less than we think (after a bit of time has passed), surely rejection by a stranger does too: It can't be personal because they don't even know you.

In a study that I ran with a team of undergraduate students, I asked people to approach a stranger sitting on a bench, who was secretly part of the research team.[37] This research collaborator rejected them. I know, I know—that sounds really mean. But all they did was politely say: "I'm sorry, but I'd rather be alone right now." After being rejected, the participants were in a worse mood than they were before. (Sorry!) But, I wanted to see just how bad rejection felt, compared to how bad it feels to experience other negative events. Being rejected by a stranger didn't feel any worse than the everyday experience of being interrupted in a conversation. Or any worse than accidentally waving back at someone who wasn't waving to them. (Maybe this isn't as benign as I think, though—I once saw a social media post that said: "I waved to a man because I thought he waved to me. Apparently, he waved to another woman. So, to get out of the awkward situation I kept my hand up and a taxi pulled over and drove me to the airport. I am now in another country, starting a new life.")

One late afternoon, I was on the Tube as it was just starting to get busy with people heading home at the end of their working day. I was attempting my usual trick of starting a conversation to help me cope with the overstimulating environment. I turned to the woman sitting on my right and asked how her day had been. I guess I was feeling lazy that day because it's not the most effective or inspiring conversation starter (see the appendix, page 235). Righty politely responded with a few words and then pulled out her phone—a classic way to signal: "I don't want to talk." It didn't feel like she was confused or concerned—just disinterested. I didn't take it personally. Instead, I turned to the person sitting on my left, who was more receptive. I'd like to think that maybe Righty overheard my pleasant chat with Lefty, and I'd like to think that she might be more willing to chat next time the opportunity arises.

## What if they think I'm hitting on them?

Ironically, we often worry not only that someone won't want to talk to us but also exactly the opposite: We worry that they might enjoy it a little *too much*. Women have told me that they're reluctant to talk to men because they don't want men to get the idea that they're flirting. Men have told me that they're reluctant to talk to women because they don't want to make women feel uncomfortable. If you're just getting started with talking to strangers, you might feel more comfortable starting with someone who doesn't trigger these worries for you. Longer term, it would be a real shame for anyone to feel that they needed to rule out half of their fellow humans as potential conversation partners.

Unfortunately, it's extremely difficult to distinguish between friendliness and flirting. An examination of fifty-four research articles found that people display friendliness and attraction in the same ways: through physical proximity, eye contact, smiling, and mimicry (i.e., imitating the other person's behavior).[38] However, unless you're in a place where it's expected (e.g., a party, the pub), flirting doesn't happen all that often. In a study by Jeffrey Hall and his colleagues that was ostensibly about how people form first impressions of each other, fewer than a quarter of people reported that they had flirted with their conversation partner.[39] And these were students, who are in a time of their lives when securing a romantic partner is a top priority. Why is flirting relatively rare? Because it's scary! It involves confronting the same fears as talking to strangers (e.g., rejection and embarrassment) but with higher stakes.

But what you really want to know is: Is someone going to think I'm flirting with them, even though I'm not? In the first impressions study I mentioned earlier, people seldom thought their conversation partner was flirting when they weren't: Only about 16 percent of women and 17 percent of men were misperceived (by their men and women partners, respectively). In another study, researchers asked people to act out scenes in which each partner was instructed to be either flirty or friendly.[40] When people watched recordings of the actors, both men and women were better than chance at detecting the difference between flirting and being friendly.

Just to be safe, if you're the one starting the conversation and you don't want to send the wrong signals, then you might want to leave a little more physical distance between you and your conversation partner. You might want to reduce eye gaze, maybe by standing or sitting side by side instead of face-to-face. You might also want to avoid talking to strangers in contexts that are sometimes associated with flirting: late at night or if either of you have been drinking. (This is good advice regardless of whether or not you're worried about being perceived as flirting.) If, on the other hand, someone starts talking to you, you could remember how bad we are at detecting flirting and assume that they're just being friendly, until proven otherwise. The only sure way to signal your intentions is to be explicit about them, and the only sure way to understand theirs is to ask.

I've tried to be honest with you. You may get stuck in a boring conversation from time to time, it's hard to completely avoid awkward silences, and sometimes you'll be rejected. All of these things have happened to me. But I honestly can't remember a single time that I've started a conversation with someone and felt like they were hitting on me. (I've had one or two people ask for my contact details, but there were good reasons for it that weren't related to romantic interest.) Of course, there are many possible explanations for this. I might be forgetting a time when this happened (my memory isn't the greatest). It might have happened without me knowing—I just shared research about how we're not very good at detecting flirting. It might be something about me and my identity as a middle-aged woman sporting a ring on that telltale finger. Another possibility, which I'd like to believe, is: People can tell that I'm just being friendly.

Just because it hasn't happened to me doesn't mean that it won't happen to you, so you might want to think through what you could do if it did happen. Attendees at my How to Talk to Strangers workshops (and women everywhere) have brainstormed answers to that exact question. They suggest changing the topic to something more impersonal/neutral or perhaps using humor to defuse the situation, if that's something that works for you. You could casually bring up your romantic partner (real or invented). You could explicitly state your intentions, in the same way that I tell people "I'm just being friendly" if they seem confused about why I'm talking to them. As with any conversation with a stranger that isn't going well, you can politely thank them for the conversation (or, let's be honest: You could make an excuse) and walk away. And if you see someone else attracting what appears to be unwanted romantic attention, you can lend your support by using your talking to strangers skills to join the conversation and help neutralize the situation.

## What will people think?

In the r/London thread on Reddit, someone asked: "Has anyone had a random conversation on the Tube with a stranger and it not been weird/creepy/awkward/an attempted pick-up? I know it breaks the cardinal rule of Tube travel, but I feel like there must be lots of heartwarming stories out there!"[41]

Jonathan Dunne, an American living in London, was clearly aware of this "cardinal rule," but he didn't like it, and he decided to do something about it. He headed to Tube stations and handed out "Tube chat?" badges that people could wear to signal that they were open to having a chat. But the "no talking" rule was more entrenched than he realized, and the reaction was not what he'd hoped for. *The Guardian* ran an article: "'Tube chat' campaign provokes horror among London commuters."[42] Londoners turned down the friendly badges and instead made their own:

- "Sod off"
- "Don't even think about talking to me!"
- "No chat please, we're British"

But that last badge maker was a bit overzealous because although many British people seem to self-identify as reserved and buttoned-up, there are well-known regional differences. British satirical news show *The Mash Report*—think a UK version of *The Onion* but with videos—"reported" a fictional news story about a man who had arrived on the train from northern England and spread terror by saying hello to Londoners. What I love about this clip is that although it's ostensibly poking fun at Northerners, who are known for being chatty, really it's poking fun at Londoners for being suspicious of someone who's simply trying to be friendly.

One Redditor is clearly aware of these regional differences because they said that their only conversations on the Tube are with Northerners or tourists. People also seem to make exceptions to the "no talking" rule to interact with dogs and their humans. I dream of one day having a story like the Redditors who told of a dog sitting on their feet or sleeping on their lap. (I know I'm not alone in this because one of the badges made in response to the Tube chat campaign was: "Wake me up if a dog gets on.")

Sometimes it's the context, rather than the identity of the conversation partner, that gives people permission to break the "no talking" rule on the Tube. One Redditor said they often have conversations "drunk or post–football match" (the latter virtually guarantees the former). Another suspends the rules when something has gone wrong with the train, say it mysteriously stops in a dark tunnel and there's an inaudible announcement (Is there any other kind?).

I wonder if the "no talking" rule and all the exceptions to it are simply a reflection of our fears. It seems to me that we make exceptions in cases where it's more likely that the conversation will be successful. Perhaps the rules are an elaborate way to protect us from possible rejection (despite the fact that it's so rare to begin with)? Maybe we make an exception for talking to Northerners because we know that they're more likely to be receptive, and therefore we don't need to worry as much about rejection. Maybe we make an exception for tourists because there's a good reason for it: to help them if they're lost or give them tips on what to see and do or where to eat. And maybe we make an exception when there's an obvious conversation starter. Redditors reported pleasant conversations that were sparked by wearing a team jersey, reading a book, or carrying a theater program, golf clubs, a musical instrument, or knitting needles. Maybe if we were more confident about our ability to have a mutually enjoyable conversation, we wouldn't need to invent so many informal rules.

All these exceptions make the rules difficult to discern, which means that you might inadvertently break them. (Or maybe you sometimes know that there is a "no talking" rule and you decide to break it anyway—you rebel!) What would happen if you broke the rules? Well, I've had many conversations on the Tube and have lived to tell the tale. I've even hugged a stranger on the Tube (see chapter 2). But it's not just me. Hundreds of Redditors shared stories of positive interactions on the Tube. Your rule-breaking conversation is likely to be as pleasant as theirs because most conversations with strangers are.

If you break the rules, you may need to confront the twin barriers of confusion and concern before you can arrive at a friendly chat. People aren't expecting your overture and don't know what to make of it. This doesn't mean you can't have a nice conversation, but you might need to be patient and work a little harder. If you capitalize on an exception and avoid breaking the rules, then you may be able to bypass the "who are you" and "why are you talking to me" questions and settle into a friendly chat more easily. In the

UK, Northerners might rarely feel confused or concerned because, for them, it's not against the rules to talk to strangers. Similarly, dog owners (or, at least, their dogs) are regularly approached by strangers, so they're unlikely to feel confused or concerned. (As one Redditor claimed: "Take a dog. . . . Everyone speaks to you then!")

One day, in a happy mood on my way to visit a friend that I don't see often enough, I was enjoying a nice conversation on the train with an architecture student who had just moved to London to start his studies. I was a bit disappointed when we reached his stop and he got off the train—it felt like the conversation had been cut short. But then another passenger on the train picked things up where the student had left off, and we carried on chatting until I got off the train. I'd love to think that we had created a new rule that day and that the conversation chain carried on without me. One Redditor shared a similar story about how they managed to temporarily change the rules. They had been reading out crossword puzzle clues to their girlfriend, and someone sitting nearby chimed in with a suggestion. By the end of their journey on the Tube, five others had offered help on the crossword too. The rules might be more malleable than we think.

## You're worrying too much

I've gone into detail about a few of the countless things that people worry about. You might worry about some of the same things or other things altogether. Whatever you worry about, I can assure you that you're not alone. I can also tell you that you probably worry far more than you need to. Over the years, I've run many studies with the same three steps: I ask people to share their worries, talk to a stranger, and then tell me whether their worries came true. The results are consistent across every study: People's experiences are much more positive than their predictions. Our worries far outstrip the reality.[43]

Let's pause for a moment and recap all the ways that we worry too much. We worry that our conversation partner won't like us, but actually they like us more than we think. We worry that our conversations will be boring, but we enjoy our conversations more than we think. We worry that we won't know what to say, but our social skills are better than we think. We worry that people won't want to talk to us, but rejection is rarer than we think. And we worry about social judgment from others, but the rules are more flexible than we realize.

All the research tells us that the negative voice in our head (aka Sid) is not to be trusted. Ignore the so-called rules. You *are* allowed to talk to strangers. Also, you *are* capable of talking to strangers. Even if you're an introvert. After all, besides blood relations, everyone you currently know was once a stranger, and you obviously managed to talk to them just fine.

If you find a way to face your fears and strike up a conversation with a stranger, it could benefit you in many and unexpected ways. As you'll see in the next few chapters, these are conversations that could result in a friendship, a career opportunity, or simply a shared moment of human connection. Conversations that help us build confidence in our social skills so that we can ask for help or revive a lapsed friendship. Conversations that make the world a little bit better.

# 2

# No Strings Attached

Despite my carefully curated playlist, my eyelids drooped as I drove six and a half long hours to the beautiful, hilly Berkshires of Massachusetts to attend a music festival. My husband usually did the driving. I was in charge of directions: If I wasn't keeping a close eye on things, he would pull out of a gas station and inadvertently head in a different direction than we'd been going before we had pulled in. But this road trip was a solo one: We had just gotten divorced after six years of marriage.

Some people seem to have everything figured out by the time they graduate high school: They know who they are and what they want their life to look like. I wasn't one of those people. Instead, I had a habit of falling into things, liking them well enough, and just carrying on, on autopilot. My mom taught me that you finish what you've started, and I took this lesson to the extreme, following through on things that maybe I shouldn't have.

I married my college sweetheart but woke up one day to realize that I felt lonely in my marriage. I felt stuck. I know that I'm not alone in having felt this way because author Edward St. Aubyn was able to perfectly, and poetically, describe how I felt in *Some Hope*: "He knew that under the tall grass of an apparently untamed future the steel rails of fear and habit were already laid. What he suddenly couldn't bear, with every cell in his body, was to act out the destiny prepared for him by his past, and slide obediently along those rails, contemplating bitterly all the routes he would rather have taken."

I didn't know what I wanted my future to look like, but I knew that I had to make space to find out. So, after our amicable divorce, I wanted to do something that I wouldn't have done with my ex, something that allowed me to explore a part of myself that I'd been suppressing. I bought tickets to the Tanglewood Music Festival, the summer home of the renowned Boston Symphony Orchestra.

I fell in love with classical music when I started piano lessons at the age of five. I remember playing with my toys in the basement when I was little, listening to Khachaturian's exciting and exotic "Sabre Dance" on the radio. In high school, I turned to pop and rock because listening to classical music made me feel uncomfortably different from my classmates. I found my way back to classical music by chance, while attending university. An acquaintance happened to mention that he was going to hear the Toronto Symphony Orchestra perform his favorite orchestral work: *Finlandia* by Sibelius. He spoke so passionately about this piece that I decided I needed to hear it, so I went to the library and found a recording. (We didn't have YouTube or Spotify in those days.) I continued to borrow recordings from the library, to explore more and more widely and figure out what music resonated with me.

My future ex-husband had no interest in classical music. After I discovered that he had attended a concert with me and spent the entire time literally counting ceiling tiles, I preferred to go to concerts on my own. That didn't bother me. In fact, when he wasn't there, I was more likely to get into a conversation with a fellow concertgoer and enjoy nerding out about music. (If *they* started a conversation, that is—I hadn't yet figured out how to start conversations myself.) What *did* bother me was the unshakable feeling that at some deep level, my husband just didn't understand me. Even worse, not feeling fully understood or accepted by my husband made me worry that I wouldn't ever feel fully understood or accepted by anyone. (Feeling different from other people is, ironically, something many of us have in common.)

There wasn't much in the way of affordable accommodation near Tanglewood for someone now living on a single salary, so I pitched a tent in a campsite on Mount Greylock. I attended concerts in the evenings, but there was plenty of time for sightseeing during the days. Mount Greylock is the highest point in Massachusetts, and at the summit is the Veterans War Memorial Tower with a faceted crystal ball on top that reminds me of a lighthouse. On the evening of my arrival, I climbed the steps of the tower to take in the panoramic view as the sun set. There at the top of the tower, I met Floyd.

I didn't make a habit of talking to strangers in those days (I was too nervous), but somehow, we ended up chatting. Maybe the beautiful view simply needed to be shared. He had a book in his hand, so I asked what he was reading. We talked about what had brought us to Mount Greylock. He didn't show any sign that he found it odd that I drove six and a half hours to hear classical music. In fact, he asked me lots of questions about the festival. For his part, Floyd was escaping Boston for the weekend to enjoy the great outdoors. When he told me that he was going for a hike the next day, I asked if I could join him. Looking back now, going for a walk in the woods with a complete stranger was probably a terrible idea. What was I thinking? (To be fair, though, doing it alone isn't the best idea either....)

The next day, I returned to the summit and waited for Floyd. I worried that he had politely agreed to my self-invitation but really had no intention of letting me tag along. But he did show up, and we did go for a hike. A five-hour hike! We had a flowing, wide-ranging, and surprisingly not-awkward conversation—one of the longest and easiest ones I've ever had with a stranger. We talked about work, of course, but also about favorite authors (I later checked out one of his), places we had traveled and wanted to visit....

I'd been so engrossed in the conversation that I hadn't noticed how far we had descended until it was time to start climbing back to the summit, where we had started. Before Floyd came along that weekend, I'd simply been planning to do an easy walk to a waterfall. I hadn't even brought a water bottle. In those days, although I enjoyed a bit of hiking and was relatively fit from playing racquet sports, I hadn't tackled anything as strenuous as this. At some point during our seemingly endless climb, when I was feeling exhausted and parched, Floyd offered me an orange. It was the juiciest, sweetest orange I've ever eaten. (There's something special and memorable about food eaten while hiking: Dad still talks about the best soup he's ever eaten; it was during a walk we did together to aptly named Iceberg Lake. There's a word for this in German: *Gipfelschmaus*. Literally translated, it means a delicious meal eaten at the summit, but according to an Instagram post, it's "that moment on a mountain-top, where even a basic snack tastes like the best meal of your life.")[1] But Floyd gave me a much greater gift that day: a feeling of newfound acceptance and the knowledge that I was going to be OK. If this stranger could accept me for who I was, then others would too. (In case you're wondering, I never saw him again. Wherever you are: Thank you, Floyd.)

## It (often) feels good to self-disclose . . .

It may seem surprising that I was able to open up so freely and have such a meaningful conversation with a complete stranger. But, in fact, sharing something about ourselves—whether it's something more sensitive and subjective (e.g., what we think and feel, or revealing a secret) or something more mundane and objective (e.g., our preferences and life experiences)—generally feels good, regardless of who our conversation partner is. (This may explain why many people seem to like talking about themselves—sometimes too much. Maybe you've noticed?)

Diana Tamir and Jason Mitchell at Harvard University have studied just how much we enjoy self-disclosure by pitting it against a financial reward.[2] They showed people two questions at a time and asked them to choose which one they wanted to answer. There were three types of questions: ones about themselves, ones about other people, and trivia. People were offered different payouts for each question. For example, people might be offered the choice between receiving $0.02 to disclose how much they enjoy singing or $0.04 to answer a trivia question about what a baby hedgehog is called. (It's a hoglet.) Participants were presented with hundreds of choices between self and other, self and trivia, and other and trivia. When the payouts were equal for both questions, people showed a clear preference for self-disclosure over the other two options, presumably reflecting the fact that they found self-disclosure more enjoyable. When the payouts were unequal, however, things got even more interesting: People had to decide between answering the question that seemed the most enjoyable or the question that paid more. It turns out that people's preference for self-disclosure was so strong that they were willing to give up money. They could have earned 17 percent more money by always choosing the highest paying task.

Why does self-disclosure feel so good? What do we gain from it? Like most people, there are times when I feel stressed and overwhelmed at work. At times like these, I get by with a little help from my friends. I might talk about what is weighing on my mind or admit that I'm struggling to prioritize the tasks on my ever-growing to-do list. (You know the one.) Without saying a word, my friends help me feel seen and understood. Sometimes a friend will give me practical advice: what I should say no to, what I should delegate, and what can wait until later. Other times, a friend will help me manage my emotions by commiserating with me and allowing me to wallow for a while, or by cheering me up and encouraging me to let something go. Inevitably, after talking to a friend, my heart feels lighter and I have a plan for moving forward.

Although the benefits of self-disclosure are, in large part, dependent on how the recipient responds to it, it's also valuable in its own right. For example, journaling involves self-disclosure in written form, and, despite not being shared with another person, can still provide benefits.[3] Or consider this story about my dad. He retired after working for thirty-three years as a high school teacher. Dad loved being in the classroom. He was popular with his students, in large part because he sees the best in people—even the kids that most teachers find annoying. (To be fair, it might also have something to do with the fact that kids like a teacher who isn't too serious, and my dad's a certified goofball.) Some people struggle with retirement—it's a transition that requires people to find new ways to spend their time and new sources of meaning and social connection. Dad was well aware of this, and in the months leading up to his retirement, it was clearly on his mind. He seemed to talk about retirement with *everyone* he met. We were at the grocery store together, and I remember Dad telling the checkout clerk: "I'm retiring soon, but I'm not worried. I have lots of activities to keep me busy."

It's not that he expected or hoped for advice or support from the checkout clerk (or any of the countless other people he told), though I imagine people did share encouraging stories of folks they knew who were thriving in retirement. Rather, I suspect that simply voicing his worries (I mean *cough* his absence of worries) helped Dad process his thoughts and feelings about retiring. After all, one benefit of self-disclosure is self-clarification.[4] (In case you're curious: Dad loves retirement, is never home because of all the activities he's involved in, and is as socially connected as ever.)

### . . . But self-disclosure can be scary

We all worry sometimes about our families, our finances, our futures. However, we often choose to put on a game face and act like everything is just fine, thank you, because opening up—about what we're thinking, how we're feeling, who we are—makes us vulnerable, and that's scary. Our frenemy Sid whispers in our ear, conjuring up worst-case scenarios about what might happen if we *did* open up. What if we admit to someone that we're going through a rough patch with our romantic partner/kid, and they think we're a bad person/parent? What if we admit to someone that we can't really afford to go with them on that fun weekend away that they're looking forward to so much, and they make us feel embarrassed and ashamed, or stop inviting us to do things together? What if we admit to someone that we're suffering with our mental health, and they see or treat us differently?

As usual, Sid's probably worrying too much. When Nancy Collins and Lynn Carol Miller looked across almost one hundred studies, they found a consistent pattern: People like us *more*—not less—when we disclose more.[5] Lest you take this as license to overshare (I'm sure you wouldn't, though), know that both conversation partners like each other more when they *take turns* opening up to each other.[6]

Why do we like people who self-disclose? Researchers at the University of Mannheim studied various scenarios that require vulnerability: apologizing after a fight, asking for help, admitting to a mistake, and saying "I love you" to a best friend.[7] People in one study were asked to imagine either themselves or someone else doing each of these things. When *someone else* is being vulnerable, we see it as admirable and courageous. (This study also revealed one reason that we might be reluctant to self-disclose: When *we* are the one being vulnerable, we see it as a sign of weakness.)

The disclosure in this study was hypothetical, but in a study by Michael Kardas, Amit Kumar, and Nick Epley, people actually revealed a secret: anything from the fact that they had never learned how to ride a bike to the fact that they had had an abortion.[8] After revealing their secret, people were surprised to report that the recipient of their disclosure had been more considerate and less disapproving than they had expected. It didn't matter whether the recipient was a stranger or a friend, family member or romantic partner. And the study participants weren't just imagining things: The person they confided in really did have a more positive overall impression of the discloser and thought they were more trustworthy and honest than the discloser had expected. Take that, Sid!

## Advantages of disclosing to strangers

Self-disclosure feels good, and, although it can be scary, it often goes better than we expect. We often disclose to people that we feel close to, that we trust. Surprisingly, however, there are many advantages of disclosing to strangers.

For one thing, you can feel confident that your disclosure won't become gossip for the rumor mill. A stranger can't share your disclosure with other people that you know because *they don't know you* or the people that you know.

When you reveal a part of yourself to someone that you know, every time you see them, you and they might be reminded of your disclosure. In one study, researchers found that when people imagined revealing a personal insecurity, the more painful they thought it would be to be reminded of their disclosure, the more likely they were to choose to disclose their insecurity to a stranger rather than a friend.[9] When you open up to a stranger, you don't need to worry about being uncomfortably reminded of your disclosure because you're unlikely to see them again.

Because we tend to spend time with people who are similar to us, the people we are close to tend to know the same kinds of things that we do. Strangers have different knowledge and perspectives. This means that they may be able to help us see things differently and give particularly effective advice.

But one of the biggest advantages of disclosing to a stranger is that strangers have no strings.

## Threads vs. strings

I like to think that we're connected to everyone we meet. At first, we're connected to a stranger by a single thread. Each interaction adds new threads. With some people—for example, the neighbor that we see regularly walking their dog in the park—we might be connected by dozens and dozens of individual threads. I love how Virginia Woolf writes about these threads in *Mrs. Dalloway*:

"And they went further and further from her, being attached to her by a thin thread (since they had lunched with her) which would stretch and stretch, get thinner and thinner as they walked across London; as if one's friends were attached to one's body, after lunching with them, by a thin thread. . . . And Richard Dalloway and Hugh Whitbread hesitated at the corner of Conduit Street at the very moment that Millicent Bruton, lying on the sofa, let the thread snap; snored."

The threads that connect us to strangers and acquaintances (like those who lunch together) are fragile and can snap when stretched by time or distance. But something happens when we really connect with someone, maybe by sharing an experience with them or sharing a piece of ourselves. When this happens, the threads wrap around one another, becoming strings. When the threads intertwine, they become stronger, harder to break. Maybe in our closest relationships, they end up as strong as the metal strings on my cello. We're bound to our friends and family, and these strings make us feel secure, make us feel that we belong.

The threads or strings that connect us to others provide a pathway for information, such as emotions, to be transmitted. For example, if a conversation partner starts laughing, it's hard not to be affected by their mirth and share in some of their amusement. When we have a stronger connection, emotions are transmitted with higher fidelity. Think about two people at opposite ends of a metal string: If the person at one end touches the string (e.g., laughs), it sets off a vibration that travels through the string and is felt at the other end. Threads, however—like the ones that connect strangers—are less taut and don't vibrate the same way. That lack of vibration can be helpful when we're self-disclosing because it can provide a sense of psychological distance.

## Strangers provide psychological distance

For years now, Al Nixon has started his day by sitting on the same seaside bench in St. Petersburg, Florida, with the same travel mug full of coffee, watching the sunrise.[10] All the locals know Al, and they smile and wave as they walk past. He's such a fixture that when he went out of town and wasn't seen for a few days, someone posted on Nextdoor asking what had happened to him, fearing the worst.* When Al returned from his trip, his bench sported a metal plate that read:

---

\* Nextdoor is a hyperlocal social media website/app that connects people in the same neighborhood.

> Al. A loving and loyal friend and confidant to many.
> Forever and always.

How does a man, who started going to the beach simply to clear his head, become such a staple in his community?

When we talk to a stranger like Al, rather than someone we feel close to, we benefit from something called "psychological distance." When something is more hypothetical or is further away from us—whether in terms of space or time or social proximity (e.g., stranger vs. friend)—we see and think about it differently, more abstractly and holistically.[11]

Sometimes psychological distance causes problems for us. It explains, in part, why we can excitedly book tickets for a show/concert/game, etc., put the event in our calendar, and look forward to it for weeks, but then on the big day when we're feeling tired or stressed from work, have to do laundry so that we can wear our favorite sweater/team jersey, and need to sort out the logistics of which bus to take or where to park, we feel notably less enthusiastic.

Although psychological distance can make some things more difficult—like predicting how we'll feel in the future—it can make it easier for us to self-disclose to a stranger, and easier for them to respond to our self-disclosure in a helpful way.

## Psychological distance allows strangers to give good advice

When my stomach rumbles, I don't get hangry, but I do struggle to make even the simplest decisions. I was on the train on my way to

London for a lovely afternoon tea that my dear friend Giulia had organized to help me celebrate, after I submitted a proposal for the book that you're currently reading. The train ended up being delayed by about an hour. Giulia managed to push back our reservation, but I was getting hungry. As usual, I had an emergency granola bar in my bag, but I couldn't decide if I should eat it or not. (Ironic, isn't it, that my hunger was impairing my ability to decide whether or not to eat something?) On the one hand, I was hungry, and the granola bar would take the edge off. On the other hand, I wanted to save my appetite for the fancy finger sandwiches, the assortment of tiny cakes and the scones (well, really the clotted cream and jam—the scones are just the delivery mechanism). I'd been chatting with a lady on the train (let's call her Oda), and she was in the right place at the right time, so I asked her for advice. Oda didn't hesitate for even a second: She told me to eat the granola bar. So, I did.

If you're lucky, you have a few people in your life that you consider wise and turn to for advice, whatever the topic. What makes someone "wise"? Psychologist Igor Grossmann at the University of Waterloo thinks a wise person is someone who can transcend their own viewpoint. They recognize the limits of their own knowledge, consider other people's perspectives, search for compromise, and acknowledge that there are many ways that things can play out.[12] Grossmann's research finds that, due to psychological distance, people make wiser decisions for others than they do for themselves (though people can learn to make wiser decisions for themselves by practicing distanced self-reflection: essentially, pretending that they're advising someone else).[13] Oda gave me wise advice, because the granola bar gave me a hit of energy, but I still had plenty of room left for cakes and scones.

The trade-offs for the "great granola bar deliberation" were trivial, but often when we make difficult decisions, there's a trade-off between idealism and pragmatism that can result in a disconnect between what we value and what we do. For example, one St. Pete resident asked Al for advice. She wanted to leave the city and try something on her own, but that would mean leaving her boyfriend, who she loved very much. As another example, we might want to apply for a new job that aligns better with our values, but the new job might involve moving to a new city, taking a pay cut, or being pushed outside of our comfort zone. When psychological distance is involved—when the decision relates to something far away, something in the future, or someone who's less close—people give advice that focuses on the ends more than the means.[14] (Advice that they admit they would struggle to follow themselves.)[15] In other words, strangers are likely to remind us of what our best self already knows is the right thing to do.

## Psychological distance dampens the emotions associated with self-disclosure

Sharing something personal can trigger a range of emotions. For example, if we talk about something that's troubling us, we might feel vulnerable, anxious, ashamed, or sad. The sharing itself can feel uncomfortable but so do the emotions that it stirs up. When we disclose to a stranger, the psychological distance allows us to focus more on the high-level meaning of our disclosure, rather than the specific—and frequently painful—details (e.g., the "what" and "why"). This bigger-picture focus gives us space to reflect more objectively, which means that we don't feel all those emotions so intensely—and neither does the person we disclose to.

When we disclose to the people who are close to us, not only do we worry about regulating our own emotions, but we often worry about helping *them* manage *their* emotions. Nothing matters more for our well-being than our close relationships.[16] They are a source of intimacy, companionship, and security, and they bring us joy. Our close others are there for us when we need support, advice, and comfort. *But* the strings that bind us together mean that when we experience intense emotions, our close others experience intense emotions too, both out of empathy for us and because of what our disclosure means for them.

When St. Pete residents share their troubles with Al rather than a close other, their psychological distance from Al means that they're less likely to feel strong emotions themselves. But they also don't need to worry about Al's emotional response in the same way that they would worry about the reaction of a loved one. Although Al is surely a compassionate person, sympathetic to people's struggles, those struggles don't impact him directly—he has psychological distance and the lower emotional involvement that comes with it. This allows Al to simply listen and provide people with the space to process their own thoughts. (In fact, Al has a rule about not giving advice unless he's asked.) Loved ones often struggle to simply listen—they want to get involved. Even when they do listen, they can struggle to hear us clearly, because of our shared history—and their personal stake. As Spanish novelist Carlos Ruiz Zafón puts it (in *The Shadow of the Wind*): "Sometimes it's easier to talk to a stranger than someone you know. . . . Probably because a stranger sees us the way we are, not as they wish us to be."

## Do people really disclose to strangers?

Psychological distance means that there are several good reasons to consider opening up to strangers. But that's just theory. You may wonder whether, in practice, people really *do* open up to strangers.

Al is not just a special case. It's a storytelling trope, but people really do open up to bartenders and hairdressers. Once, when I was waiting to get my hair cut, I overheard a woman talking to her hairdresser about her relatively recent bereavement. (I complimented the hairdresser later on how supportively and nonjudgmentally she had responded.)

I've asked a lot of people in a lot of research studies to talk to a stranger. Some have been staunchly against self-disclosure to strangers. One said: "I don't discuss private or sensitive info with strangers." This stance was itself one of the topics of conversation for another pair of strangers, who said they had talked about how: "We don't really like to share anything personal with strangers." Other people, however, have found themselves naturally self-disclosing to their conversation partners. One said: "We also were a bit vulnerable . . . and talked about some personal things." Another said: "I spoke more openly about myself than I would with most people I'd just met."

For decades, researchers assumed that when we have something important to discuss, we discuss it with the people we feel closest to. This assumption seems reasonable. Revealing something private or important to us makes us feel vulnerable, so it makes sense that we would only feel safe to open up to someone that we trust. Sociologist Mario Small at Columbia University put this assumption to the test and surprisingly found that almost half of the time that people talk about important matters (e.g., family issues, career, life goals, health), they talk to someone outside of their inner social circle.[17]

This begs the question: How do we decide who to disclose to? In Small's study, 80 percent of decisions were explained by one of three reasons. Often, we deliberately choose someone: either a person that we think has special insight about the topic to be discussed, or a person who's just generally good to talk to about any topic—maybe someone we consider wise. But surprisingly often, we don't make a deliberate decision. The third reason we choose a particular person to disclose to is simply that they're available in the moment. And, of course, strangers are perfectly suited for this because: They are there. They walk their dog in our local park, frequent our favorite coffee shop, take the same bus as us. . . .

Small's finding resonates with me. In July 2021, I had lunch with Hazel at a gastropub that was still putting up plexiglass shields between tables to encourage people to eat out despite the prevalence of Covid-19. Hazel, a clinical psychologist, had come across my research on the benefits of talking to strangers and had reached out to me (a stranger) via Twitter/X. We had chatted once online and met once in person before that lunch in July, so she wasn't a total stranger but not far from it. When I walked into the pub and Hazel asked how I was doing, I surprised both of us by bursting into tears.

I had a lot on my mind, which had been swirling and percolating as I drove to our lunch date. For one thing, I'd applied for a new job and was waiting to hear if I'd get an interview. The prospect of a new job was exciting but also a bit overwhelming (especially since this one would mean moving to a new city). In addition to the uncertainty and stress of waiting to hear about the job, I'd been working on a book proposal but had recently decided to abandon it. It hurt to give up on a project that I was so passionate about and had spent so much time thinking about. (My lunch with Hazel was two years, almost to the day, before the afternoon tea I mentioned earlier, when I celebrated submitting the book proposal.) It didn't seem like the right time, since I might soon be moving and starting a new job. Also, a book on talking to strangers had just come out the previous week, and it was hard for me to imagine that the world needed a book from me on the same topic. (Joe Keohane is an amazing storyteller and his hilarious footnotes alone are worth the price of *The Power of Strangers*.)

I was emotionally on edge before I walked into the pub—I sat in the parking lot for a few minutes to compose myself before heading inside—so my reaction to Hazel's friendly greeting shouldn't have been a surprise. Hazel didn't show any sign of being horrified by a near-stranger breaking down in the middle of the pub. Luckily for me, Hazel is both wise and kind. After I shared my worries with her, I felt much lighter. One of the delightful consequences of that lunch is that I now associate this book with Hazel, and her warmth and support in that emotionally charged moment.

Hazel was in the right place at the right time for me. I love the idea that we've all been in the right place at the right time for others' disclosures, though we may never know it. One time I may have made a difference was on the train to London, when I made eye contact and started chatting with the thirty-something man sitting across from me. He was wearing a crisp suit and was headed to an interview, in the hopes of getting a promotion. It's easy to imagine how nervous he must have been feeling. I'd like to think that having a chat with a stranger (me) helped him process his feelings and/or provided a welcome distraction. Unfortunately, I'll never know if he got the job (when you talk to strangers, you never find out what happens next), but we saw a rainbow out the train window, so I'd like to think that was a good luck sign for him.

## Strangers respond more positively than we expect

One thing that might hold you back from opening up to a stranger is your worry about how they'll react. The psychological distance between the two of you might mean that they're *capable* of providing wise advice, but are they *willing* to do so? Why would they care what's on your mind? What's in it for them?

For one thing, people are generally kind and are more willing to help than you think (see chapter 7).[18] They're likely to be willing to listen to your disclosure or to offer some advice (if you want it) because it feels good to be kind, to feel like we've made a difference to someone.[19] For another thing, although we may have the impression that we need to stick to tedious small talk when talking to strangers, research finds that we would prefer to have a more meaningful conversation—and so would our conversation partner.

You may have seen a headline like one of these, taken from *Women's Health, The Guardian,* and *The New York Times*:

"Ask These 36 Questions to Fall in Love with Anyone"

"Can These 36 Questions Make You Fall in Love with Anyone?"

"The 36 Questions That Lead to Love"

These now-famous questions were created by researchers who were interested in studying relationships. We researchers like to control as many factors as possible and then change one thing at a time to see if it has an effect. That's nearly impossible to do with relationships because they're all different: They're the product of countless conversations and time spent together in various situations. So, along with his colleagues, Arthur Aron at Stony Brook devised a way to efficiently create a relationship (albeit a nascent one) between strangers in the lab, following a consistent set of steps (i.e., asking people to answer these thirty-six questions), so that these relationships would be as similar to each other as possible.

When people spend forty-five minutes answering the researchers' carefully designed set of questions, they really do feel close to a complete stranger—substantially closer than they do after engaging in small talk.[20] If you're anything like me, there will have been times when you've spent a lot longer than that with someone and not felt close to them at all. It seems almost magical that answering a simple list of questions could "fix" this. No wonder the media made these questions so famous (though journalists might have gotten a little carried away in equating feelings of closeness with falling in love . . . ).

The magic isn't in the questions themselves. Other questions would likely work just as well. The real magic is in the *process* of answering the questions. To start, people answer mundane questions, such as: "Do you like to get up early or stay up late? Why?" Then the questions become more personal and emotional: "If a crystal ball could tell you the truth about yourself, your life, your future, or anything else, what would you want to know?" It's the process of gradually disclosing more and more personal information to another person—and them disclosing to you in return—that builds feelings of closeness. Mutual, escalating self-disclosure often occurs naturally as relationships unfold, but this "fast friends" procedure accelerates the process.

Aron and his colleagues, who developed the "fast friends" process, might be surprised to know that their process reflects what people actually want when they talk to a stranger. Researchers Michael Kardas, Amit Kumar, and Nick Epley asked pairs of strangers to discuss a set of questions drawn from the "fast friends" process.[21] Each person had two conversations, with different partners: one that involved small talk, based on the shallower questions that come closer to the beginning of the "fast friends" process, and one that was more meaningful, based on the deeper questions that come closer to the end. People felt happier and more connected to their partner after the deeper conversation. (They also felt a bit more awkward, but it's encouraging to know that people felt much less awkward than they expected to.) After having both kinds of conversations, people said they had preferred the deeper one, and they wished their everyday conversations with strangers were deeper than they usually are.

Some deep conversations can be quite sensitive, involving disclosure of beliefs or experiences that we would rather keep private. We shy away from sensitive topics because we don't want to make our conversation partner feel uncomfortable or harm our relationship with them. But even when a deep conversation involves sensitive questions, it goes better than we expect. People think that their conversation will feel more uncomfortable than it actually does and that their conversation partner will judge them more negatively than they actually do.[22]

One takeaway from these studies is that, although we might feel that we have to gradually work our way up to deeper questions (as in the gradually escalating "fast friends" process) or more sensitive questions, we might be able to dive into more interesting topics even faster than we thought, and if we do, we're likely to enjoy our conversations more.

Why do we not realize how much we would enjoy a deeper conversation with a stranger? Disclosing to someone makes us feel vulnerable, and we worry about how our conversation partner will react. Kardas and his colleagues found that people were more interested in discussing deeper questions when they imagined talking to someone who they thought was caring and considerate. You won't be surprised at this point to hear that strangers care about and are more interested in our answers than we expect. (Don't be deceived by Sid's protestations to the contrary.)

In other words, when we give our conversation partner the benefit of the doubt, and trust that they will respond in a positive or kind way, we feel safer opening up. Now, ask yourself this: How would *you* respond if a stranger disclosed something to you? I'm guessing you would listen, respond sympathetically, and show at least a little care. Is it so hard to believe that a stranger would do the same for you? We enjoy intimate exchanges more than playing it safe with small talk, but we seem to stand in our own way, blocking our own path to greater connection. Next time a stranger asks, "How are you?," you might consider challenging your instinct to respond with a perfunctory "fine, thanks" and instead be a bit more open. You're likely to get a more positive response than you expect.

## Strangers can help make the good feel even better

Psychological distance—and the objectivity it brings—doesn't just make strangers valuable allies when we're going through tough times, as I was after my divorce, when I met Floyd. They can also enhance the good times.

Whenever something great happens in my life (e.g., that book proposal I was celebrating earlier turning into a book deal), my first thought is to call my mom, who I know will respond supportively and enthusiastically. By calling her, I'm enlisting her help to do what psychologists call "capitalizing": acting to intensify and sustain an emotional response to a positive event.[23] Research on capitalization finds that positive events make us feel good but sharing them with someone who responds in a positive way makes us feel even better.[24] This might be easiest to see by considering the opposite: If something great happens, but we have nobody to share it with, it can feel a bit empty.

Sharing positive events with others can amplify our positive feelings, but it depends on how the other person responds. If they respond like my mom—expressing excitement, asking questions, showing emotions like interest, happiness, and pride—then it feels great. Married couples who endorse statements like: "I sometimes get the sense that my partner is even more happy and excited than I am [about good news]" are more satisfied with their relationship, and feel more intimacy, commitment, and trust.[25]

Unfortunately, not everyone responds as enthusiastically as my mom does. Sometimes people point out all the downsides of the positive event or act as if it's not such a big deal. When we attempt to capitalize on a positive event and the other person responds like this, we feel worse than if we hadn't told them. No surprise there. But, interestingly, even if they respond positively, we can sometimes feel worse for having told them. We want their enthusiasm to match the intensity of how *we* feel about the event, and if it doesn't, we can feel disappointed. Couples who endorse statements like: "My partner says little, but I know they are happy for me" are less satisfied with their relationship (at least in Western cultures).[26]

An ambivalent reaction like this (or even a negative reaction) might be more likely than you expect, because the strings that bind us to our close others mean that our successes have emotional consequences for them too, and those emotions may be mixed. Even if our partner/friend wants to be happy about our exciting new opportunity at work, it might remind them of how they feel stuck in their own job, or they might worry that we'll have less time to spend with them. A friend might want to be happy for us when we excitedly share the news of our engagement or pregnancy, yet find it hard to respond enthusiastically if they desperately want to get married or have kids themselves but haven't yet found the right partner.

It's simpler with strangers. Without the strings, there's no threat, no muddy ambivalence. Consider an experiment in which researchers asked people to imagine how they would feel and respond after hearing good news from a romantic partner or an acquaintance.[27] Sometimes the good news had negative implications for the study participant (e.g., their romantic partner/the acquaintance had received an offer that would require a long-distance move), and other times it didn't (e.g., their romantic partner/the acquaintance had received a large gift). People predicted that they would respond more ambivalently to the good news when it had negative implications for them, which seems natural enough. But here's the twist: The good news only felt threatening *when it was shared by their romantic partner*. When it was shared by an acquaintance, there were fewer personal implications, and people could just be happy for their acquaintance.

I shared a memorable moment with a stranger named Floyd when I was troubled and raw. I was able to process my thoughts and feelings about my recent divorce with the help of an objective listener. I shared another memorable moment with a stranger, this time when I was capitalizing on positive feelings—and it turned into something else entirely.

A few years ago, I was invited to the BBC Old Broadcasting House, a storied building in London, to be interviewed about my research for a popular radio show called *Woman's Hour*. After a brief, nervous wait in the green room with other guests who were appearing on the show, I entered the church-quiet studio and sat at a table with a very fancy microphone, notes clutched in my shaky hands. The interview was only a few minutes long, and it went by in a flash. I emerged, blinking in the sunshine, wondering if it had really happened. It was only midmorning, and I was already back on the Tube to start my journey home.

My energy high from the interview and the feeling of unreality probably partly explained why I said hello to a woman sitting a few seats away from me. I asked her how her day was going, and she responded with a simple "Fine, thanks." Not a very promising response. (I mean, I could have come up with a better conversation starter.) I thought: *Oh well, this isn't going to go anywhere*. But after a pause, her inherent politeness kicked in, and she asked me how *my* day was going. I told her about my exciting morning. She promised to listen to the show later, but I'd be surprised if she remembered because it turns out her morning had been far more eventful than mine. She'd just come from the doctor. She paused, possibly considering the consequences, then said, "I'm pregnant!" I was one of the first people to know. She was on her way back to work and was unlikely to tell anyone for months, until an ultrasound confirmed that the pregnancy was going smoothly. But it was safe for her to capitalize by telling me, a complete stranger who she would never see again. I felt so lucky to share that moment with her. We shared a hug, right there, on the Tube.

# 3

# Puzzle Pieces

"If you were both to die at the same time, who would you like to raise your children?"

The lawyer's question was ridiculous. My then-husband and I were in our twenties and unlikely to die any time soon, especially *at the same time*. We didn't have any children and didn't plan to have any. I guess these are the kinds of questions lawyers always ask when they draw up a will for you, so that you don't have to keep modifying it when your life circumstances change. I wasn't aware of it yet, but lurking beneath the surface, some part of me desperately wanted my life circumstances to change. You know by now that I felt lonely in my marriage, but I was also starting to question my career path. (Apparently, I had a quarterlife, rather than a midlife, crisis.)

I loved math in high school. The logic of it appealed to me: You learned the rules, you followed the rules, and you got the right answer. So, at university I studied math and ended up majoring in computer science. After graduating, I worked as a programmer for ten years, earning a generous salary and doing work that I found intellectually stimulating. I had a wonderful boss, who was smart, generous, and fun. He also had a terrible temper. I saw that temper directed at other people and knew that one day it would come my way. I guess I should be grateful that it eventually did because our falling out prompted me to do some soul-searching.

First things first: Did I want to keep working with him? No. But if I wanted to find a new job in the sector, I'd need to upgrade my programming skills; in the decade since I'd graduated, technology had changed dramatically. Luckily for me, I love learning. When my mostly wonderful boss, during a team-building activity, asked us what we would do if we won the lottery, I said I'd go back to school for the pleasure of learning something new. (Maybe astronomy? Archaeology? Literature?) In theory, therefore, learning another programming language is something I *should* enjoy. So, the fact that I dreaded it made me stop and take notice.

This realization led to a bigger question: What would my dream job look like? Although I enjoyed the *how* of my work (i.e., the logic of programming), I didn't like the *what* that I'd been doing so far: creating business products. I pictured myself continuing to do a similar job for decades, until I retired, and the thought of it was oppressive. What I really wanted was to put something positive into the world. But how could I leverage my training to do something more fulfilling?

As I shifted uncomfortably in a stiff chair in the lawyer's office, trying to seriously contemplate my own mortality, this seed of discontent was lying dormant in my mind. I yearned for change but couldn't imagine what it might look like. Until the lawyer inadvertently showed me.

I noticed her diploma, hanging in a burnished frame on the wall behind her desk, and I made an offhand remark about it.

"Actually, I only recently became a lawyer," she said with a proud smile.

It turned out that she had embarked on a new career in her fifties. This blew me away. Starting over in a completely new career was not something that I'd ever imagined. In my parents' era, people spent their entire professional lives working for the same company, earning a proverbial gold watch after decades of service. As for me, I'd spent four years studying at university and a decade since then building expertise. Was it really possible to throw that all away? It seemed foolhardy. On the other hand, I didn't want to live a life of regret. In my heart, I knew that I wanted to find a totally new path, like the lawyer had done.

When I arranged that meeting with the lawyer, I couldn't have known that it would change my life. When we start a conversation with a stranger, we necessarily know nothing about them (barring a few clues from their appearance and our shared context). This can make conversations with strangers unpredictable and therefore a little scary. But, if you look at it a different way, it also makes conversations with strangers exciting. We might discover something that we never expected. Rabbi Lawrence Kushner writes in *Honey from the Rock*: "Everyone carries with them at least one and probably many pieces to someone else's puzzle. Sometimes they know it. Sometimes they don't. And when you present your piece, which is worthless to you, to another, whether you know it or not, whether they know it or not, you are a messenger from the Most High."

A vision of my future was beginning to emerge as the pieces of my life's puzzle came together, but I see now that there was a gap, and the lawyer unknowingly handed me a piece that clicked satisfyingly into place.

## Humans are curious

Sometimes we feel like we *need* to learn something: a skill that will help us do our job more effectively, how something works (e.g., our new smartphone or the bus schedule), how to get someone to do what we want. Other times, we learn for sheer enjoyment—because we're curious. I'm curious about butterflies, about the lives of great composers and writers and artists, about what makes people happy.

I'm even curious about curiosity itself. One of the leading researchers studying curiosity is Todd Kashdan, at George Mason University, who finds that there are five components of a person's overall level of curiosity.[1] One of these components—which he has poetically named "joyous exploration"—represents "a general fascination with new information and experiences."

But we aren't just curious about information and experiences—we're also curious about people. For example, maybe you enjoy people-watching. In one of my studies, over 95 percent of people said that they people-watch sometimes, and more than half said that they people-watch at least once a day.[2] Or maybe you walk past a house in your neighborhood that has a bay window, through which you can see walls painted in a perfect shade of cobalt blue, and you imagine what kind of people live there. Or maybe you settle in with a flat white at your favorite coffee shop and eavesdrop on the people at the next table. These are all ways of satisfying our social curiosity (another of Kashdan's five components of curiosity): interest in other people and how they think, feel, and behave.[3]

Learning about people isn't simply a matter of satisfying our idle curiosity. It also helps us learn about the world. As eighteenth century diplomat Philip Dormer Stanhope, fourth Earl of Chesterfield, said:

"Learning is acquired by reading books; but the much more necessary learning, the knowledge of the world, is only to be acquired by reading [people], and studying all the various editions of them."

We talked in chapter 1 about the importance of belonging in Maslow's pyramid of needs. Our need for security is even more fundamental. We feel safe when our world makes sense, when we feel like we can predict what's going to happen next. One way we try to make sense of the world is by trying to understand other people. (Of course, the world and the people in it often don't make sense, and our ability to predict what will happen is limited, but to avoid triggering an existential crisis, let's not dwell on that too much....) In other words, we have good reason to satisfy our curiosity: It makes us feel safer.

No wonder, then, that we find it so hard to resist satisfying our curiosity. According to Greek myth, Zeus created Pandora—the first woman—as a punishment to mankind. (What a flattering origin story for women.) Her name means "the one who bears all gifts," and she was beautiful, charming, and clever. She was also curious, so when Zeus gave her a box and forbid her from opening it, it was only a matter of time until she did. When Pandora succumbed to her curiosity and opened the box, she inadvertently unleashed all the evils of the world.

Christopher Hsee at the University of Chicago and Bowen Ruan, now at the University of Iowa, tested just how hard it is to resist our curiosity by creating their own version of Pandora's box.[4] They built a computer screen with forty-eight buttons on it. Some buttons were labeled as "water," and if you clicked those, you would hear the soothing sound of water pouring into a jar. Other buttons were labeled as "nails," and if you clicked those, you would unleash one of the evils of the world: the sound of fingernails on a chalkboard. I don't know about you, but even reading that sentence makes me shudder. (There's no word in English for this feeling, but there is one in Spanish: *grima*.)[5] But here's where curiosity comes in: Some buttons were labeled with a question mark, and if you clicked those, you had an equal chance of hearing water or fingernails. For some people (in the labeled group), most of the buttons were labeled, and there were only four with question marks. For other people (the unlabeled group), only four buttons were labeled, and the rest all had question marks.

If people struggle to resist satisfying their curiosity, then they would want to click those unlabeled buttons—despite running the substantial risk (a 50/50 chance) of hearing fingernails on a chalkboard. Sure enough, people in the unlabeled group clicked more buttons (thirty-nine) than people in the labeled group (twenty-eight). This means that people in the unlabeled group heard the sound of fingernails on a chalkboard about eighteen times, even though they were told that they didn't need to press any buttons at all—they could just sit back and relax. They gave in to their curiosity, even though they knew it would sometimes bring pain. (An aside: I just gave in to my curiosity and spent way too much time on Reddit reading responses to the question "What is your equivalent to 'nails on a chalkboard'?"[6] One common grima-inducer is the sound of cutlery scraping on china. The sound of packing tape being removed from cardboard is grima-inducing for me.)

The story of Pandora and her box paints curiosity as a fault, something to be ashamed of. In fact, at least in moderation, curiosity is a positive trait, valued around the world.[7] After all, where would we be without people who are curious, who are driven to learn, driven to figure out how things and people work, driven to make things better? And curious people benefit from their own curiosity too: They tend to report higher well-being,[8] possibly in part because learning makes them feel more secure.

## People learn from talking to strangers

I've come to love talking to strangers, and this personal interest has also become a professional one. Fast-forward fifteen years after that life-changing meeting with the lawyer: I had returned to school, had finished a master's degree and a PhD, and was starting a new career as a psychology professor. (Oh, and I'd gotten divorced and remarried.) My research (you could call it "me-search") is all about understanding how we benefit from talking to strangers—and why we find it so hard sometimes.

I've learned so much over the years from talking to strangers: that asparagus squeaks when it grows (and it grows ridiculously fast: up to 25 centimeters/10 inches in 24 hours!); that goats love to eat bananas; that scuba divers sometimes play hangman under water when, to avoid decompression sickness, they make safety stops during an ascent; about a sport called hashing (which a man on a bus in Edinburgh laughingly described to me as "drinkers with a running problem"). Although I use my personal experiences to come up with research questions (e.g., How often do people learn something when they talk to a stranger?), I try to then put my own experiences aside and answer the questions by collecting and analyzing data.

To understand how often people learn something when they talk to a stranger, Erica, Gus, and I recruited American and British university students to participate in a study designed to test whether talking to strangers gets easier with practice (you'll read more about it in chapter 6). We were pretty confident that people would have a string of positive (or, at worst, neutral) conversations with strangers, but we didn't have any idea how much they would learn from their conversations. We didn't know whether you need to get comfortable with talking to strangers first before you can start learning from them. (As I mentioned in the introduction, I learned, in the first conversation that I remember starting with a stranger, that people can ride ostriches, but that might just have been beginner's luck.)

We needn't have worried. The nearly two hundred participants in our study had a whopping 1,336 conversations with strangers, and approximately one out of every three conversations involved learning. People got directions; tips on the best coffee shops and the most affordable places for a stylish haircut; information about upcoming social events and volunteering opportunities; advice on tattoos and keeping boots clean and whether a Canadian goose down jacket is worth the hefty price tag. Eighty percent of participants said that they had learned something from at least one conversation partner, and more than half said they had learned something from more than one partner. At the end of the study, after people had talked to strangers repeatedly for a week, we asked them what they had enjoyed most about participating in the study. Several people mentioned that the best thing was learning: "Meeting new people to learn new things." "Learning from others, hearing interesting stories."

I told you in chapter 1 about a study by Nick Epley and Juliana Schroeder that found that Chicago commuters who tried to start a conversation with someone sitting next to them on the train were rejected less often than they expected (actually, weren't rejected at all). Schroeder and Epley teamed up with Donald Lyons to run a similar study on people commuting by train to London.[9] After talking to a stranger, people reported learning more than they usually did on their commute—and they learned more than the people who sat in silence. (In both studies, people were in a better mood and enjoyed their commute more when they talked to a stranger.)

Despite this evidence that learning from strangers is extremely common, people don't seem to be aware of how much they stand to benefit. Stav Atir, now at the University of Wisconsin–Madison, along with her collaborators Kristina Wald and Nick Epley, ran a series of research studies involving more than a thousand people.[10] After talking to a stranger for ten minutes, people consistently reported learning more than they had expected, both about their conversation partner and in general.

## People are more likely to talk to strangers while traveling

For about a decade now, I've been using social media to share little stories about my conversations with strangers, in the hope that they might inspire other people to talk to strangers too. These stories have turned into a kind of archive for me. When I looked through them, I discovered that more than a third of my conversations with strangers have happened while I'm on holiday. Many of these stories involve learning:

- In Brittany (the northwest corner of France), an Airbnb host who was a retired ocean scientist taught me that the four main predictors of seasickness are: hunger, cold, fatigue, and fear (in French, they're referred to as the four F's: la faim, le froid, la fatigue, et la frousse).
- In Cornwall (the southwest corner of England), I parked my car in a small seaside village, took a taxi from there to a lighthouse, and walked back to my car along the spectacular coast. The chatty taxi driver told me the best place for ice cream along my route, for a well-earned treat.
- In Northumberland (the northeast corner of England), I found out about an active archaeological excavation when I asked a man about the drone he was flying. The dig was only a few minutes' detour from my path, but I would have missed it if he hadn't pointed it out. It was a nerdy dream come true to chat with the archaeologists, who were looking for wood fragment remains of an Anglo-Saxon royal hall (their description: "the kind of hall described in *Beowulf*").

Over the years, conversations with strangers have become more and more of a highlight of my travels.

Maybe you, too, talk to strangers while traveling? I wouldn't be surprised because I've heard lots of stories of people making new friends while on holiday. My in-laws made friends at a beach resort, and now when they book a new trip, they let their friends know, and sometimes they all holiday together again. When my sister- and brother-in-law got married, the guest list included someone they had met while traveling across Australia after they graduated from university. My parents were camping a few hours from home when they met a couple from the Netherlands who were visiting Canada. (Dad doesn't remember how he started this particular conversation, but often when he's on a walk and sees people looking tired and sweaty from exertion, he jokes that he's left them a cold beer up ahead.) They shared a campfire that night and stayed in touch for more than twenty-five years.

Between my own experiences and all these stories of holiday friendships, I started to wonder: Do people talk to strangers more often when they're traveling? So, I ran a *talking while traveling* study. I asked people to imagine that they were at a coffee shop—either in a foreign country or in their home country—and managed to secure the last free table.[11] I asked them how they thought they would feel if a stranger asked to share their table and then started chatting with them.

The scenario that I invented for the study was inspired by personal experiences. I've been the stranger asking whether I can share someone's table (I shared one story in chapter 1), but I've also been the lucky person sitting at a table, noticing people looking around in vain for somewhere to sit. The first time that I remember inviting someone to share my table was during the 2010 Winter Olympics in Vancouver, Canada. As you can imagine, all the restaurants in Whistler Village ski resort were bursting at the seams. The man who gratefully joined my husband and me turned out to be a police officer volunteering at the Olympics, who gave us a behind-the-scenes peek into how the games worked. In December 2021, returning home after visiting my dad for his eighty-first birthday, only a few of the food outlets were open at the airport, so tables were in short supply. As I ate my meal, I invited a series of people to join me as they waited for their food to be prepped and packaged for takeout. I had interesting conversations with a woman who worked at a birthing center, an estate planner who was on his way to meet the son of a recently deceased woman, and a man who worked away from his family for months at a time on a conveyor belt project.

Returning to my talking while traveling study, I found that people were more open to chatting with a stranger at a coffee shop when they were traveling in a foreign country, rather than when they were in their home country. One of the troubles (and joys) of being a researcher is that whenever you find out the answer to one question, it leads to another question. If people are more willing to talk to strangers when traveling, that begs the question: Why? Is there something about traveling that makes it easier to talk to strangers?

## Why it might be easier to talk to strangers while traveling

For one thing, I think many of us are more open to talking to strangers while traveling because we're more open *in general* while traveling. In fact, new experiences are often part of the reason *why* we travel. According to a market research poll in the UK, about one in four people say that one of the reasons they travel is to broaden their horizons.[12] On Reddit, someone asked on the r/travel thread: "Why do you travel?"[13] An answer that stood out to me was from TripPlanningNerd, who said that they travel "To feel alive!" They explained "Not that I sleepwalk through daily life, but there's so much that's on autopilot. When I travel, everything from the food to navigating public transportation is new and different, and I feel like I get a jolt of life! I get to see, do, and taste things I couldn't experience in my daily life, even if I wanted to."

It seems natural that this openness to new experiences might extend to meeting new people: One way to learn about a place is to learn about the people who live there. Maybe we feel that traveling gives us license to exercise the social curiosity that we often restrain at home.

Or maybe we seek out strangers to shake things up a bit, after being stuck for days on end with only our travel companion(s) to talk to. When we're not traveling, we tend to have quite a few social interactions every day.[14, 15] And we're happier when we have more social interactions or when we interact with a wider variety of conversation partners.[16] Maybe the reduced number and variety of interactions while traveling makes us more willing to reach out to strangers.

To summarize so far, we seem to be more open to and interested in having conversations with strangers while traveling. But I think there's a second reason why we talk to strangers while traveling: We're more optimistic about how our conversations will go. In my talking while traveling study, people expected to enjoy their coffee shop conversation more, and expected to find their conversation partner more interesting when they were abroad versus at home. After all, their conversation partner isn't just any old stranger—they're an exotic Mauritian or Estonian or Canadian stranger.

People in my study might have had rosier expectations in part because they expected *their conversation partner* to enjoy the conversation more and to find *them* more interesting. In general, we tend to worry more about our conversation partner's experience than our own.[17] Maybe while traveling it's easier to believe that someone could actually enjoy talking to us. After all, just as they're exotic to us, we're also exotic to them, aren't we? One Redditor acknowledged this: "As an American, I love meeting someone who's never met an American before. Usually leads to fun conversations."

At home, we're conscious of what other people think of us, and we worry that talking to strangers is a violation of the unwritten social code, which will be met with disapproval. Thankfully, we perceive the rules to be more lenient when traveling. (Or maybe one of the joys of traveling is the ability to forget about rules altogether?) We deduce the rules by observing others, so researchers assess people's perceptions of the norms by asking them whether people they know do (or don't do) a particular behavior. The participants in my study didn't think that talking to strangers is against the rules while traveling: They said that the people they know are more likely to talk to strangers while traveling (vs. at home).

Figuring out how to start a conversation might also be easier while traveling. When we're drinking a fruity cocktail on a sunny, beachside patio, we know that we already have something in common with the person sitting at the next table: We've both traveled to the same place to enjoy a well-earned holiday. Easy conversation openers abound. We could comment on our drinks, swap reports on how our vacations are going, or regale each other with entertaining anecdotes about past holidays.

## Asking for directions/help

We humans don't generally like *not* knowing things, but it's hard to avoid this while traveling (even if you're an overzealous planner like me). While traveling, uncertainty is certain. Because of this, it doesn't feel as threatening as usual to need help or to ask for information. We're off the hook—we couldn't possibly be expected to know everything when we're just visiting. That might explain why people in my study were more willing to ask for directions while traveling than they were at home.

Asking for directions is an easy way to start a conversation with a stranger. But, since the advent of smartphones, we have less of a *need* to get directions from strangers. When Kostadin Kushlev, now at Georgetown University, and his colleagues Jason Proulx and Elizabeth Dunn asked a group of students at the University of British Columbia to find an obscure building on their university campus, the students only talked to people 20 percent of the time. Instead of asking a fellow student for directions, they presumably asked Google Maps.[18] But when another group of students were instructed to leave their phones in the lab, they asked for directions 90 percent of the time. It took the people without their phones a few minutes longer to find the building, but I'd like to think that's because they had a bit of a chat. The time penalty might be one disadvantage of getting directions from a human rather than an app, but there are advantages to balance things out: The students who got directions from a stranger said they felt more socially connected, which put them in a better mood.

We might feel that because we *could* find our own way by using an app, that we *should* do so. We don't *need* to ask someone for directions, so wouldn't we be bothering them or imposing on them by asking for their help? Our intuition on this is wrong. In a study by Francis Flynn, now at Stanford, and Vanessa Lake Bohns, now at Cornell, students were instructed to ask someone to not only give them directions but also escort them to the campus gym, which was about three blocks away.[19] The students expected that they would need to ask seven people before one would agree to escort them to the gym. In fact, on average they only needed to ask two people.

If you're surprised that so many people were willing to help a stranger, think about what you'd do if someone asked you for directions. I'm guessing that, most of the time, you would help them find their way. When I first started to be more deliberate about talking to strangers, I got lots of practice by giving directions. I was doing my PhD at the University of British Columbia, in Vancouver, Canada, and I would take the bus to campus. Tourists would take the same bus to visit the Museum of Anthropology, with its colorful, evocative First Nations totem poles. There was a map right beside the bus stop, but even though I knew the area, I found it confusing, so I figured tourists might find it confusing too. If I got off the bus and saw someone looking at the map, I knew they were probably headed to the museum (or, sometimes, the clothing optional beach that is on campus). I'd offer to walk with them partway, along the route that I had to take anyway, to get to the psychology building. It was a great context for practicing talking to strangers because there were obvious conversation starters: Where are you visiting from? How long are you staying in Vancouver? What else are you planning to do on your trip? At the point where our paths diverged, I'd point them toward the museum (past the flagpole, down the stairs, and through the rose garden, and then left at the road), and we'd go our separate ways. I'd like to think that helping people find their way to the museum made their day a little easier. I'd also like to think that they enjoyed our chat as much as I did and as much as I've enjoyed similar chats when I've been the one on holiday.

## Asking for recommendations/advice

When we travel somewhere we've never been before, we have little choice but to rely on strangers for advice on where to stay, where (and what) to eat, what sights to visit. When I married my first husband (the one who counted the ceiling tiles), the Internet was still young. We enlisted a travel agent to book hotels for our honeymoon. We relied on a travel agent's expertise because there were few other ways to find out what options were open to us. Now, of course, we have easy access to the firsthand experiences of dozens or hundreds of people, who leave ratings online, recommending (or warning against) hotels and restaurants and attractions. Online ratings are undoubtedly a helpful source of information, but there are several compelling reasons why you might want to consider getting information from a real live human.

In recent years, when I've gone on holiday, more often than not there have been at least a few scenic walks. I'm no superathlete, so you won't find me scaling any massive peaks, but I've enjoyed walking through forests of gnarly laurel trees in Tenerife, through otherworldly karst rock formations in Spain, and along the pink granite coast in Brittany. Often, I'll take along a lunch on these walks, which means I've spent lots of time on holidays figuring out where I can get a sandwich. Reading online reviews to find a simple sandwich seems like overkill, and few people seem to bother reviewing lowly sandwich shops (not to mention that I'd rather not spend my time on holiday endlessly scrolling on a device). I've found it to be far more efficient to ask someone.

My husband and I hit the jackpot of sandwich recommendations when we were checking out of a hotel in Tenerife. The man working the front desk asked where we planned to go walking and enthusiastically recommended a roadside service area that we would pass en route, about 40 kilometers/25 miles away from the hotel. We found the place, which had the buzzing efficiency of a busy American diner. We ordered bocadillos from the take-out counter and then drove another hour or so to the start of our trail. We considered skipping the walk, since it was drizzly and overcast, but we stuck it out and the weather gradually improved enough for us to enjoy some breathtaking views of a ragged, green canyon leading out to the sea. The scenery was spectacular, but one of our strongest memories of the walk is those sandwiches. Due to language and translation issues, we hadn't known that the sandwiches would be heated. They had been wrapped in foil and were still warm and full of delicious melty cheese when we ate them, sitting on the side of the trail on that gray day.

You might be thinking: *Sure, you found a spectacular sandwich, Gillian, but maybe you were just lucky.* Why would you trust a recommendation from one particular, idiosyncratic person? What if they don't like the same things as you do? Wouldn't it make more sense to get a consensus view? Fair questions. After all, different people can have wildly different opinions. One TripAdvisor user gave the Eiffel Tower a single star, saying: "The structure itself is just a piece of old metal . . . it's very overrated." If you ask only one person for a recommendation, how do you know that it's not someone like this Eiffel Tower–basher? You don't want to run the risk of being the only person in history who goes to Paris and doesn't visit the Eiffel Tower because this outlier person told you not to bother.

You're not alone in thinking this way. In a series of studies by Casey Eggleston, Timothy Wilson, Minha Lee, and Daniel Gilbert, people made predictions about how much they would like a food item or a video.[20] They consistently preferred to make their own prediction based on a description of the food item/video (i.e., they mentally simulated how much they would like it). But if they were going to base their prediction on another person's liking (i.e., use a "surrogate"), they preferred it to be a friend's rather than a stranger's opinion, presumably expecting their own preferences to be more closely aligned with a friend's rather than a stranger's.

It turns out, though, that surrogates have more value than we expect. People made more accurate predictions about how much they would like the food item/video if they used a surrogate rather than relying on their own mental simulation. And it didn't matter whether the surrogate was a friend or a stranger—people were just as accurate either way. (In a separate study run by Gilbert and Wilson, this time with Matthew Killingsworth and Rebecca Eyre, women were almost twice as accurate in predicting how much they would enjoy a speed date when they based their predictions on a stranger's report of her own speed date with the same man, instead of basing their prediction on the man's picture and a profile description he had written.)[21]

The researchers were careful to say that we might not *always* be more accurate when we base our predictions on information from a surrogate. When there is a lot of variability in opinions, surrogates might be less helpful. But when there is a general consensus—as there is with the Eiffel Tower, for which 70 percent of reviews on TripAdvisor are 5-stars and 20 percent are 4-stars—a stranger surrogate is likely to provide valuable insight.

Talking to a travel surrogate—someone who has been there, done that, taken the selfie—can be especially useful if you carefully choose the surrogate. Let's say you're fascinated by archaeology. Who do you think would have a better idea of whether you would enjoy a particular museum: a fellow history buff, or someone who visited the museum only because it was raining but would rather have been at the beach? With online ratings, it can sometimes be hard to know which of these people is leaving the review. If you're fascinated by archaeology and you notice someone in a museum who's lingering to look at every Roman sandal or Minoan pot, why not strike up a conversation? Chances are they will have great tips on other places you'd enjoy visiting—either on this holiday or your next one.

You can, of course, also get recommendations from carefully chosen surrogates when you're not traveling. At a London Symphony Orchestra concert, the fellow music-lover sitting next to me recommended a book that was perfect for me: a memoir of an amateur pianist tackling Chopin's Ballade No. 1—a challenging piano piece that's a favorite of mine, and one that I've also attempted to learn.[22] At Regent's Park Open Air Theatre in London, I had a blast nerding out with a musical theater aficionado who was visiting from New York. He seemed to have seen every star on Broadway, in multiple productions of every musical ever made. He recommended a production of *Fiddler on the Roof* that was currently playing in London. Based on our conversation, I trusted his word, so I bought tickets and found the show incredibly moving. More mundane but more common, I've also learned about upcoming local events from people I've met on weekend walks.

One of the shortcomings of online ratings is that you only get the details that people choose to share. When you get a recommendation through conversation, you can ask follow-up questions or provide specifics about what you're looking for, what's important to you. My husband, who was born in Portugal, introduced me to fado music, which is "infused with a sense of resignation, fate, and melancholy" (according to Wikipedia). I love dramatic, emotional music, so fado is right up my alley. While visiting Lisbon, I asked the man at the front desk of the hotel to recommend a place where I could hear fado. He named a touristy fado show. These are a great introduction to the art form, but I was hoping for something more authentic. When I gave him more details about what I was looking for, he was able to recommend the perfect hole-in-the-wall place, where all the locals went. It was totally informal, not staged in any way. It didn't even have a specific start time—it started whenever the guitarist arrived. People would take turns singing, and someone who might be sitting at the next table would just go up to the guitarist and tell him what song they wanted to sing. It was a magical, unforgettable night.

Of course, not all recommendations work out the way you expect. And that isn't always a bad thing. Many travelers will tell you that their favorite, most memorable moments are the unexpected ones. We humans are complicated. We want to do what everyone else is doing (e.g., visit the Eiffel Tower) because we don't want to miss out. We also want to do what nobody else is doing because we want to feel special.

I once got an unusual recommendation when traveling in Paris. I'd read more than one novel that mentioned the Parc des Buttes-Chaumont, and I wanted to see it for myself. It's one of the largest green spaces in Paris with a lake and waterfalls and spectacular views of the city. My husband and I took the metro to a station close to the park and found a cozy little bistro where we could have lunch before exploring the park. Partway through the meal, an elegant French lady, sitting alone on her lunch break from work at a florist shop, leaned over and said hello. She had overheard us speaking in English and wanted to practice hers. She asked us about our plans for the day, then suggested we walk along the Canal Saint-Martin (I hadn't even realized that there were canals in Paris) and have a drink at a place that she liked. She couldn't remember the exact name or address of the place, but we got a detailed set of directions based on landmarks (which is how I tend to navigate too—once, when someone asked me where I attended orchestra rehearsals, I said something like: "From the south, turn on the road that has the McDonald's, continue past the train station, then turn left at the roundabout"). I didn't think we had much hope of finding the place but figured we would still have a pleasant walk along the canal as we looked for it, so off we went. And that's how we ended up at a tiki bar in Paris, drinking piña coladas topped with umbrellas, ordered from a bar shaped like a pirate ship.

The fact is that we never know what we'll remember from our travels. I suspect that many of our travel memories are of the people that we met and what we learned from talking to them. Author Elizabeth Barrett Browning said something that rings true for me, and the memories I have of my own travels: "The charm, one might say the genius of memory, is that it is choosy, chancy and temperamental; it rejects the edifying cathedral and indelibly photographs the small boy outside, chewing a hunk of melon in the dust." (Funnily enough, my husband has a travel memory that literally involves a melon.)[23]

I've spent a lot of time talking about what we can learn from strangers while traveling because we seem to be more open to conversations with strangers when we're outside of our natural environment. We also seem to think that our conversations will go better when we're traveling, maybe because it's easy to start a conversation by asking for directions or recommendations. But there's no reason for things to be much different when we're at home. In a way, aren't we traveling when we go into town for a concert or a meal? If we could figure out how to cultivate the same openness—and a bit more social confidence—at home, we would have just as much to learn from talking to strangers. And it would do us some good because we benefit in several ways by learning from strangers—ways that are less likely with our close others.

## Talking to strangers satisfies our curiosity

It's so enjoyable to satisfy our curiosity that we are willing to experience pain (e.g., hear nails scratching on a chalkboard) to do so. And yet, we resist satisfying our curiosity. If we see someone peering through binoculars, we resist asking them what they're looking at. If we see a line of people snaking all the way down the block, we resist asking them what they're waiting for. If we see someone at a restaurant savoring a bite of something that looks delicious, we resist asking what they ordered. It would be so simple to ask: "What are you doing?" or "What's happening?" or "What are you eating?" But we're afraid.

Fear is the enemy of curiosity. In Kashdan's model of curiosity, a surprising component of a person's overall curiosity is their ability to tolerate stress. If we fear uncertainty, fear the unknown, then we're unlikely to engage in the exploration needed to satisfy our curiosity. Data from one of my own studies is consistent with this idea: Participants who were more socially anxious talked to fewer strangers (and those who were more socially curious talked to more strangers).[24] Ironically, then, our fears keep us feeling insecure—they prevent us from learning, which is what helps us feel more secure. If we can find a way to talk to strangers despite our fears, it could make us feel safer and kick off an upward spiral.

Even if we could quell our fears, I suspect we'd still be reluctant to talk to strangers because I think we feel a bit ashamed of our social curiosity. We're taught that it's not polite to stare or to ask too many questions. Nobody likes an intrusive and interfering busybody. It's easy to see how, if we take this to the extreme, we might conclude that we're not allowed to be curious at all about other people. It seems to me that we often try to suppress and conceal our social curiosity. But of course, so do other people, which means that we can't easily see how socially curious they are. As a result, we think we're more socially curious than other people.[25] Trust me: They're just as curious as you are.

When I started talking to strangers, I worried about being too curious. If I asked a person with binoculars what they were looking at, or a person waiting in a long line what they were doing, would they think I was being nosy or even suspicious? According to a (very unscientific) Google search, curious people ask questions to understand, whereas nosy people ask questions to evaluate and judge. (If you're a fellow *Ted Lasso* fan, this might bring to mind the scene where Ted wins a bet, telling his opponent, Rupert, that if he had been curious instead of judgmental, he might not have underestimated Ted's skill at darts.) I came up with a way that I hope signals that I want to understand, not judge: I ask "Whatcha doin'?" (Explicitly telling someone that you're asking out of curiosity would also work.) People seem to understand my intentions, judging by the fact that they're generally happy to answer my question and tell me what they're up to. After all, people want to be seen and understood. And I want to satisfy my curiosity. Win-win.

## Talking to strangers allows us to be more creative

For most of my life, I've considered myself uncreative. When I play the piano, I don't improvise—I follow printed music. When I cook, I don't experiment—I follow a recipe. More than that, it doesn't even occur to me that I might want to try coming up with something new, that it could be fun to just mess around. It's just not how I think.

As I've learned more about creativity, I've had to reconsider. I may be uncreative in terms of divergent thinking: coming up with inventive, original ideas. (Having said that, I get frustrated when people tell me that they could never learn how to sing or learn how to cook or [insert your "never" here]—I think we sell short our potential more often than we should. I've never given myself a chance to develop this sort of creativity, so who knows—maybe with some practice, I'd surprise myself.) However, creativity can also come from convergent thinking: seeing connections between things that on the surface are only remotely associated. Noticing patterns that others don't. This type of creativity feels more accessible to me.

In other words: Creativity isn't just about coming up with brand-new ideas but combining existing ideas in new ways. After all, there are no new stories. According to literature professor Joseph Campbell, all myths follow the same structure: The hero goes on an adventure, faces challenges, is transformed by what they learn, and finally returns to where they started, the better for it. We've all read (or heard or seen) dozens or hundreds of stories that fit this mold. But we keep reading (and listening and watching) because even a story made of the same building blocks can be new and interesting if those building blocks are assembled in new ways.

Convergent thinking starts with ideas that haven't been combined before. Where do those ideas come from? One source of ideas is other people. Especially people like strangers and acquaintances.

Research finds that people we don't know well (i.e., weak ties) are an especially fertile source of new ideas. Imagine you're looking for a new TV show to binge-watch. Your first thought might be to ask a few people who are close to you (i.e., strong ties) if they have any recommendations. Let's say you ask your close friends Maren and Zihao. Chances are that they will recommend something you've already seen. Our close others tend to know the same things that we do, since our close relationships tend to grow from shared values, backgrounds, tastes, and ideas. For similar reasons, Maren is likely to recommend the same shows that Zihao does. Information gets passed around (and stuck) in bubbles.

If you want to find something new to binge-watch, you will probably have more luck asking a weak tie. Although our connections to close friends are cultivated deliberately, many of our connections to weak ties aren't. They arise from context rather than from similarity. We have weak ties with the people who happen to live nearby, the people we happen to work with, the people we happen to see as we go about our daily lives. Our weak ties act like bridges, connecting us to new people, with new information.[26]

How does this relate to creativity? Several studies have looked at creativity in the workplace: the ability to come up with new ideas and find new ways to solve problems. The people that we work with closely are likely to know the same things that we do and are likely to approach problems in the same way that we do—they're the Marens and Zihaos of the workplace. The people that we work with less closely (e.g., people who work in different departments or different organizations) are more likely to expose us to different approaches and perspectives, or prompt us to consider different angles. That's why some tech companies famously design their cafeterias to encourage chance encounters—and thus conversations and idea sharing—between people that don't work together directly. Several workplace studies have found that people who communicate with and get advice from more weak ties at work come up with more creative ideas.[27-29] And it's not just that people *think* they're more creative—their workplace supervisors think so too.

Creative ideas are more likely to come from weak ties not only because weak ties provide us with novel and nonredundant information (information that we didn't already know ourselves and that isn't known by someone else in our social circle) but also because we tend to consider their ideas more carefully.[30] When a strong tie shares an idea, we don't stop and think about it too much. It just feels right, comfortable. Maybe we don't *want* to think about their idea too much because if we discovered that we didn't like it, that would feel uncomfortable; we like our strong tie and so we expect to, and want to, like or agree with their ideas. When an idea comes from a weak tie, we don't have the same expectation. We're more open to weak ties having ideas that are different from ours, and we give their ideas more consideration.

Although much of the research on creativity has focused on weak ties, the reasons that weak ties help us be more creative should also hold true for strangers. Like weak ties, strangers give us access to novel and nonredundant information because strangers are also less similar to us than our strong ties are. In the project led by Stav Atir that I mentioned earlier in this chapter, not only did the researchers find that we learn more from strangers than we expect but that we might learn more, in general, from talking to a stranger than from talking to someone we already know.[31]

The things that we learn from strangers can translate into creative ideas. In one study, Pier Mannucci, now at Università Bocconi, and Jill Perry-Smith at Emory University asked business school students to come up with ideas for something new that could be sold at the university shop.[32] Each person had two five-minute brainstorming conversations and then pitched the idea they thought was most creative. Some people were asked to brainstorm with two close friends, and some people were asked to brainstorm with two strangers. The ideas dreamed up between strangers were rated as more creative than the ideas dreamed up between friends.

## Talking to strangers adds novelty and richness to our lives

A few years ago, I received a series of emails from someone named Sam. He had heard me on a podcast interview, talking about how conversations with strangers go better than we expect. He wasn't convinced that the same would be true in the part of England where he lived, so he decided to test it out for himself. A week later, he reported on two conversations he had started, both of which had gone well: with a package delivery driver that he had seen for years but had never spoken to and with someone while waiting in a line. But it was an email he sent me a month later that has stayed with me. He told me that most of his days are basically the same: He goes to the same places and sees the same people. He doesn't take public transit, and he doesn't have a public-facing job, both of which would afford opportunities for new social interactions. He finished his email by saying that he's started thinking about how he could vary his routine to create more opportunities to cross paths with new people.

Sam's email about routine really got me thinking. It reminded me of some research I'd read about "mobility traces." Every time we make a call on our cell phones, the location of the nearest cellular network antenna is logged. Researchers analyzed fifteen months' worth of this location (mobility) data for 1.5 million people in a small European country.[33] If they knew four places where a person had made calls from during this period, they could figure out which of the 1.5 million people it was, with a staggering 95 percent accuracy. Besides the slightly terrifying implications for the limits of our privacy, what I take away from this is: We really are creatures of habit. In some ways, habit can be positive. Doing something out of habit requires less thinking, which frees up our mental resources for more important tasks. But relying too much on habit has downsides.

Novelty and variety are important to us, though of course we differ in how much novelty/variety we desire and are comfortable with. According to a prominent psychological theory, humans thrive only when three criteria are met: We feel like we have some control over our environment, we feel connected to other people, and we feel capable.[34] Even when people imagine having a job with all of these positive qualities, they expect that they would be in a better mood—and feel more energetic and alive—if their typical day at work involved "different kinds of work and working on new projects" rather than "routine work that is well known to [them]."[35] A life that includes a variety of interesting and perspective-changing experiences is thought to be a psychologically rich life—one definition of a life well-lived.[36]

When we get together with our friends, there's often little spontaneity. We consult our calendars to find a date that works for us, and we decide where to go and what to do together. Meeting up with strangers, on the other hand, is rarely planned. We simply run into strangers as we go about our daily lives: at work, in our neighborhood, at the gym, etc. Encounters with strangers are unexpected, infusing our lives with novelty and variety, and we recognize that this makes strangers interesting.[37]

One of the first conversations I can remember deliberately starting with a stranger, just for fun, was on the subway in Toronto. (I had, of course, talked to strangers when there was reason to or when they had started conversations with me.) I'd just had lunch with a dear friend and was in a particularly good mood. The woman sitting across from me on the train was carrying a gorgeous, decadent cupcake in a clear plastic container on her lap. I commented on the beautifully decorated cupcake, and we got to talking. By the end of the conversation, she had taught me that people can ride ostriches. She had ridden an ostrich herself, on holiday in South Africa. (Years later, after I shared this fun fact in a talk, another stranger informed me that ostrich riding is not simply recreational—there are ostrich races and ostrich jockeys.)

Up until that day on the subway, it hadn't really occurred to me that there would be value in taking the initiative and deliberately starting a conversation with a stranger. Something shifted that day, when I had this unexpected, delightful conversation. I hadn't simply learned a fun fact about ostriches. Our conversation had made my world a little larger, a little richer. From that moment, I was hooked on talking to strangers.

## Learning makes conversations feel meaningful

Learning helps us satisfy our general and social curiosity, helps us be more creative, and adds novelty and richness to our lives. But, more than that, learning might be one of the key things that transforms a conversation from small talk to something more meaningful. According to psychologist Matthias Mehl at the University of Arizona, for a conversation to be meaningful, "the most important point is that you get absorbed in the conversation, there's information, there's learning."[38]

Some part of us seems to know this. When Stav Atir and her research team asked people to imagine having the opportunity to start a conversation before a lecture, on a short flight, at an art museum, or at a sporting event, the more people expected to learn, the more likely they were to start a conversation.[39] That's why it's important to know that we underestimate how much we stand to learn from talking to strangers. And learning isn't something passive that just happens *to* us. We can actively influence how much we learn by tapping into our curiosity and asking questions. One study by Kashdan and his colleagues even finds that highly curious people are able to transform a conversation that might otherwise have been a bit shallow and boring into an opportunity to develop intimacy.[40]

Motivational speaker Charlie "Tremendous" Jones highlighted the importance of learning—and reminded us that we learn from other people—when he said: "You'll be the same person five years from now as you are today except for two things: the people you meet and the books you read." I don't know if Jones included strangers in his definition of "people you've met," but I choose to include them.

I'd like to think that I learn something from each of my conversations with strangers. If nothing else, each conversation is one more reminder that I can have a nice chat with pretty much anyone and that so many people are decent. Often, it's more than that. Sometimes it's a recommendation that I can try out, or a new piece of information that I can use—or that simply delights me (like ostrich riding). Sometimes it's a story that helps me understand the world, other people, or even myself a bit better. As author Thea Astley is said to have put it: "The more you try to be interested in other people, the more you find out about yourself."

And sometimes it's even a piece of my life puzzle. I'll never forget the lawyer who unwittingly showed me a path toward a new beginning when we were supposed to be talking about my life's end.

# 4

# Sowing Seeds

It was intermission for *Madama Butterfly*, and my heart was full, reverberating with Puccini's lush, dramatic music. Act 1 ends with a love duet after Butterfly and Lieutenant Pinkerton get married. The lobby was buzzing as people, drinks in hand, shared their impressions of the performance. Across the crowded hall, I saw a man with green eyes and a contagious grin who I instantly recognized from my undergraduate days—a fellow computer science major. I went over to say hello.

I realized later that, though we had certainly crossed paths, we might not have spoken to each other before that day at the opera. (He thinks we *definitely* spoke back then, but I'm the one writing the book, so . . . ) But the passage of time casts a spell, and sometimes we feel like we know someone better than we do. Evelyn Waugh described this sorcery in *Brideshead Revisited*: "She spoke as though it were a matter of weeks rather than of years; as though, too, before our parting we had been firm friends. . . . Here she and I, who were never friends before, met on terms of long and unbroken intimacy."

This false sense of intimacy made it feel completely natural for me—in my pre-stranger-talking days—to approach my former classmate without thinking. When we were face-to-face, however, my shyness kicked in, and I said something awkward and uninspired, like: "Hey—I know you." Luckily, he recognized me, too, and was a better conversationalist than me. We shared a few laughs, reminiscing about our undergraduate days, talking about our classmates and what they were up to now. When we parted ways before returning to the second half of the opera (spoiler: Things don't go well for Butterfly), he encouraged me to get in touch and gave me his email address.

I must have had an angel on my shoulder, silencing Sid and compelling me to approach that green-eyed not-quite-stranger during the intermission because a few short years later, I married him.

Interactions with strangers can sow various kinds of seeds and/or fertilize dormant seeds so they can germinate and grow:

- seeds of connection that can develop into new acquaintances or friends—or even, as in my case, a new romantic partner
- seeds of opportunity that can enrich your life or advance your career
- seeds of possibility and change that shift your perceptions of who you can be or what you can do in your life

## Seeds of connection

Satisfying relationships are essential to our happiness.[1, 2] We are generally aware that this is the case (though our behavior doesn't always align with this knowledge). In one study, researchers asked people to imagine being eighty-five and looking back on their lives. People knew that their relationships with family and close friends would be the single most important factor affecting how well they had lived.[3]

It's easy to feel like we're failing at life if we don't have a romantic partner or a best friend, or they don't live up to our expectations—which, by the way, are probably set by the unrealistic examples we see on TV or in the movies. But our social worlds are populated by many people who can enrich our life even if we aren't particularly close.

If we think of our social network as a set of concentric circles with us at the center,[4] then our strong ties are the smallest, inner circle. These are the people we feel hard-pressed to imagine living without, the people with whom we feel the most closeness and intimacy. (It's worth noting that researcher Karen Fingerman—now a professor of human development and family sciences at the University of Texas at Austin—and her colleagues found, in a paper cleverly titled "The Best of Ties, the Worst of Ties," that these are also the people who are most likely to push our buttons.)[5]

Moving outward from the center, there are more circles, each larger than the last, with people who are progressively less important in our life, who we feel progressively less close to. Sociologist Mark Granovetter coined the term "weak ties" to describe these relationships.[6] This name can feel a bit derogatory, given how beneficial these relationships can be, but I think of "weak" as simply a relative term, to distinguish them from our strong ties.

Strangers fall outside of the set of circles—outside of our social network—entirely.

When we interact with a stranger, we sow seeds of connection that can potentially grow into weak ties. I first met Sue when we were both walking in our local green space—a mecca for dog walkers with a beautiful view of rolling hills. Sue's tiny dog, Betty, had lost her tiny ball in some long grass, after she lost interest or got distracted (even though Sue, like many dog owners, seems to have an eagle-eyed way of tracking a ball's trajectory that I, as a non–dog owner, marvel at). I helped Sue hunt for Betty's ball. When I saw Sue again a week or two later and we had another chat, we were no longer strangers, but weak ties—mutual recognition marks the thin line between strangers and weak ties. Now when we meet, I ask Sue, who's an author, about her latest children's book, and she's almost knocked off her feet by Betty, who tugs maniacally on her leash to run to me for cuddles and treats. Sue is now part of my social network.

Strangers can also develop into strong ties. After all, if you think about it, all of our strong ties (with the exception of relatives) started off as strangers. That's what happened with the not-quite-stranger I met at the opera, who eventually became my husband. For this to happen, the seeds of connection need to germinate and grow.

Turning a stranger into a weak tie requires little more than repeated exposure,[7] ideally over a short time period—I would have been less likely to recognize Sue and Betty if months had passed between the first and second time I ran into them. Turning a weak tie into a strong tie, however, requires a lot more work. According to communications researcher Jeffrey Hall (who you met in chapter 1), it requires more than two hundred hours of time spent together.[8] Assuming 7.5 hours per day, that works out to almost a month's worth of full-time work, working seven days a week. And we can't just spend that time engaging in small talk. Close friendship is fertilized by self-disclosure and responsiveness: showing that we understand, validate, and care for the other person.

## Not all seeds of connection bear fruit, and that's OK

Over time, we can grow closer to people, and they can move toward the center of our network. But just because strangers *can* turn into weak ties, and weak ties *can* turn into strong ties, that isn't to say that they *should*. Judging by the way we act, we sometimes seem to struggle to simply enjoy our relationships for what they are, and instead we seem compelled to turn them into something else. Have you ever said to someone "Let's keep in touch," and meant it but never got around to sending them a message? Or has someone said to you "Let's grab a coffee some time," and you said "Absolutely!," genuinely thinking that it would be nice but knowing deep down that it was unlikely to happen? We've all been there. I think we *want* to pursue these relationships (making new friends expands our world), but we also know that relationships take time, and time is a limited resource—the vast majority of us feel like there isn't enough time in the day to do everything we'd like to do.[9]

Instead of feeling guilty about not being able to develop and explore every relationship, perhaps we could be kinder to ourselves and simply learn to accept and value our relationships as they are. Just to be clear: I'm not suggesting that we should never make new friends or deepen existing friendships. I'm simply saying: It's OK if some (indeed, most) strangers never develop into weak ties, and it's OK if some (most) weak ties never develop into strong ties.

Just as people can move toward the center of our social network, they can also move away from the center, toward the edges. Sometimes, people we were once close to revert to feeling like total strangers and fall out of our network altogether. I think we could stand to feel less guilty when weak tie relationships lapse. When we move to a new job, move to a new neighborhood, or move away for school, it's easy to lose touch with people that we were close to. When this happens, it's easy to wonder: *Did I ever really like them?* (or *Did they ever really like me?*, if we listen to Sid). Some relationships are context-dependent and naturally lapse when the context changes. That doesn't mean that the relationships weren't real or didn't provide value while they lasted.

One reason that we needn't feel compelled to convert strangers to weak ties and weak ties to strong ties is that there's value in having social interactions, regardless of who they're with. In one of my earliest research studies, which I ran with my PhD supervisor Elizabeth Dunn at the University of British Columbia, I asked people to carry around tally counters: small, mechanical devices that are used to count things. (If I ran the study again today, I'd just use an app—times have changed.) I asked people to click a red tally counter every time they interacted with a strong tie and a black tally counter every time they interacted with a weak tie. I found that people are happier on days when they have more interactions with strong ties. No surprise there. But after accounting for interactions with strong ties, people are happier on days when they have more interactions with weak ties.[10] Both types of interactions benefit us. (Aside: This doesn't mean that we should feel compelled to have as many interactions as possible; there's probably a sweet spot, after which there are diminishing returns.)[11]

Not only do social interactions with strangers, weak ties, and strong ties all provide value, but they might each provide value in different ways. I probably don't need to tell you all the benefits we can expect from strong ties, including fun and enjoyment, appreciation and care, and emotional support.[12] We may be able to enjoy some of the same benefits from weak ties and strangers, but we may experience these benefits more fully (or be more likely to experience them) with our strong ties. On the other hand, weak ties and strangers provide psychological distance that allows for more objectivity and perspective (chapter 2) and access to novel and nonredundant information (chapter 3) in ways that strong ties can't.

The fact that different types of relationships provide different types of benefits may explain the results of a set of studies by Hanne Collins, now at UCLA, and her colleagues. Using data from more than fifty thousand people in eight countries, Collins showed that people are happier when their social interaction partners are more varied.[13] For example, a person who has four interactions with different partners, such as a stranger, a neighbor, a teammate, and a family member, is likely to be a bit happier than a person who has the same number of interactions but all of them with the same person (e.g., their spouse).

Diversification is also an issue for animals foraging for food. They need to decide between returning to a food patch that they already know or exploring in the hopes of finding new options. Exploiting a known patch takes less time and energy, and it's safer in the short-term—a guarantee of finding food. But longer-term, the food will run out at that patch and it's best to have a plan before that happens. Exploring is the only way to find a new patch, which might even end up being better than the first one. But success isn't guaranteed. The wisest course is to find a balance between exploitation and exploration.

Researchers at the University of Virginia and the University of Chicago propose that the same is true for humans and our social relationships: We need to find a balance between building new relationships and deepening existing ones.[14] They argue that many of us (because, of course, we differ in our preferences and capacity) are biased toward exploitation—toward sticking to the people we already know—but that we stand to benefit if we can find more of a balance, by complementing with more social exploration.

Over the past few decades, it has become increasingly clear just how important social connection is for our mental and physical health.[15] Having at least one person to count on in times of need—presumably a strong tie—is crucial for our well-being,[16] but imagine if you could only talk to one person for the rest of your life! During the early days of Covid-19 lockdowns, we inadvertently got a preview of what it would be like to have limited conversation partners. We were cut off from strangers and weak ties, many of whom were inextricably connected to our temporarily abandoned daily routines.[17] This deprived us of novelty and spontaneity and feelings of connection. I'm hoping that we learned just how important it is to interact with a variety of partners, to explore as well as exploit, and to find various ways to fill our need for connection.

Encouragingly, research has uncovered more and more sources of connection. We feel more connected after interacting with weak ties and strangers,[18, 19] of course, but also from:

- daydreaming about other people[20]
- one-sided (i.e., parasocial) relationships (e.g., with a favorite actor or celebrity, or even a fictional character)[21]
- feeling like a part of a group (based on identity or interests)[22]

I find this research encouraging. It means that we're not doomed to loneliness or unhappiness if we don't have a certain ideal number of close friends, or our social network doesn't have a certain ideal number of people in each circle. Each of us can find our own ways to feel connected, through whatever mix of strong ties, weak ties, strangers, and other sources that works for us.[23]

## Seeds of opportunity

When you think of networking, what comes to mind? If you're like me, you might think of an event that you don't really want to attend, in which a room full of strangers have awkward, impersonal conversations in a strategic attempt to extract something useful from one another. Or, you might think of a nepotistic group that you're not a member of (e.g., alumni from some fancy institution), who succeed in business by swapping favors. For many of us, networking "conjure[s] images of sleaze and desperation."[24]

But, at its core networking is about two things. First and foremost, networking is about building relationships. You do this in the same way as you sow seeds for social relationships. Whether you intend it or not, whether you know it or not, talking to strangers *is* networking. The topic of work often comes up in social conversations: You might discuss the type of work you do (people are always asking "What do you do for a living?") or something that happened at work.

The second part of networking is leveraging your relationships after you build them. People engage in networking for various reasons: Sometimes, people are motivated to gain status and the recognition of their peers. Other times, people are motivated to learn from others' expertise. Yet other times, people hope to advance their careers, such as by finding out about new job opportunities.[25] It's this aspect of networking—leveraging relationships—that can feel icky. It sounds like encouragement to treat people as means to an end, to be nice to people only so that you can get something from them.

But, if you think about it, don't we get something from our social relationships too? The people in our lives provide a mirror that helps us understand our own strengths and weaknesses. They go with us to a movie or afternoon tea, listen to us complain about daily stressors and grievances, make us feel appreciated and loved.[26] Why doesn't this feel icky too? Perhaps one difference is that we don't consciously build social relationships with these ends in mind.

Michael Yeomans, Maurice Schweitzer, and Alison Wood-Brooks have proposed that our conversational goals fall along two axes: relational (i.e., focused on building a relationship) and informational (i.e., focused on exchanging information).[27] Perhaps social relationships are more often motivated by relational goals and networking relationships are more often motivated by informational goals. We may have different goals than our conversation partner. This can make conversations challenging—or it can bring unforeseen benefits. On several occasions, I have reached out to a stranger for purely relational reasons and ended up benefitting in an informational/networky sort of way:

- In a professional society newsletter, I read a nice profile of a researcher that I'd never met but had once exchanged an email with. I emailed the researcher to congratulate her on the profile, and she ended up inviting me to collaborate on an exciting research project.

- While I was completing my PhD in Canada, I attended a talk given by a professor visiting from Norway. A few years later, I spotted him at a conference in Amsterdam and said hello, not knowing if he'd even remember me. I was just being friendly, happy to see a familiar face. He ended up inviting me to give a talk at the University of Oslo. That was my first invited talk and is still the only time that someone has paid for me to fly somewhere to give one.
- Browsing a conference program, I saw that a PhD student was presenting a poster that sounded interesting, on how people manage their emotions. The point of a poster session is for a researcher to share their work, usually in its early stages, and have a chance to receive feedback. Ideally, other people ask helpful questions that shape your next steps. I once presented a poster at a conference where not a single person showed any interest in my work. Because of how demoralizing that felt, I thought it would be a nice thing to do, to chat with this PhD student about her fascinating work, even though it was on a topic that I didn't know much about. She later invited me to be an early guest on a student-led podcast, giving me an opportunity to share my research with a broader audience. That podcast now has more than 150 episodes and a million downloads.

I suspect these opportunities came my way precisely because I was focused on *building* relationships, rather than *leveraging* them. Because I was offering something—friendship, encouragement—rather than asking for something. I didn't engage in any of those conversations because I expected they would help my career. Research seems to back up this hunch. In one study, by Maya

Rossignac-Milon, now at the University of Navarra, and her colleagues, people attended a networking event and recorded their impressions of the people they had met.[28] Weeks later, they were more likely to have followed up with the people who they thought had been more authentic.

Seeds of opportunity can arise when you least expect them, and they aren't always related to work. One day, on a walk, I encountered two beautiful Irish Setters and stopped to give them treats. (I carry treats in my pocket so that I can make furry friends, like Betty from earlier.) I overhead two middle-aged women talking nearby. One said something about not having read a particular book yet, and the other said something about there still being time. Although it felt awkward to admit that I'd overhead them, I asked if they were talking about a book club. They told me what book they were reading that month (which I happened to have read), and we happily nerded out about books for a few minutes. As I said goodbye, they invited me to join their book club and added me to their WhatsApp group. They couldn't have known that I was a lifelong reader and had always wanted to try a book club. I'm sure I surprised them by showing up to the next meeting. (Hi, Colchester book club ladies—and book club members everywhere!)

## Seeds of possibility

When you're a kid, people keep asking you what you want to be when you grow up. I had no idea. How could I? Nobody told me what all the options were or how to choose between them. I knew that "teacher" was an option because I saw teachers in action every day at school (not to mention that I lived with two of them). So, maybe it's no surprise that a poll conducted in 2019 found that "teacher" was a common career aspiration for eight- to twelve-year-olds in the US and the UK (though kids wanted to be a YouTuber even more than they wanted to be a teacher).[29]

When I was a kid, my world was small: It consisted of my neighborhood and my school. (And what I learned from reading stories or watching TV. I picked up a lot of Perry Mason novels at used book sales, so for a long time I wanted to be a criminal lawyer.) As I got older and gained more life experience, my world expanded. Paradoxically, this has made me ever more aware that *my* world is small, compared to the vastness of *the* world. Talking to strangers reminds us of this by continually expanding our understanding of what is possible.

You might think that as adults we would have a good idea of the employment options that are available to us. I'm not sure this is true. According to stand-up comedian Paula Poundstone: "Adults are always asking little kids what they want to be when they grow up because they're looking for ideas."

I'm still learning about all the fascinating things that people do. By talking to strangers, I've met:

- a theatrical wigmaker who crafted hairpieces for a Harry Potter movie,
- a musician in a band that welcomes foreign dignitaries at the airport,
- a volunteer who provides first aid to bats, and multiple bat counters, who sit in lawn chairs with clipboards as darkness approaches,

- a conservation specialist, who was conducting the annual calibration of devices that monitor the temperature and humidity of display cases at a museum,
- a volunteer "lookerer," who keeps an eye on the welfare of cows and sheep on behalf of a wildlife trust, and
- a sperm bank manager (my first question to him was: Do you receive a lot of thank-you cards?).

Although I'm not on the lookout for a new career (been there, experienced that existential angst), I still see each of these people as a role model. Some role models show us how to reach a specific goal, and some inspire us to set new goals. In this case, I'm thinking of a third kind of role model: one who shows us what's possible.[30] Conversations like these show me not only that a particular thing is possible (i.e., it's possible to make a living as a theatrical wigmaker) but remind me about possibility itself—that the world presents an endless array of options.

We want our role models to provide living proof that our goals are attainable, to show us that someone *like us* can achieve what they have achieved. Female students in biology, chemistry, and engineering feel more positively toward math and attempt more questions on a math test when they're told that the test was created by a female researcher rather than a male one.[31] It makes all the difference to have a living demonstration of a woman succeeding in math. As the saying goes: You've got to see it to be it.

The most effective role models are often similar to us: They come from the same background or share the same gender. If, on the other hand, a person seems too different from us, we can write off their success as something unique and special about them, something that doesn't apply to us. Because of this, strangers might serve as surprisingly effective role models. If we talk to a random stranger—nobody special, just someone that we happened to cross paths with—and find out that they've done remarkable things, it seems like incontrovertible proof that *anyone* can do remarkable things. Even us.

## Seeds of change

Talking to strangers can prompt us to think about the things we would like to do, but it can also make us reflect on who we are and who we want to be. After all, it's our experiences in the world that help us make sense of our own identity so that we're not strangers to ourselves. As poet Mary Oliver said in *Upstream*: "In the beginning I was so young and such a stranger to myself I hardly existed. I had to go out into the world and see it and hear it and react to it, before I knew at all who I was, what I was, what I wanted to be."

People change. After a health scare, we might decide to spend less time at work and more time with family. After listening to mostly classical music for decades, we might find ourselves humming the latest song by Taylor Swift. After watching a persuasive documentary, we might adopt a different stance on euthanasia. But it's not just our goals, preferences, and minds that change. Even our personalities—which can feel like the unchanging essence of who we are—evolve. The largest changes to our personality happen when we are between the ages of twenty and forty, but changes continue into old age. We tend to become steadily more agreeable and conscientious as we age, but a bit less sociable and open to experiences in older age.[32]

But we seem to forget (or maybe we're unaware) that we have this capacity to change. When you ask a group of eighteen-year-olds to predict how much their personality, values, and preferences will change by the time they're twenty-eight, they underestimate how much they're likely to change. We know that because people who are already twenty-eight say they have changed more over the past decade than those eighteen-year-olds expect to change.[33] (And the same is true at any age, up to fifty-eight- vs. sixty-eight-year-olds, which was the oldest group the researchers studied.) Strangers can remind us of the possibility of change.

While working as a clinical psychologist with the National Health Service in the UK, Mike Slade witnessed the potential for strangers to sow seeds of change.[34] He noticed that clinicians treating people with mental health issues would often recommend that their patients read an autobiographical account of a stranger's recovery from a similar issue. Nobody had ever tested if this was actually effective, so Slade secured some funding to do just that. He and his colleagues created a library of more than six hundred recovery stories that they had gathered, of people's struggles and their successes.[35] Then they recruited people who had recently experienced mental health–related distress, such as low mood, stress, and anxiety. Finally, they put the stories to the test. They gave some people access to the library of recovery stories, whereas others weren't given access until the end of the study. The people who had access to the stories felt better about their lives and felt more purpose and meaning. Reading the strangers' stories gave people hope and made them feel less alone in their struggles. (You're obviously a reader like me. Maybe you, too, have engaged in some bibliotherapy, for example, reading a novel with grief as a main theme when you're dealing with bereavement.)

When you strike up a conversation with a stranger, you're unlikely to hear a story as intense and personal as one about mental health recovery (though people often unburden themselves to strangers, so it's not unheard of). But even everyday conversations with strangers can sow seeds of change.

Melanie Tait wrote about dog park conversations in an opinion piece in *The Guardian*.[36] She tells a story about how a woman whose name she doesn't know gave her life advice that (eventually) resulted in her selling her house, moving to a new city, and leaving her safe job to be a playwright. This woman, known only as "Skippy's mum," helped Melanie envision the possibility of a new path (just as a midlife lawyer did for me).

These reminders of the possibility of change are powerful, as demonstrated in the research on "best possible selves." Dozens of studies now have asked people to: "Think about your life in the future. Imagine that everything has gone as well as it possibly could. You have worked hard and succeeded at accomplishing all of your life goals. Think of this as the realization of all of your life dreams."[37]

People who follow these instructions and envision (and write about) their life changing for the better (vs. people who write about a typical day or other mundane topics) are in a better mood afterward and feel more optimistic.[38] And these positive feelings can motivate people to take action to bring about the change they hope for. Because sowing seeds is one thing, but then we need to help them grow.

## Fertilizing seeds

When we're kids, we sow our garden with seeds of possibility: Maybe I'll sing on Broadway. Maybe I'll be a pilot and travel to exotic places around the world. Maybe I'll become a marine biologist and swim with dolphins. But most of the seeds don't germinate and grow because we don't know how (or forget) to fertilize them. Seeds planted in soil need sun and water and nutrients in order to grow. Seeds of possibility and change need sustenance in the form of information, encouragement, and inspiration.

When I learned that my lawyer had switched to a new profession midlife, it planted a seed of possibility and made me think: *Maybe I could start over too.* Deciding that I no longer wanted to be a computer programmer was the easy part. Deciding what exactly I wanted to do instead, well, that was a lot harder. I became fascinated by the relatively new field of positive psychology. Maybe it was completely clichéd—someone who had been unhappy in her personal and professional lives wanting to learn more about the science of happiness and the conditions under which people can flourish—but I couldn't imagine anything more important or interesting to learn about. I thought I might like to study for a PhD. Seeds of possibility had been sowed, but I didn't know if they were viable. (Sid, unsurprisingly, didn't think so.)

I didn't know anyone who had done a PhD, so everything I knew was based on pop culture. I thought you had to be some sort of genius to do a PhD, and I'm *not* that. Although I worked hard and earned good grades during my undergraduate degree, there were plenty of people who earned even better ones. Maybe doing a PhD was not a feasible option for me. I needed more information.

By accident, poking around online, I found out about a small psychology conference that was taking place at a university nearby, less than an hour's drive from home. (Better still, there was no cost to attend!) I showed up and, with butterflies in my stomach, found my way around the campus, which I'd carefully scoped out online before I arrived. I found the registration desk and picked up my name badge, struggling to shake the feeling that someone would figure out that I was an imposter and ask me to leave.

I took a few deep breaths to calm my nerves. I was on a mission: find someone who could help me understand what it was like to do a PhD. I worked up my courage, approached a small group of people, and asked: "Are you PhD students?"

What I didn't know at the time is that one of the main purposes of conferences is networking, and the people who attend are generally open to meeting new people. Because conferences draw attendees from many institutions, many people who attend—and PhD students in particular—only know a handful of other people. The PhD students that I approached had just met one another, so talking to another new person (me) was just par for the course.

They asked me whether I was a PhD student too.

"No," I said, "but I think I might like to do a PhD. What's your experience been like?"

They were surprised that someone would attend a conference without being a PhD student already, but they were happy to share their experiences. They told me what their research was about—and taught me that the best way to start a conversation with a PhD student is to ask "What's your research about?"

I spent the day at the conference listening to research talks. I learned about all sorts of interesting research findings (e.g., sometimes people who struggle to speak after having a stroke can communicate by singing instead, since talking and singing use different parts of the brain!)—and a few not so interesting ones. But those talks also gave me a window into what academics do, how research is done. I even learned my first lessons about how to (and how *not* to) communicate research to others.

My new acquaintances checked in with me throughout the day, curious about how well I was understanding the talks, since I didn't have any training on the topic. I could get the gist of most of the talks. I didn't understand the nitty-gritty details of the statistical analysis, but that didn't usually stand in the way of understanding the results. One talk, though, had been fairly impenetrable. It involved measurement of something called event-related potentials (ERPs), which I gathered were some kind of brain responses. The presentation contained graphs with little squiggly lines and cryptic labels like "P300." I admitted that I'd found the ERP talk confusing, but it turned out that my new acquaintances understood as little about ERPs as I did, which was reassuring.

Spending the day with these students helped crystallize my desire to do a PhD. I'd enjoyed spending time with them, which meant that I'd probably enjoy spending time doing a PhD, with other students like them. And I hadn't felt like the only ignorant person in a room full of geniuses. The fact that I had understood most of the talks—and had been reassured that my new acquaintances didn't understand everything either—made me feel that I might be smart enough to take on a PhD. This group of strangers made me feel welcome. They fertilized my seeds of possibility by providing me with additional information about what it would be like to do a PhD, by being inspiring role models, and by encouraging me to follow this new path. They made me feel like I belonged in a future I didn't yet have.

## Growing seeds to maturity

In the end, seeds only grow to maturity if we take action. It often doesn't take much—one single step in a new direction turns into another. Mountaineer William Murray talks about the importance of taking the first step in *The Scottish Himalayan Expedition*: "The moment one definitely commits oneself, then providence moves too. A whole stream of events issues from the decision, raising in one's favor all manner of unforeseen incidents, meetings, and material assistance, which no man could have dreamt would have come his way."

A series of baby steps eventually resulted in me changing careers midlife. I attended a conference and met some PhD students. I contacted a professor and started attending their lab meetings. I volunteered to help out with a study that a PhD student was running. I learned about an opportunity to apply for a master's degree, and I submitted an application. None of these steps were very large, and yet they added up to something massive: I was accepted into a master's program, and I was on my way. It took more than a decade, but when I received my first academic job offer, I finally reaped the harvest of the seeds that had been sown so long ago, during that life-altering meeting with my lawyer.

Conversations with strangers have sowed seeds of connection and opportunity for me and have fertilized seeds of possibility and change. If you're someone who hasn't thought before about talking to strangers, by writing this book (which is a very elaborate sort of conversation), I'm sowing a seed of possibility for you (i.e., a stranger), showing you that so much good can come from talking to strangers. Or, if you're someone who's already motivated to talk to strangers but haven't yet taken action, then I may be fertilizing a seed for you. Once you start talking to strangers, you'll be sowing and fertilizing seeds for others, just by being yourself and sharing your thoughts and experiences. You won't ever see those seeds grow, but you'll know that it's happening because you'll see seeds grow within you.

In my university days, I sowed seeds of connection by repeatedly crossing paths with a green-eyed stranger. Those seeds lay dormant until a decade later, when a chance encounter at the opera awakened them. Hundreds of hours of conversation fertilized those seeds. It's been more than twenty years now since I attended *Madama Butterfly* and met my husband. I'm still enjoying the fruits of my harvest.

# 5

# Feeling Seen and Seeing Together

I walked across campus feeling like an imposter. The meeting with my lawyer had planted a seed of possibility, and conversations with PhD students at a conference had fertilized it. Now, that seed had grown into a new career direction: I'd left behind a stable, well-paying career as a computer programmer to start a master's degree in psychology. Questions churned through my mind as I carried my heavy backpack around the maze of buildings on campus: *Will I be able to keep up, despite not having an undergraduate degree in psychology? Am I smart enough to be here? Did I just make a really bad decision?* (Sid was on overdrive.)

As well as being worried about my intellectual ability, I was feeling socially ill at ease. Most of the other students had started a master's directly after completing an undergraduate degree, so I had ten years' more work and life experience than they did. But it wasn't just that I felt conspicuously different on campus—I also felt very small and anonymous commuting to downtown Toronto, the largest city in Canada. I wasn't used to big cities. I grew up first on a rural Christmas tree farm and then in the suburbs of a small city. Commuting to campus meant walking through bustling crowds that invaded my personal space. It meant assaulting my ears with the cacophony that resulted from neighboring shops each playing different music. For an introvert like me, it was overstimulating. There were times when all I wanted was to retreat to my living room, dive under a cozy blanket, and shut out the world.

I slowly started to feel more comfortable about my new social environment, thanks in no small part to an unexpected source: a lady who worked at a hot dog stand. Each week, when I walked between the research lab and my supervisor's office, I'd pass a hot dog stand. One day, the lady who worked there smiled and waved at me, or maybe I smiled and waved at her—I can't recall the exact moment. From then on, whenever I walked past, we would smile and wave at each other. It made me happy to see her and to be seen and recognized by her. I hope the same was true for her, but I'll never know. (I did, however, recently receive an email from a different hot dog vendor in Toronto, who told me that they've developed lots of friendly relationships and experienced "not occasional but constant" acts of kindness.) It took me a while to realize that I always felt better after seeing her, and if she wasn't there, it was unsettling—things just didn't feel right that day. I never did buy a hot dog, and we never spoke. Not even once. But my nodding acquaintanceship with this not-quite-stranger, more than anything else, made me feel that I belonged on campus and eased my transition to graduate school.

I realized that I had other relationships that were similar to the one with the hot dog lady. There was Barry at the pet store, who knew my cat's name and would always ask after Nugget. There was Denise who worked at the reception desk at the fitness club, who I'd have a little chat with on my way to the tennis court. Even my dentist, who loved to travel, would always tell me about his latest adventure and ask me if I'd been anywhere nice. (I heard more about his travels than he did about mine because it's hard to talk while a dentist is poking around in your mouth.) These "micro-relationships" made me feel safe and at home in the world. I was woven into the fabric of my campus, my neighborhood, my community by the threads that connected me to these people.

As a budding scientist training for a career of asking (research) questions, I started to wonder if other people had their own micro-relationships, and whether they benefitted from theirs as much as I did from mine. Could these kinds of relationships be more valuable than we realized? Had I stumbled on an overlooked source of happiness and connection?

## A chat with a stranger can make us feel connected

A few years later, when I'd finished my master's degree and started a PhD, my adviser, Elizabeth Dunn, who studies what makes people happy, asked me what made *me* happy. When I told her "the hot dog lady," she looked at me like I'd just said, "licking the sidewalk." My experience with the hot dog lady felt a bit like being a "regular." When I framed it that way—asking Liz if she had a favorite coffee shop, where the barista knew her name and remembered her usual order—the hot dog lady made more sense to her. She helped me design some research studies to explore these micro-relationships. Although psychologists hadn't really studied these relationships (instead focusing their attention on close relationships), they *had* been studied by sociologists, who dubbed them "weak ties."[1]

I wanted to run a study at a coffee shop to understand what value people got from being a regular, but it proved to be tricky to study rigorously (you can't randomly assign someone to be a regular or a nonregular).[2] Instead, I asked people to *act like* a regular.

I stood on the sidewalk outside of a Starbucks in a busy shopping area and offered people a gift card in exchange for participating in my study. (I bought a *lot* of Starbucks gift cards—the cash register receipt was longer than I am tall.) Lots of people were suspicious about being stopped as they walked down the street, but plenty were happy to fill out a short survey in exchange for a free coffee. I asked some of my study participants to act like a regular: smile, make eye contact, and have a genuine social interaction. I asked others to be as efficient as possible: have their money ready and avoid unnecessary conversation.[3] Both sets of people went into Starbucks, used their gift card to buy a treat, and afterward, filled out a short survey.

It turns out that the people who had acted like a regular, by chatting with the barista, were in a better mood and felt more connected than the people who had efficiently gone about making their purchase. They benefitted from turning what could have been a businesslike interaction into a more social one. Even though this was a one-off conversation, rather than a set of repeated interactions like mine, this "barista bump" nevertheless matched my experience of feeling a bounce in my step and a sense of belonging on campus after greeting the hot dog lady.

After I did a podcast interview for the American Psychological Association in 2021, my mom did something very momlike: She emailed the link to her friend Mary. A few days later, Mary responded to share a story: "I met the FedEx lady a few weeks ago, and she was really friendly. She delivers for our area, and she welcomed me to the neighborhood when I moved in. I've seen her a few times since, and she always waves or gives a little beep. That happened today, and it made me feel much more connected to this new place. It reminded me of Gillian's hot dog lady."

Moving is often considered one of the most stressful common life events, negatively affecting our physical and mental health. Making connections, like Mary did with her FedEx lady, can make a real difference to how easily we adjust after a move. Research on a small set of newcomers found that the more weak ties people added to their social networks during their first few months in a new city, the less stress and fewer depressive symptoms they reported.[4] They even had lower systolic blood pressure.

Although conversations with strangers often leave us feeling a general sense of connection to others, sometimes they uncover a literal connection. Years ago, my dad woke up at stupid o'clock to go fishing for sockeye salmon on the Fraser River, which originates in the Rocky Mountains, squeezes through a narrow canyon at Hell's Gate, and empties into the ocean near Vancouver. I've never been fishing, but I imagine blissful solitude, water sparkling in the sunshine, the peaceful sound of water gurgling. Yet, somehow, my dad came home from fishing that day and told me that he'd met my piano teacher's brother. Of course he had.

This unexpected connection was a reminder of how it really is a small world. You may have heard the idea of "six degrees of separation"—that you're connected to most people in the world through a chain of acquaintances of acquaintances that's about six links long. This has been borne out by research: in the 1960s using postcards and in the 2000s using email.[5, 6]

The principle of six degrees of separation also holds true in Hollywood. Through the magic of word of mouth, people started to play "Six Degrees of Kevin Bacon," by finding a connection between Kevin Bacon and any other actor, via mutual costars. For example, Samuel L. Jackson has costarred with John Ratzenberger (in *Incredibles 2*), who has costarred with Kevin Bacon (in *She's Having a Baby*), so he has a Bacon number of 2. Kevin Bacon is connected to about 1.3 million actors, with an average Bacon number of 3.1.[7] Only 0.2 percent of Hollywood actors have a Bacon number higher than 6. Nevertheless, the game *should* really be called "Six Degrees of Samuel L. Jackson," because more Hollywood actors are connected to Samuel L. Jackson by 6 or fewer links than to Kevin Bacon.

All this to say: It's not a surprise that my dad had a two-degree connection to another fisherman, but it *is* a surprise (and a testament to his conversational skill) that he was able to uncover this connection during a conversation while fishing in a relatively remote location. I'll try not to be surprised if I ever find out that someone (maybe you?) ends up reading this book because they happened to run into my dad at the grocery store or the golf course or . . .

## A simple acknowledgment can make us feel connected too

Not long ago, I went to hear the London Philharmonic Orchestra perform in Brighton, where I live. I didn't want to deal with rush-hour traffic and expensive parking, so I took the bus. As I boarded, I made eye contact with the young male bus driver and said a genuine hello.

About seven hours later, after a few errands, a nice dinner, and the concert, I got on a bus to return home and was greeted with: "Nice to see you again." I was flattered that the driver remembered me; it's a busy route, and hundreds of passengers must have come and gone since he had seen me. I suspect he remembered me because I'd taken the time—mere seconds—to acknowledge him when I got on the bus. In my Starbucks study, having a chat with the barista helped people feel connected, but even without a conversation, the bus driver's acknowledgment made me feel at home in my neighborhood.

The bus driver in Brighton seemed to appreciate the fact that I'd acknowledged him, but that's not necessarily a given. It's possible that, instead, bus drivers feel that they need to manage their emotions and always be friendly with passengers, even when they're having an awful day themselves. People in all sorts of customer-facing jobs (e.g., nurses, flight attendants, waiters) perform this "emotional labor," which can negatively affect their well-being and job performance.[8] The only way to know what bus drivers think is to ask them. Luckily, I was hired by a social connection enterprise called Neighbourly Lab to consult on a project that did exactly that. We asked seventy-seven bus drivers in London, and a whopping 87 percent said that they appreciate passengers greeting or thanking them.[9] Encouraged by this, we put stickers on buses to try to encourage passengers to greet and thank bus drivers more often (which, by the way, was a success—sometimes people just need a little reminder). Afterward, we asked drivers how our sticker experiment had gone. They said things like "It's nice, it reminds passengers that we are human beings as well."

Bus drivers generally appreciate being acknowledged by passengers, but research led by Gul Gunaydin, now at Sabanci University, shows that passengers also benefit from this minimal social interaction. University-operated shuttle buses depart from downtown Ankara, Turkey, to transport students and staff to the Bilkent University campus. Gul and her colleagues asked passengers on some journeys to make eye contact with the driver and sincerely express their good wishes and gratitude when they exited the bus.[10] On other journeys, they asked passengers not to speak to the driver, which is the norm in Ankara. When passengers exited the bus, they filled out a short survey. Those who spoke to the driver were in a better mood after their commute, even though they'd only spoken, on average, three words to the driver.

Of course, the benefits of acknowledging and being acknowledged by a stranger aren't limited to bus journeys. I teamed up with Gul and her colleagues Esra Ascigil, Emre Selcuk, and Erdal Aydin to collect data from thousands of people in Turkey, using questions that would allow us to compare the data to responses from a large preexisting dataset, whose respondents were primarily from the UK. We found that, in both countries, people who regularly talk to strangers (like bus drivers) report being more satisfied with their lives.[11] Similarly, using data from a nationally representative sample in Japan, Itaru Ishiguro found that people who had more micro-interactions (e.g., greeting, thanking, or having a little chat) were happier.[12]

I think what it boils down to is: A conversation—or a simple acknowledgment—creates a moment of connection, where both people feel seen.

## Feeling unseen can be painful

Imagine you're a barista, and a customer orders a half heavy-cream/half whole-milk latte, with two Sweet'N Low, Irish-cream syrup, steamed to *exactly* 100 degrees (one Redditor's answer to "Weirdest/most specific coffee order you've served?" on r/barista).[13] Now imagine that the customer barks out this very specific coffee order while texting on their phone and doesn't look at you even once as they order, pay, and leave. On the one hand, that's just part of the job: take drink orders, serve your customers, be polite and helpful regardless of how they treat you. If someone you *knew* treated you this way, you'd be annoyed that they were ignoring you. But when it's a customer, you don't mean anything to them and they don't mean anything to you, so it doesn't necessarily feel bad. But you're also a human being, and feeling unseen, overlooked, or ignored can feel hurtful, even when there's no reason to take it personally.

Being treated as no more than a tool for someone else's purposes is the definition of objectification.[14] There's an inherent power imbalance in objectification: Someone more powerful treats someone less powerful as a means to an end. Simply remembering a time when we felt powerful versus powerless makes us more likely to focus on how others can be useful to us.[15] It doesn't feel like a stretch, then, to imagine that when people who provide services—make us a coffee, drive us to our destination, deliver a package—are ignored, they could potentially feel subordinate or used.

A few years ago, I visited Winchester Cathedral, which is the longest (but not largest) medieval cathedral in the world and the resting place of beloved author Jane Austen. A large, cheery, teddy bear of a man in ecclesiastic robes was greeting people as they arrived and providing visitor information. Knowing how bad it feels to be unseen (and, spoiler alert: how good it feels to be seen) makes me want to do more to acknowledge my fellow humans. I looked him in the eye and asked him how he was doing. He responded: "Nobody ever asks me that. It's my job to ask *you* that question. You've made my day!" His response was a heartbreaking illustration of the extent to which we overlook one another. I've had similar exchanges with several waiters, a family doctor, and a train driver (though, to be fair, train drivers are often hidden in their "offices" at the front of the train), among others. The most surprising story I heard was from a dental hygienist, who told me that one of her patients took a video call while getting their teeth cleaned. (I have so many questions. Also: Nobody needs to see that.)

Is it different when a person doesn't provide a service? Maybe not. We tend not to notice the person waiting behind us in a line or sitting next to us on the bus or at the movies. Again, because neither of us means anything to the other, being overlooked in these situations doesn't necessarily feel bad—it's just a form of polite "civil inattention." In these cases, the lack of acknowledgment is unlikely to stem from objectification—we're not focused on what we can get from the person standing behind us in the line. But there's a hidden implication: We don't think there's anything *to* get from the person standing behind us in the line. Therein lies the problem.

When we focus on achieving a goal, we evaluate who or what might help us, and who or what might hinder us. When we think someone can't help us and can't hurt us, they're irrelevant to our goal, and they become almost invisible to us.[16] Whether you're intending to or not, ignoring someone might therefore risk sending them the message that they're unimportant and have no value. And presumably, the opposite is true: When we feel ignored, it's all too easy to conclude that we're unimportant and have no value. (I can hear Sid cackling gleefully.)

## Feeling seen makes us feel connected

A story shared on LinkedIn reminded me of the power of a simple acknowledgment. At a networking event, Geri was approached by Rasheedat, who wanted to thank her. A few years earlier, Rasheedat had attended a conference and made a comment that Geri had acknowledged, with a smile and a nod. At the time, Rasheedat had been struggling with loneliness and self-doubt, and Geri's acknowledgment had made her "feel seen in a world where she felt utterly invisible." To Geri, it had been a tiny action—she didn't even remember doing it. But to Rasheedat, it had meant so much that she still remembered it several years later.

Feeling unseen can be negative, making us feel used or unimportant, so it makes sense that feeling seen can be positive. I find it moving and empowering to know that simply making eye contact with someone can have positive consequences. In a clever study by Eric Wesselmann, now at Illinois State University, and his colleagues, a researcher walked past people on a university campus, sometimes making eye contact with them and sometimes looking past them.[17] When the researcher had chosen a target person and made eye contact (or not), they gave a signal to a second researcher, who was walking behind them (and couldn't see whether the first researcher had made eye contact or not) and was tasked with asking the unsuspecting research participant a few questions. Wesselmann and his colleagues found that the people who had been visually acknowledged reported feeling about 25 percent less disconnected than the people who had been studiously ignored.

The undergraduate students who I teach can struggle to adjust to university, both academically and socially, just as I did when I started my master's degree. They often feel lonely living away from home for the first time, away from family and friends and the stability of their previous everyday routines. On top of that, students at the universities where I've worked are often taking classes with hundreds of other students, and it's easy to feel unseen, anonymous, or overwhelmed—like the woman who felt invisible at the conference or me walking through busy, noisy downtown Toronto.

For six years, I taught undergraduate statistics—a class that many psychology students dread. I loved teaching statistics because I knew that if I could do it well, it would make a massive difference for my students. I believed that the single most important thing I could do was build up their confidence. When I was able to work one-to-one with a student, I could calm them down, cheer them on, and convince them of my support and belief in their ability. But with several hundred students in my class, I couldn't do this for every individual student. I wondered whether there was something I could do that would at least help them all feel seen. I came across a solution accidentally.

To give my students practice with the course content, I created handouts with problems that they could work through in class. I'd leave the handouts in a pile near the door while I set up my slides at the front of the classroom, often getting mired in dealing with finicky classroom technology. If I sorted out all the tech in good time, I'd return to the door and give out the handouts myself, instead of having students pick them up from the pile. It was a way to pass the time, so I wasn't just standing awkwardly in front of the class, but it also gave me a chance to greet the students or say a few words, which I enjoyed doing.

One day, a senior colleague came to my class to observe and give me feedback on my teaching. When she saw me giving out handouts at the door, she commented that it was a great idea for connecting with my students. Light bulb! I hadn't been doing it with that in mind, but my colleague's comment made me realize that I could do it more systematically.

Although the students who were enrolled in my statistics class all attended the same lecture, they were broken into three groups for a separate computer lab, during which they worked independently, using software to conduct statistical analyses. I decided to run a study, doing different things in each of the three lab classes to see if I could help my students feel more connected.

In one lab class ("name tent"), I asked students to write their names on a name tent, which they would place on the desk in front of them. I'd circulate around the room to answer questions, and the name tents allowed me to address students by their names. Because there were more than two hundred students and I only taught them for five weeks, it didn't seem possible to learn all of their names, but I learned a few. In another lab ("greeting"), I stood at the door as the students entered class, and I smiled and said hello—re-creating my nodding acquaintanceship with the hot dog lady. In the final lab ("control"), students didn't receive name tents and I didn't greet them. (When I applied for approval to run this study, the ethics board clearly anticipated the results: They expressed concern that I was penalizing the control group. They had to back down when I pointed out that I was treating this group as most professors at my university treated their students in most classes.)

After teaching the students for five weeks, I asked them to fill out a survey in class. The students in the name-tent group benefitted the most in terms of feeling *known*; about 30 percent of them thought that I knew their name, compared to 13 percent of students in the greeting group and 7 percent in the control group. (I learned quite a few names but definitely not as many as they thought. However, the fact that they *thought* I did is arguably more important.) In terms of feeling *seen*, almost as many students in the greeting group as in the name-tent group thought that I recognized them (48 percent vs. 54 percent)—about twice as many as in the control group (25 percent). Both the students who thought I knew their name *and* the students who thought I recognized them felt a greater sense of belonging and were more interested and engaged in class than the students who felt anonymous.

I think my acknowledgments only made a difference because my students could tell that I was genuinely trying to connect with them. Over the years, I've been a member at various fitness clubs where I've been greeted by the people who worked at the reception desk. At one club where I played tennis, I knew Denise and the whole team who worked at reception, and their greetings helped me feel a real sense of belonging and a strong sense of loyalty to the club. At another gym, the staff greeted me not because they knew me but because they had been instructed to do so. Those greetings didn't mean anything to me—they left me unmoved.

By showing my students that I cared about them—through the simple act of seeing and acknowledging them—I helped them feel more connected to the place where they were learning and growing as people. Just as the hot dog lady had done for me.

We can't possibly acknowledge every single person we come across, but I've come to believe that it's worth doing as often as we can. As Virginia Satir, the "Mother of Family Therapy," puts it in *Making Contact*: "I believe the greatest gift I can conceive of having from anyone is to be seen, heard, understood, and touched by them. The greatest gift I can give is to see, hear, understand, and touch another person."

## Feeling seen can help when we're stuck in our heads

*Trigger warning: This subsection of the chapter includes reference to suicide, which may be unwelcome and/or distressing to some readers. If you or someone you know needs help, please see the endnotes for resources.*[18]

During the first Covid-19 lockdown in the UK in 2020, we were only allowed to leave home once a day, and only for exercise. To avoid going stir-crazy, I started going on a walk nearly every day—a habit that I've carried on to this day. Most days, as I walked my usual route, I'd feel a sense of peace as I walked through a majestic tree alley. Then I'd cross the road to get to an expansive green space, and I'd smile at whatever dogs were frolicking. (Dogs have a lot to teach us about having fun.) But one day, I was close to tears. My mind was churning and I was so stuck in my head that I hardly noticed the world around me.

I have no idea what made me so upset that day, so now-Gillian could have told past-Gillian that it wasn't all that important in the grand scheme of things. Instead, it was a stranger who put things in perspective for me, and without saying a single word. I walked past a lady who was pushing a baby carriage, and she did something incredibly simple and mundane: She smiled at me. I didn't feel instantly better, of course, but her smile was like an electric shock that interrupted the thought circuit in my head. Being acknowledged by a stranger brought me out of my head and back into the world, reminding me that the world was still turning, and I wasn't alone. Seeing her go about her day—just an ordinary, (seemingly) untroubled day for her—reminded me that everything was going to be OK, and I felt a tiny bit lighter.

Being seen and acknowledged by a stranger made a difference to me, on a gray day, but could it make a difference to someone in a much darker place: someone contemplating suicide? Samaritans, a suicide prevention charity in the UK, seems to think so. Given that there are more than two hundred railroad-track suicides every year in the UK, Samaritans teamed up with the rail industry on an initiative called "Small Talk Saves Lives."[19] They trained railway staff to be on the lookout for and then engage with people who might be struggling to cope. Samaritans believe: "A little small talk and a simple question like 'Do you know where I can get a coffee?' can be all it takes to interrupt someone's suicidal thoughts."[20]

"Would you mind taking my picture?" was the simple question that interrupted Billy Lezra's suicide attempt.[21] Billy was planning to jump in front of a subway train when a pink-haired stranger asked her to take a picture. When she shared her story in *The Washington Post* seven years later, Billy was in recovery, sober, and in therapy. Now, when she experiences dark days, she flips the lesson she learned from the pink-haired stranger and offers to take photos of other people. She says nobody has ever turned her down and that strangers "leave me with a jolt of connection that interrupts my hopelessness and makes me feel that being alive matters, just a little bit."

Having a minimal social interaction that helps someone feel seen has the potential to make a massive difference. Samaritans's twenty-three thousand volunteers respond to calls for help, twenty-four hours a day. They receive, on average, one call every ten seconds.

## Drawing attention

Feeling seen often helps us feel connected and can help us escape a negative thought spiral, but it isn't always a positive thing—feeling like you're the focus of excessive, unwanted attention can be negative. Influential sociologist Erving Goffman argued that minimizing eye contact is essential to public order. When we walk past someone, we tend to make brief eye contact but then avert our eyes.[22] According to Goffman, this "civil inattention" is a polite way of signaling respect, approval, and acceptance (at least in the Western context in which he was situated). In contrast, looking at someone for longer can signal incomprehension, disapproval, or fear.

Sociologist Ilkka Arminen, at the University of Helsinki, experienced a breach of civil inattention firsthand. While walking with a friend who wears clinical sun protection clothing due to a medical condition, Arminen noticed her friend attracting prolonged glances from passersby. She and her colleague Anna Heino decided to run a study to test the extent to which civil inattention is affected by a person's appearance.[23] One of the researchers alternated between wearing conventional clothing, an unconventional face-covering sunhat and sunglasses (in a nod to the inspiration for the study), and an abaya with a niqab (i.e., a burka), which was not common in the place where they ran the study. A GoPro camera attached to the researcher's chest recorded where passersby were looking. When Arminen and Heino crunched the numbers, they found that people looked for longer when the researcher wore unconventional clothing. Passersby breached the unwritten rules of civil inattention only 3 percent of the time when the researcher wore conventional clothing, but 45 percent of the time when the researcher wore the sun-protection clothing, and 48 percent of the time when the researcher wore an abaya and niqab.

If people notice when others look at them for longer than usual, and these longer looks can make people feel excessively seen and uncomfortably noticed, then it raises an important question: How can you acknowledge someone, which we know feels great, without making them feel uncomfortable? I suspect that much of the discomfort comes from not knowing what a look means. If you accompany a glance with a smile (and maybe a nod)—or you have a friendly chat—then you remove the uncertainty and signal that you have friendly intentions.

Canadian Mollie Kaye is flipping the script on civil inattention by deliberately inviting people to look at—and talk to—her. For the last five years, every Tuesday she dresses in vintage 1950s style, complete with a pillbox hat and white gloves. As she explains in her fun and thoughtful TEDx talk: "A few years ago, I was playing it very safe with my style. I wore the middle-aged mom uniform: black, semi-athletic 'invisiwear.' I wanted to belong, but blending in isn't the same as belonging. In fact, I was playing the world's loneliest game of hide and seek. I made myself disappear, and nobody ever found me. But when I dress like this, and someone says, 'Oh, I just love your outfit!' we've connected. Now that game is a lot more fun."[24]

Like Mollie, you can deliberately cultivate attention in your own way and give people permission—and a way—to connect with you. For example, someone who commented on Mollie's video on YouTube lamented that they would ride their bicycle around their neighborhood every day, but nobody would ever greet them—they would always have to be the first to say hello. After hearing Mollie's talk, they tried wearing a large flower in their hair while bicycling, and, sure enough, almost every single person greeted them. (See the appendix on page 235 for tips on learning to spot, and use as a conversation starter, a person's statement T-shirt or other signs of their personality and interests.)

## Seeing the world together

When we interact with a stranger, we benefit from being seen by each other but also from seeing together. Most humans are psychologists—not all of them by training like me—and most of us are interested in understanding other people and want to know what they're thinking and experiencing (not to mention that we also want to understand what *we're* thinking and experiencing). More than that, we want to know the extent to which what they're thinking and experiencing aligns with what we're thinking and experiencing.[25] We want to know whether we see the world the same way. One way to figure that out is to stand side by side and experience the world together.

Imagine being asked to eat a piece of chocolate. (Yes, please!) Would the chocolate taste any different if another person was with you, eating the same chocolate at the same time? When Erica Boothby and her colleagues asked this question, 74 percent of people were convinced that the presence of another person wouldn't matter at all.[26] But they were wrong.

In Erica's study, participants sat in a room with another person and ate two pieces of chocolate. They ate one piece of chocolate at the same time as the other person (i.e., it was a shared experience). They ate a second piece of chocolate while the other person was busy doing something else (i.e., it was an unshared experience). The chocolate was the same in both cases, though participants didn't know that. When it was delicious 70 percent dark chocolate (my favorite), people liked the chocolate *more* when they shared the experience with a stranger (vs. being the only one eating chocolate). When it was bitter 90 percent dark chocolate (yuck), people liked the chocolate *less* when they shared the experience with a stranger. In other words, whether positive or negative, an experience is amplified when we share it with another person.

Although I wouldn't have guessed that the presence of another person would affect how things taste, I can think of times that the presence of strangers has amplified how things felt. Maybe, like me, you've been in a crowd of strangers at a theater, laughing and enjoying a show even more because the people around you are laughing? Or in a crowd of strangers at a stadium, feeling even more angry about the referee's unbelievably bad call because others are booing and shouting angrily?

We want to believe that others' thoughts, feelings, and beliefs about the world are similar to ours—that we experience a "generalized shared reality."[27] For one thing, we want the world to make sense because we feel safer when we understand why someone did something (why are they looking up?) or why something happened (why did the fire alarm go off?). If others believe the same thing that we do, then our belief feels less like an opinion and more like the truth. Secondly, experiencing shared reality makes us feel connected to other people, and you already know how good it feels and how important it is for us to feel that we belong.

It's not difficult to establish a sense of shared reality—even with a stranger. In one study, by Maya Rossignac-Milon and her colleagues, pairs of strangers looked at ambiguous images together and had two minutes to discuss and answer questions like "Why do you think the man in the hooded sweatshirt and the man with the pipe are talking?"[28] Pairs who had vocalized their shared agreement or shared feelings, who had said things at almost the same time, or who had finished each other's ideas ended up feeling a stronger sense of shared reality. And people who felt a stronger sense of shared reality felt more certain that they had interpreted the images correctly and felt a greater sense of rapport with their partner.

Why would an experience feel different when it's shared? For one thing, when we're sharing an experience, we can't help but wonder what the other person is thinking and feeling. That may, somewhat paradoxically, make us pay more attention to the experience itself. There are also good evolutionary reasons for paying more attention to shared experiences: In order to coordinate to achieve shared goals, we need to be able to share knowledge, to know what one another knows.[29] It's a little bit like how when I cook with my husband, even when we try a new recipe, I know which parts he'll do and he knows which parts I'll do. Meal prep goes more smoothly because we know what each other knows.

## We see art differently when we see it together

The Tate Modern appears on many lists of the top art galleries in the world. And this despite the fact that so many people seem uncomfortable with modern art. (I count myself among this group.) This discomfort is on display on Reddit, where people have posted questions like: "I don't understand modern art. Am I missing something?," and "People who 'get' modern art, what are the rest of us doing wrong?" Lots of Redditors responded to these queries, defending modern art and explaining their fascination with it. One person said that asking what it means is the wrong question; the whole point of modern art is to elicit a reaction, an emotion. Another person said that they appreciate that modern art is about more than simply imitating reality but rather about answering a more philosophical question: "What is art?" However you look at it, modern art poses questions, prompting us to think.

Do we feel differently about modern art when we view it with others? Or is our connection to art such a personal thing that the experience can't be shared? A volunteers manager at the Tate Modern asked me to help them find out. Visitor hosts at the Tate Modern are happy to assist visitors, but they usually wait to be approached. They seldom take the initiative to approach visitors because, in typical British fashion, they wouldn't want to intrude. We decided to see what would happen if they did.

When you walk into the Tate Modern, the first thing you see (after you pass the gift shop) is the Turbine Hall. It's a massive space that used to house electricity generators: It's five stories tall and longer than a football field. In the fall of 2015, the Turbine Hall was the site of an exhibit by Mexican artist Abraham Cruzvillegas. It was called *Empty Lot* and consisted of hundreds of triangular wooden planters that contained soil collected from sites across London, including a royal residence. Nothing was planted in the soil, but it was watered and lit by lamps, and over the course of the months-long exhibit, things would grow by chance (and, as it turns out, as a result of seed-bombing visitors).

I trained a dozen or so Tate volunteers to approach visitors and have a chat. The volunteers received no special training about the exhibit; the goal wasn't to teach visitors about Cruzvillegas's work but merely to start a friendly conversation. Often the volunteers and visitors would stand side by side, looking at the exhibit together. When we asked the volunteers about their favorite conversation of the day, they told us they had talked a lot about gardening: what will happen to the soil and the planters after the exhibit's over, whether or not the lamps stay on overnight, how slugs are controlled. The volunteers also had some more philosophical conversations about art (Is it all in your mind?) and hope (Is it more powerful than fear?).

The volunteers worked in pairs, and while one was tasked with approaching visitors and having a chat, the other had the less desirable (yet crucial) task of collecting the research data. This person would wait until their shift partner had finished a conversation with a visitor and then ask that visitor if they would mind completing a short survey. They would also ask other visitors, who had not spoken to a volunteer, to complete the same survey, for comparison purposes.

We found that visitors who had a chat with a volunteer were in a better mood and felt more connected—just like the customers who talked to the Starbucks barista. More than that, looking at the exhibit together made visitors feel like they knew more—about the exhibit, the artist, and modern art—and they expected to think and talk about the exhibit more often in the next few days/weeks. Sharing their gallery experience with a fellow art lover seemed to allow visitors to engage more fully with the exhibit and reflect more deeply. (The Tate Modern visitors weren't the only ones to benefit. The volunteers seemed to enjoy having more meaningful conversations with visitors—it was more interesting than answering the usual questions about the location of the nearest Tube station or the nearest loo.)

Talking to a volunteer might have especially benefitted visitors who felt uncomfortable with modern art. A study by Hillary Wiener and her colleagues found that customers who had less knowledge about financial advising felt more comfortable and were more likely to use a financial advisor again when the advisor started with small talk rather than diving into financial planning advice.[30]

## Memories of a murmuration

At dusk, on a cool February evening, I waited on the Brighton pier, trying not to get my hopes up. During the winter months, one of the greatest wildlife spectacles in Britain takes place in Brighton: ten to fifteen thousand starlings, both natives and migrants from across Europe, fly together in mesmerizing synchrony.[31] I'd seen videos of these starling murmurations but had never seen one in person. On the bus on our way into town to visit a friend, my husband suggested offhandedly that maybe after our visit we should head to the pier and try our luck.

We didn't know where the best vantage point would be, but we staked out a spot on the pier, and as the sun set and it got colder by the minute, we settled in to wait. When I spotted a woman, bundled up in a colorful woolly scarf and hat, and carrying a camera with a huge telephoto lens, I knew that we had picked an appropriate location. I didn't really need to ask, but I did anyway: "Are you here to see the starlings?" Her name was Chloe, and she had taken an hour-long train journey from London to Brighton in the hope of witnessing a murmuration. As we waited, we talked about birds (I don't know a lot about birds, but as a nature lover, I know enough to keep a conversation going), and my husband showed her some pictures he had taken on a recent trip to Canada, of birds that she had never seen.

And then, out of nowhere, a smokelike smudge appeared in the distance. We watched, entranced, as thousands of birds danced gracefully through the sky, in fluid, constantly morphing shapes. As they turned one way, they seemed to almost disappear in a silvery shimmer. Then they would swoop another way and there would be a kaleidoscopic transformation: darker shapes would magically reappear, so close to us that it almost felt like we were part of the murmuration. Restricted as we are by the limits of our human senses, it's hard to fathom how the starlings can coordinate so well, each bird seeming to know instinctively when to change direction. Like the individual musicians in an orchestra, each bird contributes to a collective outcome that's so much more than the sum of its parts. The starlings were silent (which I didn't expect and which made the experience more magical), but when they flew close enough, you could hear the thrumming of their wings.

I was enthralled by the murmuration. Awestruck. That's a feeling that occurs less and less often as I get older. And I know that my reaction was enhanced by sharing the experience with Chloe. It's not that we talked. I know, for my part, it would have felt wrong, somehow, to do so—like breaking the sacred silence in a church or a library. We were aware of each other's presence, though: Sometimes one or the other of us would be unable to suppress an exclamation of surprise or delight, or an intake of breath. When the birds momentarily disappeared as they changed direction, we would point out to each other the location of their reappearance. As I watched the murmuration, I was absorbed in the experience myself, but I was also thinking about how Chloe had traveled from London in the hope of seeing exactly this, and I was so pleased that it had worked out for her. The experience was *mine*, but it was also *ours*. (My "us" always includes my husband, but this time it grew, to include Chloe.)

When it was over, and the starlings had flown underneath the pier to roost for the night, Chloe and I were both quite emotional. Before parting ways after sharing that special experience, we exchanged email addresses, and Chloe later shared the fantastic photos and videos she had taken with her fancy camera. We shared one more thing: a giant hug.

# 6

# Skeleton Key

I always torture myself when deciding whether to attend a conference. So, when two of my friends decided to attend a conference in 2019 and urged me to join them, I went through my usual deliberations.

Should I attend? It would let me spend an extended amount of time with my friends. I enjoy traveling to new places, learning about interesting research, and meeting new people. And conferences feel like something that I *should* be doing as part of my job.

But maybe I shouldn't attend? A conference is a busy, noisy environment that I find overstimulating and tiring. It's also very networky, and I struggle to genuinely connect with people, leaving me feeling frustrated and a bit lonely.

In this case, the location of the conference tipped the balance: There was no expensive, tiring, or environmentally unfriendly travel involved. It was only a couple of hours' drive away, at the University of Sussex, in the seaside city of Brighton. I, somewhat reluctantly, gave in to my friends and registered for the conference, bracing for the overwhelm.

Little did I know that this decision would change the course of my career.

I attended a talk given by a genial man named Robin Banerjee, who was a researcher at the host university. He talked about some research he'd done on how people define kindness and the barriers that sometimes make it hard for people to be kind. I'd been studying the barriers that make it hard for people to talk to strangers, and I wondered if some of these might be similar, so I put up my hand to ask a question. As everyone turned their eyes toward me, my heart started racing and my mind froze in panic mode, but I managed to articulate my question and Robin gave a thoughtful response.

Later, I saw him standing on his own in the teeming lobby, so I went over to tell him how much I'd enjoyed his talk. He asked whether I'd be giving a talk myself. I didn't know if he was genuinely interested in hearing more about my work or just being polite. My talk wasn't until the next day and he was unable to attend it, so I cheekily said: "I'm only a couple of hours' drive away. I'd be happy to return some other time." I assumed nothing would come of it, but a few months later, Robin reached out with an invitation. I returned to the University of Sussex to give a talk, and we kept in touch afterward. Robin added me to a mailing list he'd assembled, to bring together people doing research related to kindness.

Two years later, Robin sent an email to his kindness mailing list announcing that he was establishing a new Sussex Centre for Research on Kindness and needed a director. I imagined how delightful it would be to spend my working days thinking about kindness, and I wondered if I should apply. The idea of being the director of a center was completely out of my comfort zone, and on top of that, although I think talking to strangers can be an act of kindness and can facilitate kindness (see chapter 7), I wasn't sure others would see it that way—I wasn't sure if it was the right fit for me. But it sounded like an exciting opportunity, so I asked Robin if we could meet so that I could learn more about the position. I knew Robin was extremely busy (he was now head of the department), so I was reluctant to take up his time, but he welcomed my inquiry. After an encouraging conversation, I applied for the job.

This story is about more than simply talking to a stranger. Yes, I talked to a stranger, but I also (1) put up my hand in a room full of strangers and asked a question, (2) complimented a stranger (on his talk), (3) asked for something that I wanted (an invitation to give a talk), and later (4) asked for help/advice (about my suitability for a job opportunity). When I pause to think about this, it amazes me. Past-Gillian would have been much too anxious to do any of these things. But by the time of this conference, I'd been regularly talking to strangers for more than a decade, and the skills I'd developed were more transferable than I could have imagined.

Talking to strangers is like a skeleton key that allows you to get more comfortable with uncomfortable feelings, build social skills, and think more positively about other people. And, as if unlocking these benefits isn't enough, it can unlock doors to greater well-being.

## Practice makes progress when it comes to talking to strangers

I cut my skeleton key through hundreds of interactions with strangers, but I suspected that people would start to see benefits after even just a few interactions. I thought it might be a bit like quitting smoking. Ten years after quitting, the risk of cancer is half of what it is for smokers, but there are benefits as soon as two weeks after quitting: More than 40 percent of people feel like they breathe more easily and have more energy.[1]

Over the years, I've carried out many studies where I've asked people to talk to a stranger and then report back. In every single study, their conversations have gone not just a little but *a lot* better than they expected.[2] You might think, therefore, that people would learn from this and realize that their next conversation is also likely to go well. Alas, this doesn't seem to be the case. In two of my studies, right after people had had a pleasant conversation, I asked them to imagine talking to someone new. They thought that their next conversation was unlikely to go as well as their most recent one had. I didn't know how much practice people would need before they started to see some early skeleton key benefits, but these studies told me that a single conversation wasn't enough.

Why do we struggle to learn that there's a pattern—that conversations with strangers generally go well? When we have a successful conversation, we seem to write it off as a pleasant exception to an unpleasant rule. Instead of taking it as a positive sign about the likely success of our next conversation, we seem to think that the chips get cleared off the table after each conversation, and we're chancing a new roll of the dice every time. When we have an enjoyable conversation, we credit most of the success to our partner.[3] We underestimate how well our next conversation will go, in part because we don't (and can't) know what our next partner will be like or how capable they will be of making our next conversation a success. (If we were consistent, we'd also write off an *unsuccessful* conversation as an exception and attribute part of the blame to our conversation partner, but we have no problem generalizing when things go wrong and we readily take the blame for ourselves.) My idea was that, if people could have a few practice sessions in close succession, they would start to see a positive pattern (and have the ammunition they needed to counteract Sid's doubts and insecurities).

The first challenge was figuring out how to get people to talk to a bunch of strangers in short succession, so I could see how they benefitted over time and test whether there was a cumulative effect. How could I get people to have *several* conversations with strangers when I knew that they would be nervous having even one? I decided I needed to make it fun and came up with the idea of a week-long talking-to-strangers scavenger hunt game.[4] I'd secured some funding to develop the scavenger hunt game in the same month that I met Erica Boothby and Gus Cooney (from chapter 1) for the first time. We enjoyed working together on the liking gap project so much that we decided to work together on the scavenger hunt too.

At the university where I did my undergraduate degree, the incoming engineering students famously participated in a fiendish twenty-four-hour scavenger hunt that was concocted by the more senior students. The "missions" involved solving difficult puzzles and collecting hard-to-find objects, like traffic cones. The hunt was meant to be challenging so that new students had to work together to succeed—the purpose of the hunt was to create group cohesion.

The challenge of our talking to strangers scavenger hunt was not in the "hunt" itself. The missions in our game included "find someone wearing a hat" and "find someone drinking a coffee." Hat wearers and coffee drinkers aren't rare creatures. They aren't hard to find. The challenge of our game was that, to complete the mission, participants needed to not only find someone who matched the description but also approach them and have a brief chat. When we asked people how they were feeling before they started the game/study, some were looking forward to the challenge and expected it to be interesting and exciting, but others worried that it would be awkward, scary, or exhausting and admitted that they were nervous.

Over the course of a week, the almost two hundred participants reported having 1,336 conversations. People talked about things they had in common: classes, the weather. They talked about clothing and food, work and hobbies. Many conversations were mundane (e.g., "When the bus was coming and the weather"), but others went a little deeper. One person said their conversation topics included: "Nike shoes, customization, recyclable materials." Another person said they talked about: "Lacrosse, fashion, AI, culture." A third conversation touched on: "Efficiency, comedy, her work, airports." Participants enjoyed 90 percent of their conversations;[5] only twenty-three conversations (2 percent) were not enjoyed at all. But what we really wanted to know was whether the repeated practice was changing how people felt about talking to strangers.

Before they started the study and again at the end of the study, we asked people how they felt about talking to strangers. After a week of practicing, people were less worried about being rejected when they approached someone, they were more confident in their social skills, and they had more positive thoughts about others. Even better, when we followed up a week after the study ended, all of these changes seemed to stick, which we hope is a sign of a permanent shift in attitudes.

How much practice do people need? It's hard to say, and it will surely be different for different people. To shed some light on how quickly these attitude changes occur, we asked people every morning to tell us how they were feeling about the conversations they would have that day, and after every mission/conversation, we asked them how it went. We found that the benefits accrued gradually, day by day, conversation by conversation. At the end of the week, there was still room for improvement: People remained more worried about their conversations than they needed to be. Their morning predictions were more positive than they had been at the start of the study but were still not as positive as people's daily experiences were. We don't know yet whether it's possible to completely erase the gap between predictions and experiences, but we learned from this study that practice makes progress.

Some of the participants seemed to notice a positive pattern, just as we had intended. As one person put it: "It was a lot easier than I thought it would be to get people to talk to me. I thought it would take a few attempts, but all of my first tries worked. I enjoyed most conversations I had." Another participant shared: "I felt very nervous and aware that I might end up talking to somebody strange. . . . This didn't happen. None of the strangers were weird. They were all absolutely delightful and very inspiring."

## Getting more comfortable with uncomfortable feelings

Let's be real: For most of us, the prospect of talking to strangers provokes some anxiety. (If it was easy, everyone would do it, and I wouldn't need to write this book.) We worry about all sorts of things, including the uncomfortable feelings that we might experience during and after our conversations. We worry that we might feel the sting of rejection. We worry that we might feel the shame of negative social judgment if our conversation partner dislikes us or finds us boring or weird. And because we never know how our conversation will go or what our conversation partner will be like, we're always face-to-face with uncertainty. Rejection, shame, and uncertainty are uncomfortable feelings in themselves, but so is the anxiety that we have worrying that we might experience those feelings. We have varying thresholds for—and experience with—these uncomfortable feelings, but we all feel them to some degree.

Imagine that you decide to talk to more strangers (which I hope you will), and one of your first conversations doesn't go well. Maybe they put in some earbuds or walk away. Maybe you get tongue-tied and talk too little or get nervous and talk too much. Imagine that this uncomfortable conversation leaves you feeling rejected, ashamed, anxious. (Sorry! Bear with me. . . . )

When a positive or negative event happens in our lives, we try to make sense of it, to understand why it happened. There are many different ways to explain an event, and we differ in how we typically explain events. People with a "fixed mindset" might interpret an uncomfortable conversation like this as a sign that they have inadequate social skills.[6] They might think that some people are born with social skills and some aren't, that they just don't have what it takes and there's nothing to be done about it. (Melodramatic Sid might transmute this into: *I'm unlikable, nobody will ever talk to me again, and I'm going to die alone.* \*eye roll\*) On the other hand, people with a "growth mindset" might instead interpret the uncomfortable conversation as a sign that their social skills aren't up to snuff *yet*. They're more likely to trust that their skills will improve over time and to think about what they could do differently next time. When unexpectedly thrown into a conversation, people with a growth mindset are more likely to make the best of it, whereas people with a fixed mindset are more likely to spend the whole time resisting the conversation, trying to push all the conversational work to their partner.[7]

You probably won't be surprised to hear that people who tend to explain things in a more positive way (consistent with a growth mindset) tend to have greater well-being,[8] whereas people who tend to explain things in a more pessimistic way (consistent with a fixed mindset) have a higher tendency for depression.[9]

Fortunately, we have some control over how we choose to explain things like this (hypothetical and unlikely) uncomfortable conversation. Although our natural tendency might be to see it as a sign of social incompetence, we can choose to explain it in a different way: We can reappraise it. For example, we could choose to see it as a brave first step and an opportunity to learn so that our next conversation goes better. Reappraisal is one of the active ingredients of cognitive behavioral therapy (CBT), which is effective for treating depression, anxiety, and other mental health issues.[10] CBT works by helping people become more aware of their thought processes and then learn to challenge them and consider alternative ways of thinking. (In other words, it helps us spot Sid hiding in the shadows, notice the influence of his nasty whispers, and then stand up to him, demanding that he show evidence to back up his claims.)

Repeated practice talking to strangers helps us reappraise our uncomfortable feelings by giving us evidence that we can use to refute Sid. The first few times I deliberately talked to strangers, I was nervous about what might happen. It was easy to imagine all sorts of ways that the conversation could go disastrously wrong. But then I talked to that lady with a cupcake on the subway in Toronto who taught me about people riding ostriches. As I kept talking to more strangers, it became easier to make optimistic explanations on the rare occasions when I was rejected. If Sid tried to convince me that I was rejected because I'm unlikable and incompetent, all I had to do was point out the times when I'd had a pleasant conversation, remind him of ostriches. These examples are abundant and easy to bring to mind because I have *repeatedly* practiced talking to strangers.

## Getting comfortable with the possibility of rejection

Jia Jiang felt that his fear of rejection was holding him back as an entrepreneur, so he decided to tame his fear by deliberately and repeatedly confronting rejection.[11] He asked strangers for favors and shared videos of his "one hundred days of rejection" on social media. He asked people if he could borrow money from them and if he could give them money (not as easy as you'd think: two said yes, three said no). He asked strangers if they would give him a compliment (he returned the favor) and if he could give them a hug. And these are just some of the more routine requests.

On only his third day of confronting rejection, Jia asked an employee at Krispy Kreme donuts if they would make a set of joined donuts, in the shape of the Olympic rings. To his surprise (and presumably the surprise of the more than six million people who viewed his video on YouTube), a Krispy Kreme employee named Jackie went above and beyond to deliver his custom donut order—and even insisted on giving it to him for free because she felt like it didn't quite measure up to his specifications.[12] People commented on the video, saying things like "Someone please find Jackie and give her everything. I love Jackie." And "gotta love a problem solver, she is a legend." And "Why is Jackie making me tear up? She's so purely nice and kind and everything. I want to be her."

It's a *lot* easier to simply have a chat with a stranger than it is to ask a stranger for a loan, a hug, or Olympic donuts. But some of the lessons that Jia learned and shared in his popular TEDx talk also apply to talking to strangers.[13] He learned not to run away at the first "no," to stay engaged instead of fleeing from the discomfort of rejection. Similarly, I've learned that if I can be patient as people grapple with the understandable questions of who I am and why I'm talking to them, they will usually (eventually) get past their confusion and concern, and realize that I'm just being friendly. Jia learned to ask people the "why?" behind their no, and to provide a "why?" for his request. I've learned that sometimes it's helpful to explicitly tell people why I'm talking to them: that I'm just being friendly, that I have no ulterior motive. (I've also learned that there are conversation starters that provide a built-in "why"—see the appendix on page 235 for tips.) People granted Jia's requests more often than he expected—even Jackie, who granted his custom donut request. I, too, have been rejected less often than I first expected, and I've learned that there are many friendly, helpful, interesting Jackies in the world. If we can find the courage to talk to strangers despite the discomfort, we can give the Jackies of the world a chance to shine.

By practicing talking to strangers, we're regularly confronting the possibility of rejection and desensitizing ourselves to it. After playing the scavenger hunt game for a week, people were less fearful of social interactions in general, and less worried about rejection in particular. As one participant put it, repeated practice "made me realize that even if a conversation goes badly, it's something you can move past very easily."

For me, I think that the desensitization that has occurred over years of talking to strangers has made me more willing to ask for things that I want—like asking Robin to invite me to give a talk. The worst that can happen is that someone says no. (Why are we so scared of this tiny two-letter word?) By talking to lots of strangers, I've learned that a "no" is unlikely, and that when a rare "no" occurs, it's not as awful as Sid would like me to think.

## Getting comfortable with uncertainty

When we talk to strangers, we confront not only rejection but also uncertainty: What will this person be like? What will we talk about? Will we enjoy our conversation? We humans feel safe when we understand things and can predict what will happen, so it's natural that uncertainty makes us feel anxious. When we practice talking to strangers, we become less uncertain about it because our experience gives us a better idea of what to expect, of all the different ways that a conversation is likely to go. But maybe we don't just learn how to cope with the uncertainty of talking to strangers but with uncertainty in general.

Uncertainty doesn't always make us anxious. We enjoy reading or watching a mystery, not knowing whodunnit. We enjoy receiving a gift, not knowing what we'll find when we untie the ribbon and rip off the shiny paper. With practice, we can learn to see talking to strangers as something to look forward to unwrapping rather than something to worry about. People who played the scavenger hunt game for a week seemed to start doing this: They expected to enjoy talking to strangers more than they had before.

We don't know what to expect when we *start* talking to a stranger, but there's also uncertainty when the conversation *ends*. I remember watching a movie on a flight years ago. Just as I was getting to the emotional climax, the entertainment system abruptly turned off, and I didn't get to see the ending. Talking to strangers can be a bit like that. You never know: What happened next? Did the hikers complete the last leg of the 182-mile coast-to-coast trail and enjoy the traditional celebratory pint at the pub in Robin Hood's Bay? Did the man on the train get the job promotion? Did the pregnant lady on the Tube have a boy or a girl?

There have been several occasions when, after walking away from a conversation with a stranger, I think of something that I wish I'd said (often a joke I wished I'd made) or a question I wish I'd asked. I'm not one of those people who thinks well on the spot. There's a French term for this: esprit d'escalier. It literally means "wit of the staircase"—thinking of the perfect thing to say only after leaving the room and walking down the stairs. Most of the time, I never get the chance for closure—I just have to live with not being able to ask my question and not knowing the answer. And that's probably good for me (or so I try to tell myself). Life is unavoidably uncertain, so it seems wise to get more comfortable with uncertainty.

Every so often, I'll get a second chance. More than once, I've chatted with someone on the bus into town and then run into that same person again on my way home. One day on my way into London, I saw a man at my small, local train station with an oversize umbrella, which I used as a way to make a comment about the weather. When I got off the train on the way home, I saw him again. It hadn't rained all day. As we all know, it only rains if we don't have an umbrella, so I thanked him for preventing it from raining by carrying around that giant umbrella all day.

While doing a circular walk in the Peak District in England, I chatted with a man who was following a route in a guidebook. He told me that he was planning to do all fifty walks in the book and had done thirteen already. After we parted ways, heading in opposite directions, I wondered whether he was going through the book systematically, doing the walks in the order they were printed. Something about how he told me about his plan made me think that this was how he might approach it. Just over an hour later, I unexpectedly crossed paths with him again, and I got my chance to ask him the question. (I'd tell you what he said, but in the spirit of uncertainty, I'm going to leave you guessing. . . . )

Not being able to finish a task can be frustrating, especially for those of us who have a strong desire for closure (another trait in which people differ). We can't stop thinking about it—it continues to eat up our mental resources.[14] On the other hand, when we get closure, we stop thinking about the task and quickly forget about it. Flip this around, and it tells us that if we don't want to forget something, if we don't want to let go of something, we can deliberately choose to leave loose ends, to embrace uncertainty. Hemingway would famously finish a writing session by stopping in the middle of a sentence so that the next day, it was easy to get started.

A team of researchers at the University of Virginia and Harvard University studied the potential of harnessing uncertainty as a way to prolong pleasant feelings. They brought together groups of people online to get to know one another through exchanging messages with photos and information about their interests and values.[15] Then each person was asked to name the one person who seemed to have the most friend potential and write a paragraph explaining their choice. (In truth, there was only one person participating in the study; the photos and information about the other "people" were carefully curated.) The participant received the flattering news that three people had chosen them as a potential future friend. Some participants were told the names of the three people who had chosen them, whereas others weren't told. Everyone felt great after reading about why people had thought they'd make a good friend, but after fifteen minutes had passed, the people who didn't know who had chosen them were in a better mood than the people who did know.

I don't think I'd choose to never find out the ending to the movie that I started on the plane, but research on uncertainty suggests that I might have enjoyed the movie for longer and thought about it more deeply precisely because I *didn't* get to find out the ending. Similarly, there might be something tantalizing about chatting with a stranger and then walking away, never to see them again. After a gemlike moment of connection, they'll walk away glowing in a halo of possibility that is undimmed by reality.

## Getting comfortable with social judgment

Have you ever sat in a meeting where you wanted to speak up and share your opinion, but stayed quiet because you didn't want to disagree with your colleagues and risk having them dislike you? Or have you ever attended a talk or presentation and wanted to put up your hand to ask a question, but you worried that it might be silly or nonsensical and that people would think less of you?

My friend Alecia Carter attended an academic talk with a friend. During the Q and A that followed the talk, Alecia noticed that all the questions were coming from men. When she commented on it to her friend, he pointed out how odd that was because the audience was mostly women. Alecia, who works in the male-dominant academic subfield of behavioral ecology, cares deeply about gender equity. She knows that when younger women don't see women role models in academia, they're less likely to aspire to be academics themselves. If women aren't asking questions at academic talks, then they're less visible as potential role models to future generations.

In her research, Alecia has studied baboons, meerkats, and lizards, but she turned her attention to humans to understand whether there was something unusual about that one talk that she attended, or whether there was a pattern of gender disparity in question asking. She started collecting data at all the talks she attended, noting the ratio of men and women in the audience and paying attention to who was asking questions. I teamed up with her to add a psychology perspective and to help her figure out how to scale up the study. We enlisted the help of dozens of friends and colleagues at universities around the world, and together we collected data at almost 250 talks, at 35 universities in 10 countries. We found that when there's an equal number of men and women in the audience, men ask about two and a half times as many questions as women.[16] (And this phenomenon isn't unique to academics—we later found evidence of the same gender disparity in question asking at a public science festival.)

When someone puts up their hand and asks a question, all eyes are on them. The fear of social judgment gets in the way of people asking questions. We found that people worry about all sorts of things: that they aren't clever enough to ask a good question, that their question will reveal that they misunderstood the content of the talk, that their question isn't appropriate. Men worry about all these things, but women are more worried about every single one. This may be because certain types of question-asking behaviors are judged less positively (e.g., stating an opinion instead of asking a question; taking up space by speaking for longer).[17] Women might be more aware of the nuances of social judgment than men are, and might therefore worry more about delivering their question in the wrong way and being judged negatively for it. One woman told us they felt that women question askers are "judged more harshly," and another thought women were "afraid of sounding 'bitchy' if they ask a question that seems assertive."

After doing this research, I feel like I need to do my part to speak up and ask a question when I have one—like I did at Robin's talk about kindness. I still dislike having all eyes on me, but I feel like all the practice I've had talking to strangers has made it easier for me to speak up and ask a question, by forcing me to confront my fear of social judgment. (It also helps when sometimes a person thanks me for asking my question because they wondered about the same thing.)

It's natural to worry about social judgment because being accepted and valued is so important to us. However, we often worry too much. People don't even notice us as often as we think. In a classic study by Tom Gilovich, Victoria Medvec, and William Savitsky, undergraduate students who walked into a room wearing an embarrassing T-shirt (with the face of 1970s/1980s crooner Barry Manilow) overestimated how many people noticed it; they thought twice as many people had noticed compared to how many actually did.[18]

Even if people do notice us, they don't judge our failings as harshly as we imagine. In a study by Savitsky, Gilovich, and Nick Epley, people who imagined accidentally triggering a fire alarm in a library or being the only guest to show up to a party without a gift thought that others would judge them more negatively than they actually did.[19]

Students who were instructed to wear the embarrassing T-shirt may have worried that people would laugh at them. Nobody likes to be laughed at, right? Actually, it turns out that some people do. There's even a word for these people who consider laughter to be a sign of appreciation: *gelotophiliac* (*gelos* is Greek for laughter). When I stopped to think about this, I realized that my dad's a gelotophiliac. He absolutely relishes making people laugh, often at his own expense. Dad's an extremely athletic retired physical education teacher. He once earned a day off (sadly, a rare thing for a teacher) for helping with timetabling over the summer. His idea of the best possible way to spend that day was: drive to a lake, go for a swim, follow that with a run, then finish things off with a round of golf. (I'm sure he talked to strangers at every point of that day too.) He has competed in so many running races that he could fill his closet with nothing but race T-shirts (which are great conversation starters—he has started many a conversation with a stranger by commenting on theirs).

Although Dad took his running seriously, tracking his times and setting targets, he sometimes did races more for fun than to achieve a running goal. (One of these fun races was called the Turkey Trot, and he always seemed to win a draw prize—maybe a pumpkin pie.) On these more casual occasions, he sometimes wore a very special pair of shorts that he got as a practical joke gift. They had vertical red and white stripes, and on the back, there was a rubber insert that was intended to look like a person's bum. He loved to hear people gasp and snicker as he ran past them in these shorts. I'd like to think that all those years of talking to strangers helped him get to the point where he not only doesn't worry about social judgment but flips the script and invites it (a bit like Mollie Kaye dressing in her 1950s outfits).

Maybe one day I'll worry as little about social judgment as my dad does. In the meantime, I'm still a work in progress. I read a post on LinkedIn from someone who brings a bowl of tiny plastic giraffes when they facilitate a workshop. Any time someone says something brave, bold, or different, they get a giraffe. Giraffes aren't just awarded by the workshop facilitator—people can award them to one another. More and more tend to get awarded as the workshop continues. I love this idea! I don't always stick my neck out as much as I'd like, and I'd welcome the encouragement.

I can think of a time when I deserved a giraffe. I was at a multiday event, and the facilitators asked the thirty-five or so attendees to come up with topics for breakout groups. We would spend our final afternoon with whatever group we chose. Several people proposed topics—the usual suspects who had seemed most comfortable speaking up throughout the event. I listened to all the topics in dismay. None of them appealed to me. I started thinking: Should I join a breakout group I'm not interested in? That didn't seem like a good use of my time. Maybe I should just go home early? The idea was tempting, but I knew that I'd regret it, that later I'd be disappointed in myself for not taking the opportunity to connect with all the interesting people who had come together at the event.

Just before this call for breakout group topics, I'd been having an interesting chat with a woman named Wing. I felt like we had really connected, had been on the same wavelength. I mustered my courage, put up my hand, and in what felt like an inarticulate, uncontrolled burst of words, I proposed my own idea for a breakout group topic, which was inspired by my conversation with Wing. Later, several people (including Wing) came up to me and thanked me for speaking up, and we enjoyed a stimulating conversation in our breakout group that afternoon (which a good number of people chose to attend). What sticks with me from this event is the powerful reminder of how worthwhile it can be when we're brave enough to channel our inner giraffes.

Repeated practice talking to strangers can help us get more comfortable with uncomfortable feelings, but we're unlikely to banish them altogether. After a week of playing the scavenger hunt game, people were less worried than they had been about negative judgment from their conversation partners, but they were still more nervous than they needed to be. I'll keep working toward Dad-level fearlessness, but for now, I'll settle for less fear than I had before I started talking to strangers. I take heart from something that Mark Twain said: "Courage is resistance to fear, mastery of fear; not absence of fear."

## Skill development

After hundreds of conversations with strangers, I feel confident in my ability to start a conversation with pretty much anyone. (I still find it challenging sometimes to end a conversation; some people have a tendency to go on and on, and it feels impolite to interrupt. . . . ) After only one week of practicing, scavenger hunt players also felt more confident in their conversational abilities.

One said that, over time, "it made me more confident, and I realized I have better conversational skills than I thought." Another noticed that "as the week went on it got easier to start and carry a conversation."

These improvements in conversational skills likely make it easier to talk to nonstrangers too. Although many of us get a bit anxious at the prospect of talking to people we don't know, sometimes we also get anxious when talking to people we *do* know. For example, we might worry about a friend rejecting us—or, at least, thinking less of us—if we were to admit to something that we're ashamed of. We might worry about not having the right words to comfort a friend who's struggling. Even in less emotionally fraught situations, feeling more confident in our social skills might help us do the things that strengthen our relationships: open up (i.e., engage in self-disclosure) and ask for/offer advice or help.

But conversational skills aren't the only skills that we develop or improve by talking to strangers. We also get better at paying attention to the world around us and better at enjoying the moment.

### The skill of noticing

Until I reached my thirties, when I walked past someone, I'd briefly make eye contact and then immediately look down at the ground. It wasn't simply a matter of civil inattention (i.e., a polite acknowledgment followed by politely respecting someone's privacy). I was nervous about other people, and dropping my eyes made me feel safer. It took time and effort to break this habit, to retrain myself. I couldn't notice other people—and opportunities to talk to them—until I did.

The scavenger hunt study challenged people to talk to strangers, but there was another challenge baked in. Before starting a conversation, participants had to choose someone to talk to. The missions were designed to help people narrow down the possibilities, from literally anyone to specifically a hat wearer or a coffee drinker, for example. Nevertheless, some of our participants struggled, at first, to figure out who to talk to.

After playing the scavenger hunt game for a week, people noticed more opportunities to talk to strangers than they had before. One participant realized "how many strangers we actually meet every day and don't notice." Another particularly thoughtful participant said that they eventually realized they didn't need to try so hard to find people to talk to because their everyday activities naturally provided opportunities or their friends would introduce them to people. They said that by the end of the week, "I didn't think of it as a scavenger hunt, so much as a self-challenge to open up more and notice who I speak to."

It doesn't seem like a stretch to think that when we start to notice other people more often, we might also start to notice the world around us more often. And this has a surprising benefit: It might bring us good luck. After all, what *is* good luck? Psychologist Richard Wiseman believes that much of what people refer to as luck is instead the natural result of their thoughts and behaviors.[20] He thinks people can learn how to be lucky, and one of the key skills is attentiveness.

In one study, he asked people who consider themselves lucky and people who consider themselves unlucky to count the number of photographs in a newspaper. On the second page of the newspaper, there was a message in a large font that took up half the page telling people to stop counting because there were forty-three photographs. The people who considered themselves lucky were more likely to notice this message, whereas the unlucky people were so focused on counting the photographs that they didn't notice it.

As Wiseman puts it, "unlucky people miss chance opportunities because they are too focused on looking for something else." He believes that people can learn to be "luckier" by noticing (and creating) chance opportunities, listening to their intuition, nurturing positive expectations, and adopting an attitude of resilience (which sounds a lot like getting comfortable with uncertainty and rejection).

Paying attention underlies every aspect of our lives. The "father of American psychology" William James, in true academic fashion, wrote about attention literally: "My experience is what I agree to attend to. Only those items which I notice shape my mind."

But the same is true metaphorically, as stated so poetically in a quote attributed to Mary Oliver: "This is the first, the wildest and the wisest thing I know: that the soul exists and is built entirely out of attentiveness."

### The skill of enjoying the moment

On a walk in my neighborhood, I noticed a man in his garage, which had more than a dozen paintings hung on the walls. I made a comment on his garage gallery, and we ended up chatting about how long he's been painting, the various places that he has painted, etc. I was enjoying our conversation when, with a jolt, I remembered that I had a dentist appointment to get to—I'd been so caught up in the moment that I almost forgot. (Like father, like daughter—Dad would head out to run a simple errand, and we'd never know when to expect him because he'd always end up chatting and lose track of time.)

There are many reasons that I regularly talk to strangers, but one of the simplest is: I enjoy it. It's fun to discover that some people have turned their garages into galleries (and that people can ride ostriches). After a week of practice, the people who played the scavenger hunt game also enjoyed talking to strangers more than they had before. By developing the ability to enjoy a fleeting, everyday moment with a stranger, we might also learn to enjoy other kinds of life's small joys.

People walking through a town in California were handed flyers that urged them to stop and smell the roses, in a study by Andrew Gregory and his colleagues.[21] Although the roses in this expression are often metaphorical, in this case they were literal: Down the street, volunteers associated with the research study waited with a bouquet. The flyers that people had received before they came across the table offered one of two reasons why people should savor the moment: "Life is unpredictable" or "Life is constant." People who were prompted to think about uncertainty were more than twice as likely to stop and smell the roses (26 percent compared to 11 percent of people who received the other flyer). The researchers concluded that when we feel unsure about the future, we pay more attention to pleasurable experiences in the present moment. In the same way, the uncertainty that comes with talking to strangers might also make us more mindful and able to enjoy the moments.

## Thinking more positively about other people

Many of us have been warned since childhood about "stranger danger" (though this term has been retired and kids are now being taught a more nuanced message).[22] At the same time, we're motivated to believe that others are generally good and trustworthy—these beliefs help us feel that the world is safe and predictable. If our belief in the goodness of others is shattered—through trauma, for example—our ability to cope hinges on our ability to rebuild that belief.[23]

E.M. Forster wrote, in *Howard's End*, about the tension between trust and suspicion: "The confidence trick is the work of man, but the want-of-confidence trick is the work of the devil."

He thought that even if we sometimes go wrong by placing too much confidence in others, "It's better to be fooled than to be suspicious."

Forster was on to something because research finds that when we believe in the goodness of other people, we feel safer and happier.[24]

The extent to which we believe that there's more good than bad in the world, and that people are generally good and trustworthy, can change. It changes as a result of experiencing trauma, but it also changes as we age: We find it easier to believe in the benevolence of people, and the world more generally, as we age.[25] In my experience, it also changes when you repeatedly talk to strangers.

It's hard for me to remember how nervous past-Gillian used to feel about other people, when I used to drop my eyes to the ground as a way to feel safe. I've learned that I feel safer if I connect with strangers rather than shutting myself off from them. Now, after having so many positive conversations, I walk through the world differently, believing that people are generally friendly and kind, and knowing that I could have a nice chat with pretty much anyone. For me, this is the single biggest benefit of my now-habit of talking to strangers.

People who played the scavenger hunt game also noticed a shift in their perceptions. By the end of a week of talking to strangers, they felt more warmly toward strangers and trusted strangers more. One person realized that "people are generally nicer than [they] expected," and another that "strangers are generally friendly and helpful" (which reminds me of Jackie, from Krispy Kreme).

Even a single conversation with a stranger is able (at least temporarily) to change our perceptions about strangers. In a study I ran with Erica and Gus during Covid lockdowns, I paired up strangers to talk to each other online.[26] They arranged when to meet each other and what technology they would use, and they talked for as long as they wanted (which turned out to be, on average, about forty minutes!). After that single conversation, people felt a greater sense of trust in others than they had before, and they could recognize the goodness of other people.

Research by Taylor West and her collaborators at the University of North Carolina at Chapel Hill suggests that this might go both ways. In our Covid study, we found that after people had a (presumably positive) chat with a stranger, they reported more trust in others. Taylor and her collaborators found that people who felt more trust in others also felt more positive after interacting with a stranger.[27] In one study, the researchers asked people to imagine moving to a new town and losing their wallet. Some people were asked to imagine that their wallet was returned and that a neighbor said: "That's not surprising, people tend to look out for each other around here." Other people were asked to imagine that their wallet wasn't returned and that a neighbor said: "That's not surprising, people tend to look out for themselves around here." When people imagined interacting with a stranger (e.g., a store clerk or a person at the park), those who had the impression that people in their new community were trustworthy (vs. not) expected to have a more positive conversation.

## Cutting your own skeleton key

How can you cut your own skeleton key so that you can get more comfortable with rejection and uncertainty and social judgment, develop the skills of noticing and enjoying life's small moments, and learn to see the goodness in others? You don't need to play a scavenger hunt game (but you could, if that appeals to you; I've made the list of scavenger hunt missions available on my website[28]). In theory, it's very simple: You just need to find people to talk to and then talk to them. In practice, it's not always so simple. You may need to channel your inner researcher and experiment with different approaches until you find what works best for you. (The appendix on page 235 provides some tips on how to get started.)

The results of the scavenger hunt study provide reassuring evidence that most people can learn to enjoy talking to strangers. Unfortunately, I can't promise you that it will be easy. It will take time, practice, and patience. You may experience setbacks. I hope you'll approach talking to strangers with a growth mindset: as a challenge rather than a pass/fail test that defines you forever as a successful stranger-talker or an unsuccessful social misfit. Many of the regular people who played the scavenger hunt game—people just like you—were nervous but grew more confident over time and enjoyed the experience. There's no reason to think that the same won't be true for you.

The scavenger hunt study was my way of giving people a taste of what I've experienced through talking to hundreds and hundreds of strangers. This now-habit of mine has proven to be a skeleton key that has opened doors that I wouldn't have expected—including the door to a new job that I love. Two years after I met Robin at the conference, he called to offer me the position and I joyously accepted.

# 7

# The Kindness of Strangers

In the lead-up to the Brexit referendum in 2016, my husband and I took the Eurostar train from London to Paris and spent a glorious long weekend eating pains au chocolat, drinking wine, and riding rental bikes along the Seine. When it was time to return home, we arrived at the train station ridiculously early because we knew that the customs officers were scrutinizing passports extra carefully, to make a point about how Brexit would cause delays. We couldn't believe our eyes: There was an endless line of people, snaking all the way around the cavernous entry hall of the station. We joined the end of the line and resigned ourselves to a long, tedious wait.

We stood in that line for hours, and much of the time it felt like the line wasn't moving at all. At first, we commiserated with the people near us in the line. But it doesn't take long until I get tired of complaining about things that can't be changed—and besides, we didn't want to ruin our postgetaway warm glow. Instead, we chatted about other topics, particularly with an older couple who'd been visiting their grandchildren. We talked about family, work, and places we had all traveled—in France and beyond. It would be an exaggeration to say that the time flew, but at least it didn't drag.

As we continued to wait, it became more and more likely that we wouldn't leave on time, and we started to think about how the delay would affect our travel once we arrived in London. Normally, we would have simply transferred to a local train to get home, but that day, the first part of our route was closed due to track repairs. Instead, we would first have to take an agonizingly slow bus replacement service past the section of the tracks that was under repair before we could switch to the local train. It was shaping up to be a long, exhausting evening.

When we mentioned all this to our new acquaintances, providence intervened. They lived in a town on our local train line (Chelmsford), and they offered to drive us forty-five minutes from the Eurostar station to the Chelmsford train station. Chelmsford was past the point where the track repairs were happening, so we wouldn't have to take the bus replacement. Even better, they weren't going all the way into London but were instead getting off the Eurostar at an earlier stop (Ebbsfleet), which would also save us some time.

We eventually boarded the train in Paris and went our separate ways, to our assigned seats. (It felt so wonderful to sit down, after standing for so many hours in that line.) The journey itself was uneventful, and it took less time to travel to Ebbsfleet station than we had spent waiting in line in Paris. When my husband and I were two of only a handful of people to get off the train at Ebbsfleet, I felt a brief stab of anxiety. What if we couldn't find the nice older couple? How would we get home from here? But then we spotted them, appearing on the platform like our gray-haired guardian angels. They safely delivered us to Chelmsford station, and we only had to wait a few minutes for our local train. I had a warm feeling in my chest as I sat on those familiar blue cushions, full of gratitude for the kindness of strangers.

We had talked to this nice couple for hours, and they no longer felt like complete strangers by the time they made their kind offer, but strangers have often lent me a listening ear, given me directions, provided helpful tips, etc. Once, on my daily walk, I said hi to a woman in dirt-smudged clothes outside a local allotment garden and commented on the gladioli she was carrying: They were my late grandfather's favorite flower. She insisted I take some of her excess summer vegetables, which I turned into a tasty ratatouille. At the Wimbledon tennis tournament, in a line for the ladies' toilets (why is there always a line for the ladies' toilets?), a woman who was heading home near the end of the day gave me her tickets. I was visiting with my dad, who's a huge tennis fan, and we had a grounds pass that let us watch the lower-ranked players up close on the smaller courts. This woman's ticket allowed my dad the priceless experience of sitting on Centre Court at Wimbledon and watching the end of an exciting match between higher-ranked players. While walking in England's Lake District, I learned that strangers might be performing acts of kindness that I wasn't even aware of: A walker told me that he always greets people on the trail as a way of unobtrusively checking that they have enough water and aren't lost or disoriented. The kind couple on the Eurostar were clearly not an exception.

## People are kinder than you think

Consider a study that was conducted at a botanical garden.[1] Researchers Xuan Zhao and Nick Epley put up a sign offering visitors a free photo, taken on a Polaroid instant camera. The only catch was that visitors needed to ask a stranger to take the photo. People underestimated how many strangers would be willing to take photos for them (96 percent of the strangers agreed) and how good the photographers would feel after helping. They also thought it would be more of an inconvenience to the photographers than it was. It seems like strangers are kinder than we expect and happier to help.

Acts of hate and aggression make headline news, but quiet acts of kindness occur far more frequently. Just before I started my new job at the University of Sussex, I worked on a public science project called the Kindness Test,[2] which was spearheaded by Robin Banerjee at Sussex and Claudia Hammond at BBC Radio 4 (who has written a wonderful book sharing some of the results of the project[3]). Over sixty thousand people from across the UK and around the world kindly answered our lengthy questionnaire. The results show that kindness happens all the time; about 60 percent of people said that someone had been kind to them within the last day (16 percent of people said they had received an act of kindness within the last hour). Many of these acts of kindness were between strangers; 5,607 people (10 percent) told us that the most recent time someone had been kind to them, it had been a stranger.

Kindness is the norm. When people around the world report their strongest-held values, benevolence (i.e., being helpful, honest, forgiving, loyal, and responsible) consistently comes out first—above values like security, power, achievement, and hedonism.[4,5] But we're not simply kind because we feel compelled to follow the unwritten rules imposed by societal values. We're also kind because it feels good.

Kindness is an example of what researchers call "prosocial behavior": behavior intended to benefit others (e.g., cooperating, volunteering, donating time or money). A review of twenty-seven research studies involving more than four thousand participants found a consistent pattern: After people do a prosocial act, they're happier.[6] (Even simple everyday niceness—acting in a warm and friendly way, such as smiling and greeting people, or giving someone a compliment—makes people happy.)[7] This connection between kindness and happiness seems to be universal. According to a study by Lara Aknin, now at Simon Fraser University, people all over the world, even in places that are economically deprived, are happier when they use their money to benefit others rather than themselves.[8] And being kind doesn't seem to be something that we simply learn to enjoy, because in another study led by Lara, even babies are visibly happier when they give goldfish crackers to a friendly monkey puppet rather than keeping the treats for themselves.[9]

There's something special about how kindness makes us feel. In general, we get used to things and they start to provide less pleasure than before. Maybe you've had the experience of listening to a favorite song so many times that instead of making you want to dance, it makes you want to stick your fingers in your ears? Or maybe you've regularly returned to a restaurant for their delectable four-cheese gnocchi, but the last time you ordered it, it was sadly underwhelming? We may not get used to kindness as quickly. In a study by Ed O'Brien at the University of Chicago and Samantha Kassirer at Northwestern University, people played a word-search game ten times. After each game they were either given a small amount of money to keep for themselves or the same amount was donated to a charity of their choosing.[10] Although everyone's happiness declined over time (people were happier after the first game than after the tenth game), those who earned money for charity stayed happier for longer. By the tenth game, their happiness had declined only half as much as it had for people who had earned money for themselves.

## Barriers to kindness

Since it feels so good to be kind, you'd think we'd be kind more often. But, of course, it's not that simple. There are social forces pushing us toward kindness but psychological forces pushing in the opposite direction, making us second-guess our better instincts. It's not hard to remember a time when we were inclined to do something for someone but then decided not to. Just as we can come up with lots of reasons for *not* talking to a stranger, we can come up with lots of reasons for *not* carrying out an act of kindness. When we're inclined to be kind to a stranger, one of those reasons might be that, in order to be kind to a stranger, we usually need to talk to them.

When I looked through all the stories that people shared in the Kindness Test, I realized that acts of kindness between strangers often involved a conversation between strangers. There are some exceptions, of course: Bus drivers waited to let passengers board, people held doors open for others or let others ahead of them in traffic. But in many cases, a conversation was the means to carry out the act of kindness: People complimented strangers, thanked them, asked if they were OK or needed assistance, helped them find their way, or taught them how to use a ticket machine. (There were *so many* stories about getting help with ticket machines. I don't know what kind of intensive training is required to figure out these devices, but I *can* tell you from personal experience that getting a PhD isn't sufficient.) Other acts of kindness didn't *require* a conversation but likely involved an incidental one; it's possible for someone, without talking, to offer up a seat on the bus or wave someone ahead of them in a line at the grocery store, but it's more likely for a few words to be exchanged.

If, in order to be kind to a stranger, we also need to talk to them, then those of us who are worried about talking to strangers might choose to withhold our kindness and instead wait for an opportunity that doesn't require us to talk. There are some hints that this may be the case, at least in the stories that people shared in the Kindness Test. We asked people whether their act of kindness had involved saying something to the other person, doing something for them, giving something to them, or providing them with information. When people showed kindness to acquaintances, friends, and family, saying something was the most common way to be kind (35 percent of the stories). In contrast, when people showed kindness to strangers, doing something (38 percent of the stories) was the most common way to be kind, and saying something (21 percent of the stories) was less common. These data might be a sign that our concerns about talking to strangers are limiting our ability to be kind—or at least to be kind in certain ways.

When we consider being kind to a stranger, we worry twice: We worry about having to talk to a stranger, *and* we worry about carrying out the kind act. Some of our concerns about being kind to strangers are similar to our concerns about talking to strangers.

For one thing, we worry that we don't know what we're doing, that we're not good enough. We worry, for example, that we won't be able to compliment someone without sounding patronizing or that we won't find the right words to support someone who's struggling and might instead make things worse. Secondly, we worry about what the other person will think of us, about how our kindness will be received and perceived. Will a stranger be pleased by our compliment or will it just feel awkward for both of us? We worry about these two things—our competence and how we'll be judged—even when we're delivering a compliment or providing support to someone we know,[11, 12] so it's no surprise that we have similar worries when we do these things for a stranger.

However, as with our worries about talking to strangers, our worries about being kind to strangers are unwarranted. Competence doesn't seem to matter all that much when we're on the receiving end. If someone gives us a genuine compliment, we don't get hung up on the exact words. We just feel flattered that a complete stranger noticed us and went to the effort of saying something nice. This seems to be a general pattern across various kind acts: The person who does something kind worries about their competence—whether they did it well enough—whereas the person on the receiving end simply appreciates the gesture, and the warmth that it conveys.[13] Knowing this has helped me trust my instincts a bit more. I find that I'm better able to push past my worries and do something kind if I can remember that the other person cares about my positive intentions more than my eloquence (or, according to Sid, my lack thereof).

We worry more than we should about our own competence, but also about how others will respond to our attempts to be kind. Researchers Amit Kumar and Nick Epley gave free cups of hot chocolate to people who were ice skating in a public park in Chicago. Then they asked those people if they would be willing to give it away to a stranger of their choice.[14] Ninety percent agreed because people really are generally kind. These "givers" realized that people would enjoy the free treat, but they underestimated just how much. The recipients thought it was a much bigger act of kindness than the givers did. (Children as young as four years old underestimate how good another child will feel after receiving a free pencil/pen and how much they will value the act of kindness.)[15]

It seems likely, then, that the skeleton key that we cut by learning how to talk to strangers allows us to open yet another door: the ability to be more kind.

## Learning to talk to strangers allows you to be kind

Most of this book has focused on the surprising ways that *we* benefit from talking to strangers, but if we flip that around, it becomes clear that we can help *others* benefit in those same ways: We can offer support with no strings, we can hand someone a puzzle piece or plant a seed for them, we can help someone feel seen, we can share a laugh. And these acts are noticed and appreciated as acts of kindness—even when they come from a stranger.

### Offering no strings

I met Floyd while attending a classical music festival, and he helped me gain perspective when I was adjusting to life after divorce. People who took part in the Kindness Test told us similar stories of strangers listening to them, encouraging them, and offering them support and advice:

- "I was in tears, and they asked me how I was and listened to me."
- "A stranger said some encouraging words to me when she could see I was in a stressful situation."
- "The grocery clerk listened as I told her I was sad that my dog died. She asked details about him, talked about her own loss, and told me it's OK to mourn."

The fact that people told us these stories when we asked them to tell us about a time someone had been kind to them suggests that people often appreciate strangers' attempts to provide support. However, you might worry about what would happen if *you* were to offer support to a stranger. What if you said the wrong thing? What if they think it's inappropriate, intrusive, or presumptuous for you to even attempt to be supportive?

By now, you can guess what I'm going to say: You're probably worrying too much. James Dungan, David Munguia Gomez, and Nick Epley brought together pairs of strangers and asked one person to describe an issue they were currently dealing with and could use some support for.[16] These "recipients" described issues related to employment and finances, family and romantic relationships, health, etc. Their partner was asked to express support in whatever way they felt was appropriate. Supporters worried that recipients would feel uncomfortable receiving support from a stranger, but recipients felt less awkward than supporters feared and more cared for than supporters expected. They also thought supporters did a better job than they thought they'd done—the support came across as sincere, warm, and articulate. This study tells us that not only do strangers appreciate our support more than we expect, but we're also better at providing it than we realize.

I think author Paula Hawkins in *The Girl on the Train* beautifully described the ability of strangers to extend support and kindness through a lack of strings: "It's impossible to resist the kindness of strangers. Someone who looks at you, who doesn't know you, who tells you it's OK, whatever you did, whatever you've done: you suffered, you hurt, you deserve forgiveness."

You might feel more comfortable offering support to a stranger if you knew what the right words are—and the wrong ones. Researchers would love to know this, too, but they have unfortunately come to little agreement on what those things might be—or if there even are "right" or "wrong" things to say.[17] (Well, there are a few "wrong" things, but it doesn't take a scientist to know what they are. Sometimes we say the wrong things anyway, maybe because we feel so anxious and uncomfortable in the situation that we panic. Hopefully our warmth and positive intentions make up for these very human blunders.) Instead, what researchers *do* agree on is that we shouldn't let our anxiety about what to say result in us not saying anything at all. Avoiding contact or avoiding a tricky topic can be upsetting and unhelpful to someone who's in distress.[18, 19] Perhaps the best thing we can do for someone is to ask them what kind of support they want. An article in *The New York Times* suggests that one way to do this is to ask someone whether they want to be helped, heard, or hugged.[20] (Hugging a stranger is a bit next level, but there were a few stories in the Kindness Test of hugs between strangers. I've hugged a handful of strangers over the years—like the pregnant lady on the Tube and the woman with the fancy camera after the starling murmuration. After asking permission, of course.)

We probably worry too much about exactly what to say because we can offer support with no words at all, by simply listening (like Al, from his bench in St. Petersburg, Florida). Effective listening involves giving someone our full attention and showing them that we understand their perspective—and doing these things genuinely and with positive intentions.[21] We show people that we're listening through nonverbal signals like maintaining eye contact and nodding our head, but also by paraphrasing, reflecting back what we've heard, and asking open, nonjudgmental questions[22]—especially follow-up questions that dig deeper on responses to earlier questions.[23] When we listen well, we show the other person that we care about them and value them. (Added bonus: We feel better, too, when we listen well.)[24]

Our objectivity might also allow us to be kind in another way: providing feedback that has the potential to help someone (i.e., constructive feedback). In one study, researchers asked students several questions, ostensibly to see if they were eligible to participate in a paid study.[25] The real purpose of asking the questions was to get the students to look at the researcher, to test whether the students would tell the researcher that they had a chocolate or lipstick smudge on their face. Quite a few people (57) claimed they hadn't noticed the smudge, but of the 155 who admitted that they *had* noticed, only 4 people mentioned it to the researcher. We withhold feedback because we don't want the other person to feel uncomfortable and we don't want it to harm our relationship. Maybe it's easier to give feedback to a stranger because there is no relationship to harm, and the lack of strings means both parties feel less emotionally involved. (Which isn't to say that we are more *willing* to give constructive feedback to strangers; the researchers found that another major impediment is that we underestimate how much our constructive feedback will be valued, and we do that with strangers as well as with people that we know.)

## Presenting puzzle pieces and planting seeds

When I met a lawyer who had changed professions midlife, it opened my mind to the same possibility for myself. People who took part in the Kindness Test also learned from strangers:

- "I was following written instructions for a walk and got lost. A stranger went out of his way to show me the right path."
- "A bus service had been canceled without notification and a kind reverend gentleman stopped and told me, and gave me the number for a taxi service."
- "[A] gentleman helped me to understand the complexity of paying for a car parking ticket from a machine that required a degree!"

These examples are, admittedly, more mundane than my experience with the lawyer, but the Kindness Test asked people about the most *recent* act of kindness they had experienced, not the most memorable or meaningful.

Sometimes the things we learn from talking to strangers plant seeds of connection, opportunity, possibility, and change. It's hard for a third party to judge whether a seed has been planted, but some of the stories from the Kindness Test, involving strangers providing information, seem seedlike to me:

- "A customer stopped for a chat in my shop and then later called me to give me the phone number for a support group that she thought I could use."

- "While on a dog walk, an older gentleman stopped to chat. We talked about our love of Devon and he recommended his favorite place there."
- "I am new here and was invited for coffee with a neighbor I had not met. She made a list of everyone's names in the road. Very helpful."
- "A lady unknown to me crocheted some hedgehogs, put them in boxes with instructions on how to care for real hedgehogs, and hid them on the estate."

When we provide strangers with information, we avoid some of the worries that come with other ways of being kind. We might worry that we don't know the right words to say to someone who's struggling, but we either know how to use the ticket machine or we don't. The information that we hold is the source of our competence. Similarly, we might worry that someone who's struggling won't appreciate us trying to provide emotional support, but we know that someone will appreciate finding out that the bus they were waiting for has been canceled. The fact that we don't need to worry as much about our competence or social judgment from the other person means that providing a stranger with information is an especially nonscary way to be kind to a stranger.

### Helping others feel seen

When I returned to school after working for ten years, that smile-and-wave relationship with the lady who worked at a hot dog stand made me feel like I belonged on campus. People who took part in the Kindness Test also shared stories of feeling seen by strangers:

- "I was alone in a group of strangers on a wildlife walking tour and one woman made the effort to make conversation with me and ask me about myself."
- "People chatted to me and made me feel welcome in a new exercise class."

We've all had times when we were the new person, feeling uncertain and somehow simultaneously overlooked and conspicuous. I started playing tennis in my late twenties. (I hate going to the gym, so I needed to find another way to get some exercise.) As with any new skill, there was a steep learning curve. (It took me about seven years before I didn't dread when it was my turn to serve.) Shortly after taking up tennis, I attended a drop-in session, where a tennis pro arranged foursomes, changing up the partners every half hour or so. I found attending this session intimidating because I didn't know anyone, and I didn't play tennis well enough to be there. But, in order to improve, I needed to play more, and this session was meant to be social rather than competitive. I'll never forget one woman, who *really* didn't want to be stuck in a foursome with me. Her frustration and animosity shook what little confidence I had mustered just to have the courage to attend the session—and probably made me play worse too. Thankfully, during the next rotation, I was placed in a foursome with a woman called Sarah. She noticed that I was feeling nervous, and she encouraged me throughout our match. I'm sure she wouldn't remember doing this, but it meant the world to me. I might not be playing tennis today if it weren't for Sarah making me feel welcome that day. I hope that the skeleton key skills of attention and mindfulness that I've gained from talking to strangers improve my ability to notice newbies and pay forward the gift that Sarah gave me.

People who took part in the Kindness Test told us stories of being not only seen but also appreciated by strangers:

- "Chatting to a customer at work who talked about crochet and gave me a lot of compliments and treated me like a real human being instead of just a cashier."
- "Someone was kind enough to stop as they walked by and say how my garden improves their mood and life as they walk by each day."

Although most of us enjoy receiving compliments, we often worry about delivering them. As with providing support, we worry about getting the words just right—even when complimenting someone we know.[26] But this is yet another case of us worrying more than we need to. The people we compliment think we're more articulate and capable than we give ourselves credit for.

When delivering compliments, we also worry about how our compliment will be received. A study by Erica Boothby and Vanessa Bohns finds that this worry is also overblown.[27] The strangers we compliment feel more pleased and flattered than we expect and less uncomfortable. I know that I, for one, love getting compliments from strangers because they feel more genuine. It's easy for me to shrug off a compliment from a friend or family member as them simply being nice because they care about me, but a stranger has no such reason.

In December 2024, I attended a small-town Christmas tree festival. While we walked around the church admiring the trees that had been decorated by various community organizations and businesses, an elderly gentleman entertained us with music on the organ. When he took a break, I took the opportunity to compliment and thank him for his playing. He told me he had particularly enjoyed playing a piece called "Carillon de Westminster," which included the tones from Big Ben's chime. It had been written by a man called Louis Vierne, who was the resident organist at Notre Dame Cathedral in Paris. The day of the Christmas tree festival was the day of the grand reopening of Notre Dame (after the fire in 2019). Without taking the time to compliment the organist, I wouldn't have learned the music's backstory and would have missed out on the significance of that thoughtful moment of tribute on that hopeful day.

## *Sharing a laugh*

Because this book has focused on *surprising* benefits of talking to strangers, I haven't talked much about one unsurprising benefit that I'm sure you've spotted between the lines: It can be a lot of fun. People who took part in the Kindness Test told us about conversations with strangers that made their days a little brighter:

- "A stranger made a lighthearted comment about the weather, while I was waiting at the bus stop. It was just a little bit of light in a dark world."
- "I was having coffee and I'd [showed up on] the wrong day and the person on the next table began chatting to me. She was thoughtful, listened, and we laughed together."

These stories tell us that even when there are no tangible benefits, simply having a friendly chat can make someone's day.

One of the most memorable conversations I've had with a stranger happened while I was on holiday with my husband in Wales. It started in the same way as hundreds of others: I spotted a cute dog and went up to say hello to the dog and its human. The human turned out to be fascinating—he had spent his career making wigs for theater and film productions. He clearly loved talking to strangers because he invited us over to his house for a drink, and we later learned that we weren't the first strangers he'd invited over. (Note to my mom: I know that I also told you about going for a walk in the woods with a stranger, but I promise that I don't make a habit of this sort of thing, and I wouldn't have gone into a stranger's house alone.) We had a lovely chat, and he and I even ended up playing a duet on his piano. When my husband and I left to rush off to our dinner reservation, I could hardly believe what had just happened! This man, through his warmth and hospitality, left me with a special holiday memory.

You might not ever invite a stranger over for a drink (the only invitations I've extended have been in public places), but we can all leave someone with happy memories by simply having a friendly chat. We can all offer support, share information, plant seeds (of connection, opportunity, or possibility), and give someone a compliment. We can all notice when somebody is new and help them feel seen by showing them around, making them a cup of tea, or simply saying hello. These stories from the Kindness Test show us just how much strangers tend to appreciate small acts of civility and kindness. This is articulated in one of my favorite quotes attributed to professor and author Leo Buscaglia: "Too often we underestimate the power of a touch, a smile, a kind word, a listening ear, an honest compliment, or the smallest act of caring, all of which have the potential to turn a life around."

If Sid tries to convince you that you shouldn't ask someone if they're OK, help someone find their way, or deliver a compliment, please remind him that you're more competent than he thinks. Remind him, too, of how good it feels to be on the receiving end of these actions and that the action matters more than the exact words.

## Kindness between strangers is less complicated

As you can imagine, since becoming the director of a center for research on kindness, I've talked to a lot of people about kindness. I get the sense that many of us feel that we don't measure up: We're not as kind as we think we should be, not as kind as we'd like to be. One reason that we might doubt our own kindness is that we seem to think that kindness doesn't count if it benefits us in some way.

The problem in only allowing ourselves credit for "pure" altruism is that kindness almost always benefits us (as well as the person we're being kind to, of course). When we do things for our relatives or to benefit members of a group that we belong to, it helps our family/group (and therefore us) to survive and thrive. When we're kind to someone that we expect to meet again, we're likely to benefit from that person reciprocating at some point in the future. Regardless of who we're being kind to, when others see us being kind it enhances our reputation because kindness is universally valued. And finally, as we saw at the beginning of this chapter, doing things for others generally makes us feel good.

The way I see it, if benefitting someone else is genuinely your primary motivation, then you're acting out of kindness. Motives are the key. Although we generally feel good after we do things like help or spend money on someone, we don't feel as good when we do those things for selfish reasons, like self-improvement, self-enhancement, or self-protection.[28] That may be because different parts of our brain are activated when we're aware that our act of kindness will have payoffs for us rather than only benefitting someone else.[29]

It's easier to trust the purity of our motives when we do an act of kindness for a stranger rather than someone we know. In a project that I ran with Mia Brady and Taylor West, we asked participants to imagine seeing one of several acts of kindness (e.g., someone offering to carry a heavy bag at the supermarket, or someone giving a compliment to a person who was trying on a jacket at a clothing store).[30] We asked some participants to imagine that people were doing these acts for someone that they knew, and others to imagine that people were doing these acts for strangers. Participants thought that the people who were kind to strangers had exerted more effort and were more selfless (and less likely to benefit) than the people who were kind to known others. That may be why, in the Kindness Test, people felt just as happy, but prouder and like a better person, after being kind to a stranger versus someone they knew.

Doing something kind for a stranger not only feels especially meaningful to us but also has advantages for them because it comes with no strings. Imagine that you're at work, and your colleague Sammy pokes their head in your office and offers to help you with a report that you're working on, a report with a tight deadline that's stressing you out. You accept their kind offer, but then you might start to wonder if you made the right decision. You might start to worry that this act of kindness comes laden with hidden messages: Maybe Sammy only offered to help because they felt sorry for you.

Maybe they didn't think you'd do a good job on the report and that they could do better. (And Sid, of course, will try to turn this into: *Sammy's better than I am, I'm terrible at my job, I'm going to get fired....*) The joy of receiving an act of kindness dissipates if we attribute it to pity,[31] feel like it calls our competence into question,[32] or feel indebted and worry about being unable to reciprocate.[33]

Now imagine that a stranger sees you struggling to figure out how to use a parking machine. They ask if you need help, and you accept their kind offer. You won't be able to return the favor, but they don't expect you to. You might, as in the workplace example, wonder if they feel sorry for you or question your competence. However, these thoughts are less threatening because you're less likely with a stranger to let these thoughts snowball into: *They think I'm useless; they're right; I'm never going to drive anywhere again because there's no way I'll ever figure out parking machines.* Chances are, you're left simply thinking: *How kind of them!* And: *Maybe people are kinder than I thought....*

## Making the world a little kinder

I think many people would agree: The world could use more kindness. One simple way that each of us can make the world a little better is by talking to strangers. Beloved writer Maya Angelou is quoted as saying: "Good done anywhere is good done everywhere. For a change, start by speaking to people rather than walking by them like they're stones that don't matter. As long as you're breathing, it's never too late to do some good."

Once you feel more comfortable talking to strangers, your skeleton key will help you feel more comfortable doing acts of kindness for strangers too. You'll notice opportunities for small acts that take little time or effort but have a big impact. Because kindness toward strangers comes with fewer strings, it can feel especially good—for you *and* them. I hope that being kind toward strangers will help you realize that you *are* kind—probably more kind than you give yourself credit for. I also hope that being kind to strangers will help you realize that other people are more kind than you gave them credit for but may be held back by the same concerns that (used to) restrain you.

There's another, somewhat counterintuitive way that I believe you can add a drop of kindness to the world's bucket: Allow others to be kind to you. It can feel uncomfortable to be on the receiving end of kindness. We might doubt the other person's intentions or simply not want to impose on them. I was invited to an event to lead a session on kindness in the workplace. Afterward, my host asked me if I'd like a cup of tea. My first thought was: She's busy running this event and has more important things to do than make me a cup of tea—I can just make my own. But then I realized that she genuinely wanted to do something kind for me, maybe to thank me for coming to the event. I thought about the research (occupational hazard) and realized that she would likely feel good after making me a cup of tea and might instead feel bad if I turned down her kind offer. So (after an embarrassingly long pause while I considered all this) I said: "Yes, thank you, I'd love a cup of tea."

You could even take this a step further and ask others for help. Instead of struggling to reach that item on the high shelf at the supermarket, you could ask someone to help you. Instead of pulling out your phone and trying to figure out if this is right place to catch the bus heading downtown, you could ask someone who's already waiting at the bus stop. By asking for help, not only will you kindly give someone the opportunity to exercise and enjoy their own ability to be kind, but you might end up having a nice chat too.

You might be surprised at just how kind strangers can be. My dear friend Traci was on sabbatical, staying with her husband, Steve, in an apartment in Paris for several months, when they were given an unusual opportunity to be kind to a stranger. Here's how she told the story on social media, accompanied by a picture that she had taken: "Meet Sebastian, staying in the apartment below ours. He just arrived in town to attend a ball, but when he opened his suitcase, alas, his dress shoes were not there, and the ball is starting now. So he knocked on our door and asked if anyone had dress shoes size 41 to 43. Suffice it to say, Steve's shoes are attending a ball in Paris."

I think that Traci and Steve did a wonderful thing by lending a pair of shoes, though I'm sure they would say it was no big deal. I'd wager that, years from now, Sebastian will remember not only that time that he went to a ball in Paris, but that a stranger was kind enough to lend him a pair of dress shoes. (In case you're wondering, the shoes appeared outside the apartment door the next day, along with some chocolate. They refuse to divulge any stories about their adventures.)

## Ripples of kindness

This is a book about small things, everyday moments. It's easy to discount small things, but one of the life lessons my mom taught me, that I've taken to heart, is that small things add up to bigger things. Small acts of kindness can kick-start a virtuous cycle. When we do something kind for someone, however small, we feel good (and, by the way, possibly less lonely too).[34] And when we feel good, we're more likely to do another kind thing.[35] (Talking to strangers likely kicks off a similar process. Talking to strangers feels good, and these good feelings might make us want to talk to strangers even more often.)

Kindness between strangers is goodness squared—the good feelings are intensified for both the giver and the receiver. But the good feelings ripple further: People who see you being kind to a stranger also feel good. In the Kindness Test, we found that the people who noticed more kindness around them tended to be happier and less lonely. Psychologists have coined a term for the positive emotion that we feel when we see others do something virtuous, such as an act of generosity: elevation.[36] In addition to feeling uplifted, we sometimes feel an opening in the chest or a lump in the throat.

Elevation doesn't just feel good. Others' goodness makes us aspire to more goodness ourselves. In one study, people watched an uplifting video in which a "musician pays tribute to his mentor and former music teacher, who had saved him from a life of gang activity and violence."[37] The more elevation people felt while watching the video, the longer they volunteered to help the researcher with a boring task.[38] By talking to and doing acts of kindness for strangers, not only can you personally make the world a little better, but you might even inspire others to do the same.

That couple on the Eurostar offered an act of kindness that meant a lot to my husband and me. They saved us about an hour's worth of time late at night and some hassle too. If you look at it objectively, the act itself was small—they only had to go a few minutes out of their way to drop us off at the train station on their way home. But the bigger act of kindness was the trust they showed by letting complete strangers in their car. They gave us living proof of how much kindness there is in the world. I'll never forget it.

# Conclusion

In January 2023, I read an article in *The New York Times* called "Future Cringe." People from various walks of life were asked to weigh in on the question: "What are the things we do today that will seem embarrassing or otherwise regrettable to our future selves—the stuff that will make us cringe when we look back on how we lived our lives in the early 2020s?"[1] The respondents proposed things like wearing Crocs, pushing domestic pets in baby carriages, and drinking from plastic bottles. Bill Schulz, TV writer and journalist, said: "You know how the very idea of a phone conversation, regarding anything that can otherwise be texted, seems rude at this point? I think we'll feel the same way about face-to-face conversations 20 years from now, whether it be a random interaction on the street or having dinner with actual friends. It will seem offensive to 'future us' if a person attempts actual verbal contact."

At first, I thought it was satire, poking fun at our current obsession with technology. But when I thought about it a bit more, my heart skipped a few beats. If you were to look objectively at our current behavior, it really does seem that we're walking obliviously along a path toward the future that Schulz describes. It chilled me to realize that it's not all that implausible that Schulz's dystopian vision could become our reality.

It doesn't help that there's some obvious appeal to a world with fewer face-to-face interactions. It's often cheaper and more efficient to interact with machines instead of people. And machines are, at least in theory, more straightforward than humans (with the clear exception of parking machines). We don't have to make small talk with a machine or pretend that we find a machine interesting. We don't have to worry about forgetting a machine's name or wonder what a machine's thinking about us. It's a huge relief to be able to avoid the social judgment and confusing rules of face-to-face interactions—especially for those of us who are socially anxious or on the autism spectrum. But it's worth thinking about what we're trading away in order to save money and time—and to avoid facing our overblown social fears.

I was prompted to rethink my own efficiency trade-offs after listening to computer scientist Daniele Quercia's thought-provoking TED talk.[2] He explains that, like many of us, he used a mapping app to plot the most efficient cycle commute to work. One day, after months and months of cycling along a colorless, car-clogged street, for some unremembered reason he took another route. His commute that day took two minutes longer, but the new route allowed him to cycle along a quiet, tree-lined street, which was far more enjoyable. He makes a powerful case that there are drawbacks to thoughtlessly prioritizing low cost and efficiency, and we might want to factor in other qualities, like beauty and happiness. If his mapping app had not only showed him the most efficient route but also the most beautiful route as an alternative, he could have avoided months of dreary commutes, knowing that it would only cost a few minutes of extra time.

It seems to me that our overprioritization of low cost and efficiency to the detriment of joy and connection is at least partly responsible for luring us down the path that Schulz described. When it comes to talking to a stranger, although it could take a few minutes of precious time, often we don't even need to sacrifice efficiency for enjoyment. Imagine you're at work, you pop out to your favorite place to buy a quick bite for lunch, and the line is tediously long. You might start thinking about how frustrating it is to wait in line, especially given that your to-do list is a mile long and you didn't get as much done in the morning as you had hoped (because, spoiler alert, nobody ever does). You might succumb to the siren call of social media and spend your time doomscrolling, which isn't going to do any favors for your mood. Instead, you could have a chat with someone else who's waiting in line. (You could even start the conversation by complaining about the length of the line.) It wouldn't take any extra time to have a chat. You're stuck in the line either way. There's no efficiency versus enjoyment trade-off. In fact, it's likely to make the waiting time pass more quickly and therefore feel *less* inefficient.

## Rosebushes

In some vineyards, rosebushes are planted at the end of a row of vines. Roses are highly susceptible to certain fungal diseases, meaning that they act as a sort of early warning system, allowing viticulturalists to intervene before the disease spreads to the vines. I think the fact that we seem to be having fewer interactions with strangers, the fact that we struggle with (and, more important, give in to) fear and anxiety and mistrust, could be an early warning that our broader social ecosystem is at risk.

How does a person become skilled at a sport or a musical instrument? We all know that part of the answer is: lots and lots of practice. Why would we expect social skills to be any different? Indeed, practice seems to help, as we saw with my talking-to-strangers scavenger hunt game (in chapter 6). So, it's worrisome that changes in our lifestyles (online shopping, working from home, etc.) are resulting in fewer opportunities to practice. I'm reminded of Sam from chapter 3, who was inspired to talk to more strangers but realized that his daily routines didn't provide many opportunities to do so, and he first needed to change his routines.

To make things worse, many of us feel that we lack a natural ability to talk to strangers, that we're less capable than other people (see chapter 1). It's not true but that's irrelevant—we feel what we feel. Although not essential, natural ability helps with skill-building: If the basics come more easily to us or we're able to learn more quickly, then we're often more motivated to practice.

Practice is required not only to develop skills but also to maintain them. If we have fewer opportunities to practice talking to strangers and we're not especially eager to do it in the first place, then it's no wonder if we start to lose confidence in our skills. Feeling unskilled makes us even less interested in talking, and voilà: We have ourselves a negative spiral.

And here's the scary part: The negative spiral might not stay restricted to our interactions with strangers. Our lifestyle changes might limit our opportunities to interact face-to-face with our acquaintances and friends as well as strangers. Believing that we lack the skills to talk to strangers is only a small step away from believing that we also lack the skills to talk to our acquaintances and friends. (And where will our acquaintances and friends come from, anyway, if we don't talk to strangers?)

The whole point of planting a rosebush is to provide a warning in time to intervene. If we can remember how good it feels to connect with and feel seen by other humans, maybe we can avoid Schulz's vision for the future. A future without these small, human interactions may be more efficient, but it's also bleak and lonely.

## Why talking to strangers matters

Most of us are lonely from time to time. According to Gallup survey data, about a quarter of the world's population feels very or fairly lonely.[3] Feelings of loneliness are a signal that we need to reach out and connect with others—just like a rumbling stomach tells us that we need to eat. If we can find ways to restore feelings of connection, then our loneliness is soon quelled. But unchecked, loneliness can change how we think about ourselves and others.[4] First, we become more fearful and anxious. Then, this changes how we act around others, and how they respond to us—ironically, we might elicit the very response that we fear. Loneliness, therefore, can become entwined with chronic stress, and that's when it gets under our skin and starts to affect our physical as well as mental health.

Thankfully, the world is starting to wake up to the importance of social connection, and lots of clever people and dynamic organizations have put their energy into coming up with solutions to help relieve chronic loneliness. Many efforts focus on helping people build new relationships. This aligns with popular advice. When asked what helps us feel less lonely, people who participated in a public science project called the Loneliness Test suggested joining a social club or taking up new social activities.[5]

However, Loneliness Test respondents also said that this is one of the most *un*helpful things that other people suggest. I think that's because it's easier said than done. Let's say you love to sing and decide to join a local choir that rehearses at a church, or you like to fix things and decide to volunteer at the local repair café. Sounds great in theory, but in practice, you need to go to the church or the repair café and walk into a room full of strangers. Most of us would find that pretty scary. If the people in the choir or at the repair café all seem to know one another already, it's even harder. If you've made it a habit to talk to strangers, however, walking into that church or repair café is a little easier. If you've made it a habit to talk to strangers, you'll have learned through repeated experience that people are generally friendly, and you'll have learned how to use your shared interest in music or tinkering as a built-in conversation starter. (And once you've settled in and gotten to know a few people, your habit of talking to strangers will allow you to reach out and welcome the next new person who comes along, making it a little easier for them to transition from stranger to valued member of the group.)

Building new relationships is one way to tackle loneliness, but it's hard work to build new relationships. As we saw in chapter 4, it can take two hundred hours to make a new friend, which equates to years and years of choir practices. Another thing we can do to tackle loneliness is take stock of the relationships we already have and think about whether there are any that we could reinforce or revive. There may be people who we were once close to but lost touch with for no particular reason: We got busy, they got busy, someone had a kid, someone moved to a new house.... Time passes and then it feels too late, somehow, to reach out. It may surprise you to hear that making it a habit to talk to strangers can help with this too.

I met my dear friend Lara Aknin during graduate school, and we've continued to work together ever since. We enjoy dreaming up research projects together, but what we love even more is the fact that working together gives us an excuse to meet regularly and catch up on each other's lives before diving into whatever our ongoing project is. Our most recent project had wrapped up several months earlier when Lara emailed me on New Year's Day in 2022, saying that she missed me and would love to meet up. She said it would be great to have a chat, but she also wanted to float an idea for a new project that we could work on together.

Lara told me that she had wanted to reach out to me for a while, but despite us being friends and working together for fifteen years, she felt that she needed some kind of excuse—like New Year's Day or a new research project that we could work on together. One of the joys of being a social psychologist is that we sometimes get to turn our personal experiences into research studies. Lara's research idea was to figure out why it had been so hard for her to reach out to me, and how to make it easier next time. We started collecting data and soon found that most people (at least three quarters) could think of someone they had lost touch with.[6] However, people generally felt the same reluctance to reach out that Lara had. Even when we gave people time to type a message and used various strategies to encourage them to send it, fewer than a third of people reached out. It's not that people don't want to reconnect—it's just that they don't want to be the one who reaches out. Instead, they want their old friend to reach out to them. But of course, their old friend is thinking the same thing. . . .

We eventually realized that reaching out to an old friend might feel a lot like talking to a stranger. For one thing, when people considered whether or not to reach out, they seemed to worry about some of the same things that people do when they consider talking to a stranger: What if they don't want to talk to me? What if we don't have anything in common (anymore)? We found that the more an old friend felt like a stranger, the less willing people were to reach out to them. In fact, people were no more willing to reach out to an old friend than they were to talk to a stranger (or to pick up litter!). If reconnecting with an old friend feels like talking to a stranger, then the skills that we maintain and strengthen through talking to strangers might also help us revive relationships from our past.

Talking to strangers isn't going to cure loneliness. But it might help us develop social skills and even a little bit of social confidence. It might be a good place to start.

## Taking the next step

My goals with this book have been to remind you of all the reasons why it's worthwhile to talk to strangers and to reassure you that it's likely to go better than you think. Now it's time for you to take the next step, whatever that is for you, and however small it may be.

You may be a beginner who identifies with past-Gillian, who couldn't maintain eye contact with a stranger, let alone imagine talking to one. You may be an inveterate stranger-talker like my dad; I know there are others out there because I once received an email with the subject line "Never knew we were related," that started with "Gillian, I learned recently that we are siblings because we have the same dad." Or, more likely, you're somewhere between past-Gillian and her/my irrepressible dad.

If you're not yet an inveterate stranger-talker, then your goal might be to talk to one stranger. If this feels like something you could do right now, then by all means, jump right in. If, on the other hand, this feels like a distant dream, then take a baby step. As civil rights leader Martin Luther King Jr. said, "Take the first step in faith. You don't have to see the whole staircase, just take the first step."

You could start, as I did, by making eye contact with people. (It took me ages to do this consistently.) You could smile at people (and nod, if you like—I find that helps people understand that your smile is directed at them). You could scope out the contexts that feel safest or easiest to you. You could choose a person and imagine how you would start a conversation with them. Take as long as you need to slowly work your way up to a greeting and eventually a brief chat. You can find some tips in the appendix (including some from my dad, see page 235), but I encourage you to experiment and find what works for you.

Once you've talked to one stranger, talk to another one. Your first conversation is likely to go well because most conversations with strangers do. There is, however, a good chance that it won't go as well as you'd hoped: Sid will berate you for anything less than exceptional. It would be irrational to expect your first conversation with a stranger to go as well as my dad's conversations do. My dad's an expert now, but he has fine-tuned his opening gambits and honed his skills over many decades. It would be irrational, and yet it's hard not to have unrealistic expectations, hard not to compare ourselves to experts and then feel disappointed when we inevitably fall short. It's also hard to see our own progress. As (double!) Nobel prize-winning scientist Marie Curie said, "One never notices what has been done; one can only see what remains to be done."

But progress *will* happen. The trick is to keep going. The more conversations you have, the easier it gets to talk to strangers. The more conversations you have, the more likely you are to have a particularly interesting, informative, or fun one. The more conversations you have, the more it will change how you see the world and your fellow humans. I'm not suggesting that you should talk to all the people, all the time. I'm simply encouraging you to talk to strangers a bit more often, regularly enough that you keep your stranger-talker muscles strong and toned.

If you're already an inveterate stranger-talker, this book may serve a different purpose for you: helping you articulate all the ways that you benefit and helping you celebrate the joy of talking to strangers. (In other words, if someone in your life finds it incomprehensible or embarrassing that you talk to strangers, like I did with my dad, feel free to use this book to justify your behavior.)

Even if you're already, or eventually become, an inveterate stranger-talker, there's a next step available to you. Once you've become comfortable starting conversations, you can be more deliberate and inclusive about who you start conversations with. When it comes to friendship, we tend to connect with people who are similar to us: people who have similar interests and values and demographics (age, income, education, ethnicity). You may find that when you talk to strangers, you also naturally default to talking to people who appear to be similar to you.

It probably feels a bit scarier to talk to someone who appears to be dissimilar to you. When postdoctoral research associate Caitlin Kelly and I asked people to imagine talking to a stranger, the worries they had about talking to a stranger who was similar to them were somewhat different from the worries they had about talking to a conversation partner who was of a different race or was living with a physical disability.[7] Worries about how to start a conversation and keep it going were in the top five regardless of the conversation partner. Worries about the stranger taking something the wrong way or taking offense were in the top five when the imagined stranger was different (in terms of race or physical disability) but not when the stranger was similar. Worries about saying the wrong thing or saying something insensitive were in the top five when the imagined stranger had a physical disability but not when the stranger was similar or differed in terms of race.

It's worth repeating: Your goal needn't be to banish all your fears but rather to talk to strangers despite your fears, remembering that your fears are overblown. You might take inspiration from this quote attributed to American essayist Ralph Waldo Emerson: "He who is not everyday conquering some fear has not learned the secret of life."

If you have learned to talk to strangers who are similar to you, you can also learn to talk to strangers who are dissimilar.

I haven't talked much about my mom, who's an introvert like me. She also talks to strangers, though less inveterately than my dad does. She feels strongly about making everyone feel included and welcome. It's been several decades since I was in primary school, but I can still vividly remember more than one occasion on which she urged me to be nice to some new kid in my class. Mom knows that some people, including people who appear to be different in some way (like the new kid in class), might struggle with feelings of isolation or exclusion. She likes to counteract this by sending her own message of inclusion, by extending a greeting or having a friendly chat. Once you're comfortable with talking to strangers, you might consider whether you can widen your circle and offer a message of inclusion to someone who could especially benefit from it.

## Patience and progress

Before I started my first academic job, I found myself with two months of freedom. A dear friend encouraged me to really make use of this time and asked if there was something I'd always wanted to do. This is the kind of question that I normally find challenging, so it surprised me when an answer to his question immediately sprang to mind: I wanted to take cello lessons so that some day I could play in an amateur orchestra.

As I was considering my friend's "no time like the present" advice, the universe worked its magic. I was getting on the Tube in London one evening when I saw a woman carrying a cello case. I sat beside her and said, "I'd love to play the cello someday." (Ah, the classic "someday" that we imagine will magically appear and make all our wishes come true.) At some point during our brief conversation, she said that, because I had a base of musical knowledge from my many years of piano lessons, I'd probably pick up the cello quite quickly. It wasn't until she said this that I realized how disheartened I was by the idea of all the years of painstaking practice that would be necessary before I could achieve any level of proficiency, let alone play in an orchestra. She unknowingly assuaged this concern that I didn't even know was holding me back. Shortly afterward, I rented a cello from the local music store, found a teacher, and took my first lesson. (In case you're wondering: I joined an amateur orchestra four short years later. Although I don't always play every note, with a lot of practicing I can get by, avoid unintended solos, and experience the absolute joy of making music in an ensemble.)

When I learned the piano as a child, I took lessons and worked toward formal, graded exams, so when I started learning the cello, I did the same. When I started working toward my grade four cello exam, my teacher suggested that I record myself playing each of the songs that I'd chosen to prepare. Months later, on the day before the exam, I listened to the recordings. In between, despite practicing those songs hundreds of times, it didn't feel like I'd made much progress: The songs hadn't improved as much as I'd hoped, as much as I'd wanted them to. (It's unavoidably frustrating to be a beginner, especially as an adult.) When I listened to the recordings, I was shocked. I was playing the songs more quickly, the intonation (i.e., pitch) was better, and whereas the earlier recordings sounded hesitant, my playing now sounded surprisingly confident. One of my favorite quotes is from eighteenth century British thinker Samuel Johnson, who said in his periodical *The Rambler*: "Men more frequently need to be reminded than informed."

Taking cello lessons was a much-needed reminder that progress often happens imperceptibly.

It was at a performance of *La Boheme* in 2022 that I became aware of how much progress I've made in terms of talking to strangers. Every summer, Glyndebourne stages a world-famous opera festival. Performances include a ninety-minute intermission between acts so that men in tuxedos (and a few kilts) and women in flowing summer dresses can eat fancy picnic dinners, replete with champagne, on the lawns around the lake. When I moved to Sussex to take up my new job, Glyndebourne became only a short drive away, and although it's a splurge, I decided that I wanted to experience it at least once.

When I returned to my seat after the intermission, I turned to the couple sitting to my right and asked how they were doing. People generally tell you they're fine even when they're not, so when this couple could barely muster a "fine, thanks," I knew something was amiss. The man must have sensed that I'd picked up on this. He admitted: "My wife has Parkinson's and isn't feeling well."

She was worried that she might need to leave during the performance, but she also worried that if she did, she'd be disrupting the six people seated between her and the aisle, not to mention everyone sitting behind them. I asked: "Would you like to sit on the aisle? I'd be happy to ask people if they're willing to move."

He told me it was too much trouble, but at the exact same time, she told me how much more comfortable she'd feel if she could sit in an aisle seat. So, I asked the two couples sitting to my left if they would mind moving over to accommodate this woman, who was feeling unwell. I wasn't at all surprised that they were happy to comply.

As the couple living with Parkinson's moved past me to get to their new seats, the man turned to me gratefully and said, "I could never have done that. Thank you."

When he said that, I realized: Past-Gillian could never have done that either. Without me really noticing, talking to strangers has become second nature to me.

## What talking to strangers has meant for me

I grew up bewildered by my dad's compulsion to talk to strangers. I honestly couldn't understand why he did it. I felt embarrassed whenever I saw him strike up a conversation because I knew it wasn't a "normal" thing to do and I worried about how people would respond. (Now, however, I love that it's something that we share.)

I didn't recognize it at the time, but I know now that my dad gave me a gift—and this book is my attempt to share that gift with you. Talking to strangers has transformed my life. Some of that change was catalyzed by a few specific conversations, but life-changing conversations are the exception. In many ways, the accumulation of pleasant, everyday conversations has made the biggest difference to me. I know now that I can have a nice chat with pretty much anyone, and knowing this has fundamentally changed how I see other people, how I see the world.

But becoming a stranger-talker hasn't changed everything. I'm still decidedly an introvert. I get overwhelmed by noisy environments and crowded social gatherings. If you give me the choice between sitting on my couch with a book and a cup of tea (and ideally a cat, but that depends on the whims of the cat . . . ) or going out to a social gathering—even one where there will be lots of people that I know and like—my heart's pretty much always going to choose my living room. (My head, on the other hand, knows the importance of human connection and will sometimes convince me to attend the social gathering. I'm usually glad that I went.)

And although I generally find it easy now to start a conversation with a stranger, that doesn't mean that I'm some kind of paragon of social skill. Far from it. In the fall of 2022, I was invited by a former student (who I'll call Ana) to attend a celebration. I thought I'd know a couple of people at the party, but they didn't show up. Given all the practice I've had, I wouldn't have thought it would be so hard to chat with the strangers at my table. No matter what I tried, I couldn't get a conversation going. Just as I was beginning to despair, Ana introduced me to a few people sitting at another table. We immediately hit it off. I spoke for longer with these new people than I had the whole time I'd been sitting at the other table. The question of why some people click and others don't is the holy grail of relationship and conversation researchers everywhere (not to mention dating apps). I don't know what happened that day, but Ana's party reminded me that, regardless of how far I've come, sometimes I'm going to strike out, and that's OK.

These days, when I go to a social gathering, although I feel more confident in my social skills, I still haven't banished all my worries. I worry about freezing because I don't feel comfortable thinking on my feet. I worry that I'm not a good storyteller—and stories often seem to be the most valuable social currency. I don't trust that my stories are interesting enough for people to listen to, so I skip the details and rush to the ending. (Writing's so much easier for me than talking. Thanks for "listening" to my stories.) Finally, I worry that I do too much listening and not enough talking. I still find it hard to get over the idea that I need to be invited to participate in a conversation. Of course, I probably worry too much and pay too much attention to Sid's laundry list of my shortcomings. But none of this troubles me as much these days. Sid can't convince me that I'm completely socially inept because I have the comfort of knowing that I've become really good at talking to strangers.

## What talking to strangers could mean for you

I really do understand why you might be reluctant to talk to strangers. Your worries are natural, but they're overblown and out of proportion. It's hard not to listen to that the negative voice in your head (hello again, Sid), which has an overactive imagination and a tendency to fear-monger. The good news is: You don't need to eliminate fear. Instead, you can talk to strangers despite your fears. When you do, it's likely to go better than you think—and you'll be better able to confront Sid the next time he starts whispering. And you might even unlock some of the hidden benefits of talking to strangers: the objectivity that comes from the fact that there are no strings attached; access to pieces of your life's puzzle that you didn't even know you were missing; seeds of possibility/opportunity/change/connection that might eventually yield a bountiful harvest; or simply the calm sense of well-being that comes from feeling seen, feeling human.

For a long time, I wasn't sure if my message would resonate with others or if it could help others. There were a few positive signs. A student emailed me once to share her story: "I was on the train when someone sat next to me watching one of my fave Marvel shows. In this moment I really wanted to strike up a conversation, which is something I would typically never do. But then I thought, what would Gillian do? Inspired by your #Talking2Strangers tweets, I started a convo about the show and we chatted until I reached my stop. This one, short convo w/ a stranger really lifted my spirits and boosted my confidence and I have you to thank for that."

But maybe students are especially likely to be influenced by their teachers. Maybe most people are dead set against talking to strangers and won't be open to an encouraging message. Maybe learning about the psychological barriers that prevent us from reaching out isn't enough to help people get over their fears.

I was in the midst of writing this book when I received an incredible sign of encouragement. It's a long story, but luckily I'm writing it rather than saying it out loud at a social gathering, so I feel that I can take my time. This is a story told in three acts.

Act one, April 2022: I was attending a conference (at which I learned that seals have a sense of rhythm!). When I left the conference at the end of the day, instead of hopping on the Tube, which would have been faster, I decided to walk through St. James's Park to get to Victoria train station. It was a beautiful spring day, the gardens were bursting with color, and there were even some cute fuzzy ducklings meandering around. I noticed a tall young man watching the ducklings, so I used them as a conversation starter. It turned out that he was visiting from Germany, traveling on his own for the first time and still getting used to it. We walked together for about fifteen minutes, past Buckingham Palace and toward the train station. He asked what I was doing in London, so I told him about the conference and about my research on talking to strangers. The value of talking to strangers seemed to especially resonate with him because he was traveling on his own and hadn't really talked to anyone for a few days. I've come to love talking to strangers while traveling (more than a third of the #Talking2Strangers stories that I've posted on social media have been conversations I had while traveling), so I was happy to offer this young man an opportunity for some human connection. When we reached the train station, we exchanged first names, shared a hug, and parted ways. I mentally added this conversation to my ever-growing collection of pleasant interactions with strangers.

Act two, July 2024: After a chamber music concert in London, my husband and I hurried to the Tube station in the hopes of making it to Victoria station in time to catch a particular train. We descended the escalator to the platform, knowing that it would be a close call, only to find the platform overflowing with people. Obviously, it had been a while since the last subway train had come through, and even if whatever problem had occurred was now resolved, it would take a while to clear out the backlog of people. There was no chance we'd make it to Victoria station in time for our preferred train, which meant that we'd have to wait half an hour until the next one. It was a nice evening, so I suggested we skip the Tube and walk to Victoria station instead. As we walked through St. James's Park, we passed Duck Island Cottage where, two years earlier, I'd seen the fuzzy ducklings and met the German tourist. I smiled, reminiscing about our pleasant conversation, and shared the memory with my husband as we walked past Buckingham Palace.

Act three: Less than three weeks after attending the concert, I received an email from someone named Pedram who said he had come across an article that I'd written. I've been fortunate to receive quite a few emails like this over the years. It's not unusual for the email sender to refer to something that I've written or a media article that I've been quoted in. The email continued: "Over the past two years my life has changed quite a lot—but in a good way. I've met wonderful friends who I'm grateful for every time I see them and I only met my current girlfriend because I worked up the courage to strike up a conversation with a stranger."

OK, so this is going to be one of those lovely emails where someone tells me about their own experiences talking to strangers—an "I love talking to strangers too!" email. But then . . .

"For the past two years, colleagues and friends have been complimenting me on how I'm able to talk so openly to random people as if I've known them for years, and asking me how I learned to do it.

"And each time I've told the same story about the time I traveled to London in 2022, and how I was standing in St. James's Park at Duck Island Cottage, watching the baby ducks with my coffee, minding my own business, when suddenly someone walked by and just said, 'Cute, aren't they.'"

Wait—what? Is he talking about me? He must be, but how is this possible? My heart started racing, and I kept reading. . . .

"That someone turned out to be a psychology teacher who specialized in talking to strangers, and who tried to strike up a conversation with a stranger every day."

Yep, definitely me. The article he referred to was one I had written myself, rather than one I was simply quoted in, and so it had my name (which he had remembered after two years?). Unusually, it also had a picture of me, which might have helped him recognize me.

"A psychology teacher . . . who taught me that we're too self-conscious about our flaws, and that other people won't notice and will see us in a more positive way than we could ever imagine, and that we need to overcome those fears."

Well, I guess I don't need to sum up the book now because Pedram has done an excellent job. But the best part of the email was his assertion that learning these messages from me had made a difference to him: "I wanted to say thank you from the bottom of my heart for choosing me as your random stranger of the day, for giving me the courage to talk to strangers, for giving me all those new friends. I honestly can't even put it into words. Thank you, Gillian, for being the stranger who changed everything, who gave me the gift of connecting with other strangers, and of believing in myself again."

Pedram's message is surely one of the best emails I will *ever* receive, and I cry happy tears every time I reread it. I even cried while writing it up to share with you (which I've done with his permission). The thought that I might be able to make a difference to someone—to *you*—was what drove me to write this book, and Pedram's email provided powerful confirmation that this is possible. I truly hope that talking to strangers will be as transformative for you as it has been for Pedram—and me.

## The power of small things

The world can often feel like a dark place, full of violence and pain, disease and destruction. I know I'm not alone in asking myself existential questions: Why am I here? How should I spend my life? It's easy to feel hopeless. It's easy to feel that we don't have the time, money, or expertise to make any difference. Two beliefs give me solace: (1) We can each do small things, and (2) small things add up. Benjamin Franklin talked about watching our pennies, and Mother Teresa talked about drops in the ocean, but I find American historian Howard Zinn's words especially heartening: "When change takes place it takes place as a result of large, large numbers of people doing little things unbeknownst to one another. And that history is very important for people to not get discouraged. . . . History is instructive. And what it suggests to people is that . . . anything they do, however small, becomes part of a much, much larger sort of flow of energy. And when enough people do enough things, however small they are, then change takes place."

Over the years since I started talking to strangers, I've benefitted from helpful recommendations and advice, shared many a laugh, and most important, I've felt a sense of shared humanity. These interactions have been meaningful to me, so I think it's not too presumptuous to assume that they have meant something to my conversation partners too. I believe that learning to talk to strangers has allowed me to make a small difference in the world (I'm so grateful to Pedram for telling me that I made a small difference to him), and I know that it will help you do the same (as I'm sure that Pedram has). We may not be able to do much, and certainly not all that we wish we could do, but we can all make the world a bit more human, a bit friendlier. It starts with something as simple as: "Hello."

# Acknowledgments

Woodrow Wilson wrote: "I not only use all the brains I have, but all I can borrow, and I have borrowed a lot." This book was only possible with the brains—and hearts—of so many people.* (I hope I haven't forgotten anyone!)

This book would not exist without my agent, David Doerrer (The Platform), who planted a seed by reaching out to offer an "innocuous chat about book prospects." I'm so glad the reports of your "death" were greatly exaggerated. (What are you reading?) Thanks also to Caspian Dennis for finding the book a home in the UK.

To my editor, Maya Alpert, for embracing my vision. And to Daniella Wexler and Nicky Ross, who believed in this project from the beginning.

The journey to publication starts with a book proposal. I was fortunate to receive expert coaching and advice on mine from

---

\* For the record, it did not require any artificial "brains"; I didn't use AI to generate, improve, suggest, correct, or anything else.

Aaron Shulman at Splash Literary. Thanks for your advice on storytelling (and on restaurants in Granada) and the line about "licking sidewalks," which lives on in the book. I'm grateful to the following role models, who not only went first and showed me that it could be done but also kindly shared their book proposals: Angela Duckworth, Ashley Whillans, Celeste Headlee, Joe Keohane, Traci Mann, and Vanessa Bohns. Their proposals (and books) served as helpful models at various stages. Thanks to Jules Pretty and Andy Field, who went first at the universities where I have worked and who helped me understand my universities' perspectives on book writing.

Thanks to Jay Hosking, who always believes in me more than I believe in myself and acted as if me writing a book was a question of "when" not "if." You've been there from the start: I might not have replied to David's initial email if it hadn't been for your encouragement. I will always be grateful that you said yes to that first waffle invitation.

Despite finding enough words to fill a whole book, I'll never find enough to adequately thank Giulia Poerio and Traci Mann, who gave me generous feedback on every chapter and helped me celebrate milestones along the way. They always made time to read this book and give me speedy feedback, even if that meant doing so from a plane on the way to a conference in Japan (GP) or at an outdoor café in Paris (TM, who was "interrupted by my lovely conversation with the stranger next to me"). Seeing the book through their eyes helped me make this book better, as did their wise advice. It meant so much to me that they laughed at my corny jokes, making me feel safe to be silly and to be vulnerable. More than anyone, they made me believe that I could do this crazy thing. I honestly don't know how I'm lucky enough to have such wonderful friends.

I'm also grateful to the experts who sanity-checked and gave me feedback on sections of the book: Angela Duckworth, Erica Boothby, Hazel Harrison, Jeffrey Hall, Lara Aknin, and Veronica Lamarche. Any errors that remain are mine.

Since this is a book about talking to strangers, I would be remiss if I didn't thank all the hundreds (thousands?) of strangers who have enriched my life, usually without me ever learning their names. Most shared only a moment, though a few changed my life. I'm particularly grateful to all the strangers who listened to me on *Hidden Brain*, looked me up, and sent me emails to tell me how much this topic resonated with them. I had put this book on indefinite hold, but it was your messages, more than anything, that convinced me that it needed to be written.

This book contains primarily my own stories, but I've shared a few that belong to other people. I'm grateful to Susan Cross for sending along news stories that she thought I'd be interested in, and to Mary Tucker for allowing me to share her story. Special thanks to Pedram Imanian for allowing me to share his email, which will stay with me as long as I live. I am so grateful that you tracked me down online and took the time to send your beautiful message.

My research on strangers and weak ties wouldn't have been possible without the open-minded admissions committee at Ryerson (now Toronto Metropolitan) University, who welcomed me as part of their inaugural cohort of master's students despite my unconventional academic background. I'm grateful to my academic advisors: Frank Russo (who took a chance on me and generously came up with the perfect research project to meld our interests), Liz Dunn (who taught me how to ask interesting research questions and made me a better writer—I still hear your voice in my ear when

I'm writing), Toni Schmader (my fun academic aunt, who pulled back the curtain on this job and made it look easy, and who adopted me in her lab and offered friendship), and Jason Rentfrow (who lured me to the UK).

I've had the good fortune of working with (and learning from) fantastic collaborators. They include Lara Aknin: Where would I be if you hadn't hosted me for my master's placement? Your creativity, ingenuity, enthusiasm, and kindness inspire me. (Long live the dream team.) I hit the jackpot when I sent an email to Erica Boothby. Working with you and Gus Cooney has been a highlight of my research career. Thank you for collaborating instead of competing on the liking gap. (Go EGGs!) Thanks to Alecia Carter, Alyssa Croft, Barb Fredrickson, Ciara Atkinson, Emre Selcuk, Esra Ascigil, Grant Donnelly, Gul Gunaydin, Jane Ebert, Kathryn Buchanan, Taylor West, and all my other past and soon to be coauthors. A nod to fellow talking-to-strangers researcher Nick Epley, who has also offered friendship and support instead of competition.

I am grateful for generous funding for my postgraduate studies from Ryerson University, the Social Sciences and Humanities Research Council (Canada), the University of British Columbia, the Government of British Columbia, and the Izaak Walton Killam Memorial Fund for Advanced Studies. The research reported in this book was funded by the University of Essex, the British Academy, the Economic and Social Research Council (UK), and the University of Sussex as well as a National Lottery Community Fund grant to Neighbourly Lab. My position at the University of Sussex was initially funded by the Pears Foundation.

Research requires not only financial but also human resources. The hidden backbone of my research is the team of enthusiastic undergraduate and graduate research assistants who volunteered their time and energy to do fun stuff like acting as a confederate, but also boring stuff like coding videos. I've included some of your names as aliases in the book. Sorry I didn't have room to name you all, but I couldn't have done this work without all of you. Thanks, also, to postdocs Caitlin Kelly and Joshua Moreton.

Real-world experiences inspired my research, so I've always hoped that my research would make its way out of the ivory tower and back into the world, into the hands of people who would benefit from it. It's been an honor to work with and learn from the passionate people at organizations like Talk to Me (who inspired and hosted my first How to Talk to Strangers workshops), the Campaign to End Loneliness, the Cares Family and Generations United, and the Relationships Project. I spent a memorable day with Matt Smith (who contributed the book's working title) from the Community Waffle House, and I am regularly energized by Georgie Nightingall, whose self-reflection always inspires me. A special shout-out to Neighbourly Lab, who saw the potential of minimal social interactions between residents and the essential workers who serve their communities and welcomed me on board when they got funding years after our initial conversation. And another special shout-out to force of nature—and epic hugger—Pete Bombaci, for making me an unofficial ambassador for GenWell and taking inspiration from my work to launch a Talk to a Stranger Week (www.talktoastrangerweek.org).

My research has found its way to these people and organizations primarily thanks to dozens of journalists around the world who have helped me share my research/stories. These include Allie Volpe, Claudia Hammond, David Robson, Elizabeth Bernstein,

Elizabeth Weingarten, Emma Beddington, Jennifer King Lindley, Jochen Metzger (who have all interviewed me more than once), and many others. Special thanks to storyteller extraordinaire Joe Keohane, who featured my work in his book (our theater outing will not soon be forgotten), and Celeste Headlee (who flew to the UK to see the scavenger hunt in action). Extra special thanks to Julia Furlan for interviewing me for NPR *Life Kit* (by far the biggest source of traffic to my website) and providing the fun opportunity of doing a Reddit AMA (Ask Me Anything); and to Shankar Vedantam, Autumn Barnes, and Kristin Wong at *Hidden Brain* (who really know how to tell a story and have attracted the most amazing listeners).

I'm so grateful to everyone who checked in with me and cheered me along, including: Alecia Carter, Alyssa Croft, Dan Campbell-Meiklejohn, Grant Donnelly, Hazel Harrison, Kristy Larson, Lara Aknin, Willa Harasym, tennis friends at the Weald (thanks for sweeping the courts for me and not giving me a hard time when I didn't stay for tea), orchestra friends (especially Ali Wicks), and Robert Barnfield, who asked about the book *every single time* he cleaned my windows. Thanks also to everyone who supported my #Talking2Strangers stories on social media, especially Andrew Beer (who, at the time of writing this, is still a stranger—I need to fix that!). To Jill Murray-Dimic, for inspiring the book cover. And to everyone who was understanding when I said: "I can't—I'm writing."

And finally, my family. To Paulo, my rock, for supporting me in every way when I unexpectedly decided to give up my nice computer programmer's salary to go back to school, and for moving across Canada and then across an ocean to allow me to pursue my career dreams. Thank you for taking care of so much life stuff so that I can do everything that I do. And for tolerating all my conversations with strangers. I love seeing you starting to have some of your own.

To Mom, who provided my first research training when I did an elementary school project on penguins—she taught me how to use the card catalogue at the library (how retro!) and how to digest what I read and say it in my own words. You were my first writing coach, giving me feedback all through my school years. I appreciate all that red ink now, but back then, I really wanted to write something that was good enough that I didn't need any feedback. Maybe I got closer this time?

What do I say about Dad that I haven't already said? Thank you for showing me a way to live that is joyful, kind, and meaningful.

# Appendix
# How to Talk to Strangers

This book has been a celebration of talking to strangers. Now that you know just how valuable and meaningful it can be, I'm sure you're feeling motivated to try it out yourself. But how do you get started? Who's easiest to talk to? What exactly should you say to start a conversation? You will have gleaned a few ideas from the stories that I've shared throughout the book, but this appendix is intended to address these questions more explicitly. I'll share some tips and tricks that I've learned through trial and error (but since you've already read an entire book, I'll try to be brief).* Everyone's different, and you'll need to experiment and find what works for you.

In addition to sharing my own tips, I interviewed my favorite

---

\* My expertise is in understanding the psychological benefits of talking to strangers and the psychological barriers to doing so. I don't consider myself an expert conversationalist or a conversation expert. The latter exist, of course, and have written whole books about this stuff, some of which I've included in the resources (page 291).

talking-to-strangers expert: my dad. In some ways, Dad wasn't very helpful at all. He said that asking him how he does it is like asking him how he breathes. But Dad shared some of his conversation starters—and his advice and encouragement—which I've sprinkled throughout the appendix. (Mom was also part of the interview, and I've included some of her thoughts too.)

I started sharing some of my #Talking2Strangers stories on social media at the end of 2015. I hoped that others might read these little moments of connection and be inspired to create their own. I wanted to show people that it doesn't need to be complicated—that there are opportunities all around and lots of ways to start a conversation. Little did I know that these social media posts—numbering in the hundreds now—would one day serve as a database of memories that I could mine for this book. Of course, these account for only a subset of my conversations with strangers—and perhaps an unusual subset, since I posted the most unique and interesting ones—but I thought it would be helpful, nonetheless, to comb through them (I love a good spreadsheet!). I'll tell you about some patterns that I noticed.

You can read through this appendix as if it were simply one final chapter in the book, or you may want to jump straight to the parts that you find most helpful. I'll start by talking about how to find opportunities to talk to strangers: which people and situations might be easiest, as you start out. Then I'll give you some tips on how to start, maintain, and end conversations. Finally, I'll offer some suggestions for troubleshooting: (1) what to do if you need more time to work yourself up to starting a conversation, and (2) what to do if something goes wrong.

## Finding opportunities

A few years ago, I was invited by BBC radio presenter Claudia Hammond to record a segment about talking to strangers. She proposed that we walk from the BBC Broadcasting House in London to Regent's Park. I'd find some strangers to talk to in the park, and she'd record me doing it. I was thrilled to have the opportunity to show how much fun it can be—and how easy it can be—to talk to strangers. But it ended up being much harder than I expected, to talk to strangers *on demand*.

My experience in Regent's Park reminded me that, although we may be surrounded by opportunities, some are more conducive to conversation than others—especially as a beginner. Over time, I've become better at noticing conducive opportunities, I've learned to make use of a wider range of opportunities, and I've even learned to create opportunities. But that doesn't mean that I find it easy to talk to strangers in every situation.

When we talk to a stranger, it's only natural for them to ask themselves: "Who are you?" and "Why are you talking to me?" Depending on who they are and the context of the interaction, they could ask themselves these questions in a puzzled or bemused way, or an anxious way. Upon reflection, I realized that one reason it was so hard to talk to strangers on demand in Regent's Park was because I usually choose opportunities that allow me to circumvent—or at least minimize—people's confusion and concern. It was hard to force one of these opportunities. Knowing that people will ask "Who?" and "Why?" helps us understand which people might be easiest to approach and which situations might make it easiest to start a conversation.

## Selecting a person

I regularly work from home and spend much of my day sitting in front of my computer. To counteract all that sitting, on most days I go for a midafternoon walk. On a good day, I'll get to pet a few dogs. The vast majority of dogs seem to enjoy "talking" to strangers. Some are nervous, and some are too distracted by smells to take any interest in people (spaniels—I'm looking at you), but most seem to want to, at the very least, come over and have a sniff.

Because dogs enjoy interacting with strangers, **dog owners** are accustomed to talking to strangers. In a study by June McNicholas and Glyn Collis at the University of Warwick, a male researcher stood, as if waiting for someone or something, in various places around a small city in England, following instructions *not* to interact with people.[1] In the eight hours (in thirty-minute shifts) that he stood *without* a dog, fifty-seven people interacted with him, either nonverbally (e.g., smiling or nodding) or verbally. In the sixteen hours that he stood with a large black Labrador dog, 1,113 people interacted with him—almost ten times as many.

I'm not a dog owner. I live with two cats. (I can't bring myself to say I'm a cat owner—anyone who lives with a cat knows that nobody *owns* a cat.) Nonetheless, a substantial proportion of my conversations with strangers involve dogs—about one in five of the #Talking2Strangers stories that I've shared on social media. I've met a sheepdog, descended from working sheepdogs, that is scared of sheep; a dog that eats snails; a dog that picks and eats blackberries; a dog that climbs trees and swims for miles alongside his human paddling in a kayak; and several dogs that love sitting in puddles, tide pools, and mountain tarns.

Assuming you're not afraid of dogs, I think talking to a dog owner is the single easiest way to start a conversation. Dad agrees: "The easiest people to talk to are people with a dog, because 'What a beautiful dog,' or 'What kind of dog is it?' And I mean that's the floodgate opener." I carry dog treats in my pocket (an idea that Dad has adopted too). When I ask someone for permission to offer their dog a treat, they understand why I'm talking to them—I bypass that common conversation killer: confusion. (People sometimes get confused about the fact that I carry dog treats but don't have a dog, but that's a different type of confusion.) I often return home covered in fur and muddy pawprints, but I think that's a small price to pay.

In addition to dog owners, these "targets" are also less likely to get confused or concerned:

- **Parents** are used to people lavishing attention on their babies (or sharing tips about parenting).
- **Small children** are Dad's favorite. ("If I have a choice, definitely I'll go with the kids.") He loves to make them giggle. Sometimes they're shy at first, but after using one of his outlandish conversation starters, Dad can usually get them to open up, and then they're often more open to talking to strangers than their parents are. Be sure that a parent is present and seems comfortable—you don't want to make anyone worry about their child's safety.
- Talking to strangers is part of the job for **service providers**. This includes people like the bus driver on your regular route, the cashier at the grocery store, the barista at your favorite coffee shop, or the volunteer at the art gallery. Make sure you're not keeping them from doing their job (ahem, Dad!).

- In one of my studies, **older adults** were far less worried about talking to strangers than younger adults were.[2] Maybe because they're no longer busy working or raising kids, they're better able to stop and enjoy moments of human interaction. (Mom said when she was busy working and running errands with two kids in tow, she never seemed to have the time.)

When you're starting out, you want to do everything you can to ensure that your first conversations are a success, so you might want to try one of these options. Once you've built up your confidence and feel more comfortable, you can branch out. People who don't, at first glance, seem very approachable are often more receptive than you think, and we benefit from talking to people who are different from us. (My mom loves talking to people who weren't born in Canada and learning about their culture; she thinks "we're all people" and we have so much in common, even with people who speak a different language, look different from us, or have different beliefs.)

### Selecting a situation

If you're just starting to talk to strangers, think about what situations would make you feel most comfortable. First and foremost, choose a context that feels **physically safe** (e.g., in a public setting, in daylight hours, with other people nearby). Depending on your preferences and specific concerns, you may wish to choose a situation with one of the following features:

- You may find it more comfortable to sit/stand **side by side** rather than face-to-face.

- If you're worried about others' judgment, you may want to choose a situation in which other **people are unlikely to overhear you.**
- If you're worried what your friends and family will think if a conversation doesn't go well (though that's unlikely), you may feel more comfortable talking to strangers when you're **on your own**. Alternatively, you may prefer to have a **trusted person with you for moral support**. Both Dad and I talk to strangers more often when we're on our own. I feel like I'm more aware of my surroundings and more willing to take the time to stop, knowing that I won't be inconveniencing the person I'm with.
- If you're worried about talking to someone once, in case you see them again and feel obligated to talk to them again, you may want to choose **someone that you'll never see again**. This may be one reason that many people feel more comfortable talking to strangers while **on holiday**. (Personally, I love having repeated encounters with people like the hot dog lady.)
- If you're worried about running out of things to say, you can choose a **time-limited** situation with a clear ending that allows you to just walk away (e.g., with a service provider or while waiting for a bus).

As well as considering what situations make you feel the most comfortable, you may wish to consider choosing a situation that makes it easy to start a conversation. People may be less likely to wonder why you're talking to them in the following situations:

- You're **attending the same event** (e.g., concert, festival, show, exhibit) **or doing the same activity**. Often, I'll turn to the person sitting next to me and ask them why they chose to attend that particular performance, if they've seen the show or performers before, or what other events they've been to. Other times I'll go first and tell someone how excited I am about the performance.

- You experience **an unusual, shared situation**. This could be an extreme weather phenomenon, such as a heavy snowstorm. When traveling on transit, it could be a delay or mechanical issue—or something more whimsical, like a person breaking into song.
- **When we feel uncertain** (e.g., waiting for an interview or a medical appointment), we seek reassurance, and we get it from talking to others.[3]
- Talking passes the time while we're **waiting** (or **bored**). I often talk to people when I'm standing in a long line or sitting on a bus. Dad recognizes that many people don't like grocery shopping, but he "make[s] it an adventure" by talking to people while browsing the shelves or waiting in line. He enjoys talking to checkout clerks too much to ever use a self-checkout.

These situations may be more comfortable than others, but in truth, no situation will feel completely comfortable when you're starting out. Don't let your search for the perfect situation become a barrier because the perfect situation may not exist. At some point, you need to just start experimenting in the best conditions you can find. And then, keep pushing the boundaries so that you feel comfortable in more and more situations. (Dad thinks there's no place where you can't do it.)

## My go-to opportunities

When I looked through my #Talking2Strangers social media posts, there were clear patterns in terms of the situations that I use as opportunities to connect. As you might expect, a good number of my stories came from close to home: time spent **in my neighborhood and around town** (23 percent). Besides dog owners, I've talked to people who were working in their gardens, washing their cars, taking bicycles or golf clubs out of their car, building snowmen, or, once, getting into their car in beekeeping regalia. In two different cities, I've talked to people sitting in lawn chairs on the side of the road just before dark, with clipboards on their laps, monitoring bats.

It tells you a lot about me that almost a quarter of my stories came from conversations I had **while hiking** (24 percent). I often spend the weekend exploring the beautiful English countryside, and many of my holidays in recent years have involved long walks with scenic views. There are easy conversation starters: I ask someone about their route or how far it is to the summit or viewpoint. One fellow walker in the glorious Lake District told me that stopping to exchange a few words is part of walking etiquette: It's a way to check that the other person has enough water and isn't disoriented or lost.

My remaining stories generally came from four sources: (1) **on transit**, with fellow passengers (18 percent), (2) with **service providers** and **volunteers** (14 percent), (3) with fellow customers at places that serve **food and drink** (13 percent), and (4) with people who are attending the same **event** (8 percent).

## Starting a conversation

Once you learn how to spot the endless opportunities to start a conversation, it's time to make use of those opportunities and start talking. (If you're not quite ready for this step, then skip to the section called "What if: you need more time to work yourself up to starting a conversation" on page 261.) Over the years, I've been asked countless times for tips on how to start a conversation. First, the bad news: There's no perfect way to start a conversation, no magic words that I can teach you. But there's also good news: It's less complicated than you think, and you already know how to get started. I know this because each time I've taught my How to Talk to Strangers workshop, attendees have come up with long lists of ideas, starting with the most basic: smile, be friendly, say hello.

Instead of focusing on what to say, my best advice is to think QUICK: ask a **QU**estion, find something **In C**ommon, or extend **K**indness.

### Ask a question

Probably the single most common way I've started a conversation is by asking **"Whatcha doin'?"** I ask this question playfully, to convey that I'm curious—I don't want someone to think I'm accusing them of something. This question is how:

- I got the opportunity to visit an archaeological dig, when I asked a man about the drone he was flying (see chapter 3).
- I got a peek at the inside of the ticket machine at a train station, from one of only fifty engineers across the UK who can maintain these feats of German engineering.

- I found out about the Santa Skate, in which hundreds of people roller skate together through London, dressed in over-the-top festive attire.

Along similar lines, you can ask someone about **something they're wearing**:

- I once asked a woman on the Tube about a pin she was wearing on her cardigan. She was a nurse, on her way to Westminster Abbey for a service commemorating the centenary of the funeral of Edith Cavell, a nurse who helped several hundred Allied soldiers escape from German-occupied Belgium. This was especially interesting to me because I'd recently read a novel about female spies during the First World War and had learned a bit about Cavell (who has a mountain named after her in Canada).
- One evening in late December on the Tube, I noticed the lanyard around a man's neck. He had just been setting up the fireworks for New Year's Eve and had formerly worked on the opening ceremony for the London Olympics. Now, whenever I watch the fireworks on TV, I think of this conversation.

Elias Weiss Friedman (aka @TheDogist on social media) has taken more than fifty thousand photos of dogs over the last dozen or so years. He approaches people and asks a standard set of questions. My favorite is whether they have **any funny stories to share** about their dog getting into mischief. I've used a similar strategy:

- While on holiday in Northumberland, getting a ride to the start of a one-way walk along an endless windswept beach, I asked the

taxi driver about his longest ever fare. He once drove a woman 375 miles because she doesn't like trains.
- While checking out at the grocery store, I noticed that the woman in the next aisle had nothing on her belt except a giant stack of tea. She must have emptied the shelf. When I asked, she told me that she was on her way to France for a few months and couldn't get her favorite tea there.
- I asked the pest control man, who helped us get rid of more than a dozen rats from our attic, about the most rats he'd ever had to deal with, which pests are the peskiest, etc. (You don't want to hear the story shared by the man who inspected the sewer pipes to help us figure out how the rats were getting into the house!)

I've visited a lot of historic houses since moving to England, many of which employ volunteer room stewards. I've started asking them about their **favorite** object in the room:

- A volunteer at Dover Castle pointed out the bedspread made from squirrel pelts.
- A volunteer at one of Winston Churchill's homes showed me stuffed animals that children gave to Churchill during the Blitz.
- A volunteer at Glasgow Cathedral pointed out a tiny ladybug that soldiers had carved into the canopy of a chair to commemorate a ladybug that had brought them luck.

I would never have noticed any of these things without someone drawing my attention to them.

A variation on this is to **ask for a recommendation**. People love sharing their favorites:

- Shortly after moving to Brighton, I went on a walking trip in the Lake District. I chose most of my walking routes from a spectacular website (i.e., I got recommendations from a digital stranger),[4] but some were suggested by people I met while walking. (While enjoying the breathtaking view of Derwentwater from Walla Crag, about 360 miles away from Brighton, a stranger recommended that I try his favorite Indian restaurant in Brighton.)
- Every spring in the UK, I marvel at the lush purple carpets of bluebells. They're particular about where they grow, so you have to know where to find them. Strangers have helped me find spectacular bluebell woods.

If you learn how to tap into your curiosity, you can come up with endless questions. To a person with binoculars or a camera around their neck: What are you hoping to see? What have you spotted today? To a reader (but maybe don't interrupt their reading): How's the book? Read anything good lately? To someone with a suitcase or giant backpack: Where are you traveling? While on holiday: What sights have you seen so far? What are your plans today? Dad—a retired teacher—often asks kids how they like school and what their favorite subject is. When Mom hears someone speaking with an accent, she likes to ask how long they've been in Canada and where they're from. (I asked her if anyone takes offense to these questions, but she says, on the contrary, that people are generally pleased that she's interested in finding out about them and learning about their culture.)

### Find something in common
It would be a lot easier to start a conversation with a stranger if you magically knew what you had in common with them. Imagine you

could know that someone shares your love of historical fiction, your devotion to *Ted Lasso*, or your passion for Taylor Swift. Sometimes this is possible, without any magic, because sometimes people's **interests are visible**. If you notice someone reading the latest Kate Quinn novel, watching a video clip of Ted saying "barbeque sauce," or wearing an Eras Tour T-shirt, then you already know that you have something in common, and you can use that as a conversation starter. Dad often approaches people who are wearing a T-shirt or hat from a sports event or somewhere he's traveled.

Hillary Wiener at the University of Albany, along with James Bettman and Mary Frances Luce at Duke, has studied the power of the **statement T-shirt**: a T-shirt that says something about the person wearing it. In one study, people who approached someone with a statement T-shirt had deeper conversations and enjoyed their conversations more than people who talked to someone wearing a plain shirt.[5] Presumably the T-shirt helped people find common ground more quickly. In another study, the researchers pitted statement T-shirts against another thing people have in common: the weather. They asked all participants to approach someone wearing a statement T-shirt but asked some people to start the conversation by talking about the T-shirt, and others to start by talking about the weather (though many couldn't resist and eventually talked about the T-shirt). People who used the T-shirt as a conversation starter enjoyed their conversations more and got to deeper conversation topics more quickly than people who started with the weather.

Talking about **the weather** is a cliché, but we all do it. (Even my dad uses the weather as a conversation starter sometimes—though he usually turns it into a joke.) And it's not a new thing. In the 1750s, English writer Samuel Johnson wrote: "When two Englishmen meet, their first talk is of the weather." According to a poll commissioned by Bristol Airport, the average Brit will spend 4.5 months of their life talking about the weather.[6]

We talk about the weather because it's an experience that we share. But we have other things in common with our conversation partners:

- At times, your **location** reflects shared activities or interests. I've talked about music with people sitting next to me at a concert, about food and evening plans with people sitting next to me at a pub or restaurant, about art with people standing next to me at a gallery, and about trails with people I cross paths with while hiking. While traveling, I've talked to fellow tourists about sightseeing, food, etc.
- When you take **public transit**, you necessarily share a location with fellow passengers. When I get on the bus at the stop near my house to head into town, I'll often ask someone about their plans (e.g., "Are you doing something nice in town today?").
- It's hard to get a conversation going with "How are you?," because people can't tell if you're really interested or just being polite. Instead, I'll often customize my greeting based on the **time of day**. In the morning, I'll ask "On your way to work?," and in the early evening, I'll ask "Heading home from work?" In the later evening or on a weekend, I'll ask "Doing something fun this evening?"
- You can bring someone's attention to something in your **shared environment**. On holiday in Devon, I chatted with an older man who had pointed out a seal. (It was fun to see excited kids wave back when the seal "waved" its flipper at them.) I've

drawn people's attention to spring flowers starting to appear in a garden, dogs frolicking in the park, and fuzzy ducklings.

### Extend kindness

When I interviewed my parents for this appendix, I knew that Dad loves talking to strangers, and I knew that he loves making people laugh. What I didn't know, somehow, was that he sees talking to strangers as a calling—something he's been placed on this planet to do. He knows that life can be hard, that people struggle, and he knows that his conversational skills give him the ability to **offer a moment of lightness**. He feels that he's doing something important (and kind) by talking to people and bringing a little happiness to their day.

My dad has a well-honed list of conversation starters designed to elicit a chuckle. (He told me that the outlandish conversation starters that he uses with kids were inspired by my mom. She is a retired school librarian, and she told him that the more outlandish a story was, the more the kids seemed to like it.)

- To kids, he'll ask: "How old are you?" If they hold up fingers to show their age, he'll slowly count them and pretend that he can't count, so that they have to correct him. Once he knows their age, he'll say: "Same as me." Other times he'll ask little kids who look six or eight: "How old are you? Sixteen? Seventeen?" He also likes to ask little kids if they're married and if they have a pet alligator or hippopotamus.
- To someone walking a tiny dog or some sweet-natured breed, like a Golden Retriever, he'll ask: "What kind of dog is that—a pit bull?"

- To someone who looks a bit tired and sweaty, say on a hiking trail, he'll say: "I left a cold beer for you just around the corner."
- He'll even make a joke out of commenting on the weather. He'll say something like: "Beautiful day, but then again it never rains in these parts." (He lives near Vancouver, which, like Seattle, is famous for rain. He used this one while I was on a walk with him, and someone joked back: "Yep, only on the weekends.")

I can attest that these conversation starters work like a charm because I've borrowed them from time to time. I might have to stop using the one about the beer, though, because one man had such a hopeful look on his face when I said it that I felt a bit guilty.

Cracking jokes doesn't come as naturally to me as it does to my dad, but I occasionally give dad humor a try. I once joked with a young man on the Tube about his "breakfast of champions": a packet of cookies. On a recent walk in my neighborhood, I saw two men who'd been trimming a hedge, and I asked if they were offering free haircuts.

One of my rare talking to strangers failures came from attempting a joke. I was on holiday and had stopped at a grocery store to buy a big jug of bottled water. I saw a woman pushing a shopping cart that was loaded with drinks and snacks, so I lightheartedly asked whether I could come to her party. The problem was that this grocery store was in France. Although I'm theoretically bilingual, I don't get much practice speaking French and I stumbled over my words. The woman could see that I was trying to be friendly, so I don't think she was concerned, but the conversation was killed by confusion. (I had a lovely conversation later that day, thanks to a dog, which restored my confidence enough to allow me to make further, mostly successful, attempts to talk to strangers in French.)

I share my dad's belief that talking to strangers is a way to spread kindness and often start conversations with that intention:

- I've **offered people a seat**. Once, when I was attending a concert alone, I had a cup of tea during the intermission. I noticed someone looking around for a table and invited them to join me. We had a lovely chat about music.
- I've seen people sitting on their own and **offered them some company**. Sitting at a restaurant waiting for a friend, I overheard a man talking to the waiter. He was in town for work, and I know that can be lonely, so I struck up a conversation and talked with him until my friend arrived. He turned out to be a sperm bank manager, and I asked him a million questions.
- I've **thanked** volunteers for their service (e.g., helping out with municipal elections, clearing brush from walking paths). Once, I thanked two young girls for litter-picking in my neighborhood. They said they do it to help wildlife, especially hedgehogs. I told them I'd never seen a hedgehog (though I've seen one—and only one—since that conversation). They hadn't ever seen one either, but their uncle had given them a hedgehog house, and they were hoping a local hedgehog would soon take up residence.
- If I see someone who looks lost (looking at a map or their phone), I'll ask if they need help, and I'll **provide directions**. I've come to realize that providing someone with directions, information, or help is an especially easy way to start a conversation because it bypasses confusion.

One of my mom's favorite ways to start a conversation is to give someone a sincere **compliment**. You might be reluctant to do this, for fear that the compliment will be misinterpreted. "You have such a nice smile" can come across as creepy or as a sign of attraction. Instead of complimenting physical features, I recommend that you stick to complimenting expressions of a person's individuality: clothing (Mom will say "the color of your blouse looks great on you"), accessories, tattoos, nails. Or avoid the personal altogether, and compliment someone on their well-behaved child or dog, or their beautiful garden.

It's taken me a while to realize that compliments often elicit self-disclosure, which makes them especially good conversation starters. I once complimented a waitress on her sailboat earrings. She told me that she collects earrings wherever she travels. These ones were from Edinburgh and were made from wood reclaimed from an old sailboat. Another time, I complimented a waitress on her cow necklace. She explained that she loves cows and was training to be a farm vet, waitressing at night to make ends meet. In both cases, my compliment was interpreted as an invitation to tell me about their jewelry, to have a more meaningful conversation.

I love delivering a compliment to a stranger, in part because I know how good it feels to receive a compliment from a stranger. If a friend compliments me on my new glasses, I don't know if they really mean it—they might just be telling me what they think I want to hear. There's no reason, however, for a stranger to compliment me (and they're low-key breaking norms by talking to a stranger to do it), so their compliment feels more authentic.

As well as extending kindness, you can also start a conversation by **requesting a kindness**. People are generally happy to help you reach something at the grocery store, give you directions, or take your picture (see chapter 7), and your request serves to allay your helper's confusion and concern about why you're talking to them.

## Helping people start conversations with you

Starting conversations is one way to talk to more strangers, but you can also flip around some of the things we've been talking about and make it easier for strangers to start conversations with you:

- **Look up and look around you.** Even my dad—who essentially claims that he'll talk to anyone, anywhere, anytime—doesn't talk to people whose heads are down.
- This means you need to **put your phone down**. In one study, people who were asked to wait for ten minutes alongside a stranger were more likely to chat if their phone had been confiscated—and they spent about 30 percent more time smiling.[7]
- I wear earbuds when I go on my regular afternoon walks. I'm ready to press pause in an instant, and I preemptively pause when I'm approaching someone, to make space for a conversation to occur. Although **headphones** don't hinder your ability to initiate conversations, they might make it less likely that others will talk to you.
- **Leave some extra time**, so you're not rushing. (I'm still working on this one—I've got the whole "last minute" thing down to a science.) It will give you more time to look around, and it will leave you time for a quick chat, if the opportunity arises.
- Give people an easy conversation starter by using your clothing and accessories to **express your identity**.

Many university teachers spend hours agonizing over their course syllabi, which explain our policies, rules, and regulations. We provide the syllabus to our students, we spend lots of time going through it on the first day of class, and we repeatedly refer to it in lectures. All this can leave us feeling more than a bit frustrated when a student comes up to us after class and asks a question that is answered in the syllabus. It's one of several pet peeves that academics rant about (riveting, I know). My perspective on this completely changed when someone posted on social media: "It's time for my annual reminder that students ask questions that are answered in the syllabus because they want to talk to you." I had never considered that maybe students just want to connect and don't know how.

Similarly, strangers may be trying to talk to you, and you're just not noticing. They might be asking you a question about the bus schedule even though they could check an app. They might be telling you how to use a parking machine even though you've already figured it out (you genius, you). You can choose to interpret these kinds of interactions as an offer of conversation and respond with something QUICK.

## Maintaining a conversation

With strangers, you might be happy to just have a short exchange and walk away. That's absolutely fine. Some of the benefits that I've described in this book are available through even the shortest conversations. Dad regularly gets into longer conversations, but he says most of the time it's just superficial—he makes a joke, gets people feeling good about themselves, and then he walks away.

Your conversation partner might prefer a short exchange too.

They're likely to feel confused or concerned at first. If you're patient, you can usually help them past those barriers. (According to my mom, it only takes about three seconds for people to realize that Dad is harmless and just being friendly.) But sometimes a conversation partner can't get past those barriers. Or they do but just aren't interested in talking. Or they *are* interested in talking but have other things they need to do. Whatever the reason, you don't want to be a nuisance or make anyone feel uncomfortable. A conversation takes two people, and if they aren't interested, just walk away.

On the other hand, they may turn out to be an interested and engaged conversation partner, and both of you may want to keep the conversation going. After all, some of the benefits that I've described in this book are only likely to manifest after a slightly longer conversation. This can raise new worries for you: You confronted your fears and figured out how to start a conversation, and your reward is that now you need to figure out *more* things to talk about? But, let me remind you of a study from chapter 1: People worried that they would run out of things to say or lose interest, but they talked for twenty-five minutes and continued to find plenty to talk about, continued to enjoy their conversations.[8]

If you're stuck in your head (battling Sid), worrying about running out of things to say, worrying about what you should or shouldn't say or do next, then you're stifling spontaneity, the magic that takes a conversation from cupcakes to riding ostriches (see chapter 3). For that reason, I worry that providing too much advice about how to keep a conversation going could actually backfire. Ideally, you'll immerse yourself in the moment and work together with your conversation partner to unspool the threads that weave a meaningful moment. The words will come more naturally once you develop and improve two (not so) simple skills: listening and talking.

Effective listening is hard. You can't give your full attention to your conversation partner when you're thinking about how to respond or what to say next—or what they might be thinking about you. Eye contact and nodding signal attention to some extent, but we show people that we're really listening—and care about what they have to say—by reflecting back what we've heard. This can be done by paraphrasing what they've said or referring back to something they said earlier.[9] It can also be done by asking follow-up questions. In a study by Karen Huang, Michael Yeomans, and their colleagues at Harvard University, some people were instructed to ask their conversation partner a lot of questions (at least nine), and others were instructed to ask only a few questions (no more than four).[10] People liked partners who asked more questions because they seemed more responsive. According to Yeomans, now at Imperial College, good follow-up questions go deeper on feelings, goals, and processes (e.g., "That sounds frustrating," "What made you change your mind?," "How did you manage that?"), or they provide a narrative shape (e.g., "And then what happened?").[11]

I used to feel a lot more anxious when I talked to people. Asking questions felt easier than doing the talking. I still do a lot more listening than talking, but now it's less as a coping mechanism and more because it's by listening and asking questions that I learn something new. My mom and I share that thirst for learning—and one study suggests that it might help us put Sid in his place. In this study, after talking to a stranger, less curious people had been more focused on being accepted and liked (i.e., they were listening to Sid), whereas highly curious people had instead been more focused on enjoyment and learning (which presumably directed their attention away from Sid).[12]

Listening and asking questions allows us to learn from a conversation, but a great conversation is reciprocal: We also want to feel that our conversation partner has listened to and learned from us. That means we can't just do the listening—we have to do some talking too. (I still struggle with this, even when I'm talking to the people I'm closest to—sometimes I'm too reactive and could stand to be more proactive.) And that means figuring out what to talk about.

I've given you some tips on how to get a conversation started, but once a conversation gets going, it naturally flows from one topic to another. Emma Templeton, Luke Chang, and Thalia Wheatley at Dartmouth College have done some clever work looking at the topics that students discuss when they first meet each other—and how conversations transition from one topic to another.[13] They found that people talk about different topics at different points in time. First, there are introductory topics that people discuss at the beginning of a conversation and never return to. Next, there are topics that they call "conversational launch pads": topics of general interest that everyone understands, that can take us in multiple directions. In their student sample, these topics included hometowns, classes, professors, exams, and sports. We may stay on these topics for a while, or leave and return to them later. Conversational launch pads help us to quickly find common ground, which we then use to transition into the third type of topic: the ones that we tend to discuss only later in conversations, that allow us to go a bit deeper. In their student sample, these topics included: recap of the week, upcoming/future/professional plans, and hobbies. These may be the sorts of topics that are referred to in popular small talk methods like FORD (family, occupation, recreation, dreams),[14] or the more modern HEFE (hobbies, entertainment, food, environment).[15]

This study reminds us that conversations are dynamic, always moving from one topic to another. It's normal—and there's good reason—for a conversation to start with more mundane topics. The trick is to find common ground quickly so that you can transition to, and spend more time on, interesting topics. Here, it's worth a reminder that people are more willing to discuss deeper, more personal topics—or even sensitive topics—than we expect, and we both tend to enjoy our conversation more when we do.[16, 17]

## Ending a conversation

Ending a conversation can be tricky, regardless of who our conversation partner is, and why we want to end the conversation (e.g., we're not enjoying it, or we just have something else we need to do). We don't want to be rude or hurt our conversation partner's feelings (even if they're a stranger). And, because of our *need* to belong, we care what they think about us, so we want to leave them with a positive impression.

I'm not the best person to give advice on ending conversations. Over time, I've become adept at starting conversations with strangers (if I do say so myself), but I'm still learning how to end them. Maybe that's because I've had less practice actively ending conversations. Most of the time, I talk to strangers in a time-limited context or a context that makes it easy to just walk away. Most of my conversations don't last long enough to make me want to (or feel like I need to) end them. (My dad said the same thing: Most of his conversations end naturally, due to the context.) I do, however, remember once striking up a conversation with a man on a train who droned on and on, complaining about work. I couldn't walk away, so I just let him talk, and I hope it did him some good.

Nobody wants to get stuck in an unpleasant conversation. As with most worries, it can help to come up with a plan ahead of time, about what you'll do if the dreaded eventuality occurs.

What can you say to end a conversation, that's both effective and kind? I asked attendees at my How to Talk to Strangers workshops for their advice. Their top tip? Lie. They **invent excuses**, like wanting to get a drink or some food, needing to use the toilet, or being late for a meeting. (Mom suggests the more generic: "I've got to get going.")

Another idea is to **change things up**. You can invite another person to join your conversation. If you're at an event with lots of people present, you can introduce your conversation partner to someone else (ideally someone who you think they'd have a great conversation with).

In every workshop, there's one person who advocates using a more **direct approach**: They use a stock phrase, to ensure their partner is left feeling good about the conversation (e.g., "Great meeting you," or "It was nice talking to you," or "I've taken up enough of your time"), and then they walk away. I did this while I was writing this book. On my habitual afternoon walk, I was having a fun and engaging conversation (I had learned that a long-married couple had met at university when he asked to borrow a hairdryer), but I felt like it had run its course and that I should get back to my desk (This book didn't write itself!). I can't remember exactly what prompted it, but I spotted an opportunity and said something like: "That seems like the perfect ending to our conversation" (and "I really enjoyed chatting with you").

I'm starting to think that it may be an act of kindness to accept the responsibility of actively ending a conversation. If we both avoid the responsibility, then our conversation might just stagger along even though neither of us is really enjoying it. Instead, we both stand to benefit if the conversation is ended kindly but deliberately. Someone has to do it—why not you?

## What if: you need more time to work yourself up to starting a conversation

This appendix has offered advice on how to notice and then use opportunities to talk to strangers, but you might not be ready to start talking quite yet. Instead, you may prefer to work your way up to it, one small step at a time. If someone has a phobia, treatment might include graded exposure therapy.[18] They might confront their fear of snakes by first talking or reading about snakes, then seeing pictures or watching videos of snakes, and after many, many steps, eventually holding a snake. A similar approach could help you work your way up to talking to strangers. After all, we *learn* to fear both snakes and strangers—and we should be able to unlearn these fears too.[19]

The first step for me was to learn how to **maintain eye contact**. When I passed people on the street, I used to cast my eyes to the sidewalk. When I got divorced from my first husband, I realized just how much I'd been hiding in his extroverted shadow, and I knew that I wanted to learn to be more social. After repeatedly catching myself dropping my gaze uncomfortably, I started to deliberately practice keeping my eyes up. It took a lot of practice to get over the compulsion to look away, and I still have to fight it sometimes. But it got easier when the rewards started coming: People would sometimes smile at me.

Once you lift your gaze, you can start to **notice other people**. In our scavenger hunt study, some people were asked to talk to strangers and others were asked to simply observe people.[20] Essentially, we gave them permission to **people watch**. At the end of the study, the people watchers showed some signs of being more open to talking to strangers (though not nearly as many as the people who had talked to strangers). You may find that when you start watching people, they start to seem less scary and more friendly and approachable.

The next step is to **acknowledge** people. A friendly smile directed at a stranger sends the message that you're not a threat.[21] I often accompany a **smile** with a **nod**, so that people know that I'm smiling *at them* and not simply because I'm happy. I've made it a habit, when I descend on an escalator into the bowels of the London Underground, to see if I can get anyone heading up on the other escalator to return a smile. It's surprisingly difficult. If I succeed in making eye contact (which is rare), then I'll smile and nod. Some people smile back, but others don't know quite what to make of my friendliness and look away, presumably in confusion or discomfort (as past-Gillian might have done). A few years ago, when my dad visited from Canada, I suggested a friendly competition, inspired by this escalator habit: Which one of us could induce the most people to smile back at us, during a long journey on the Tube? We're still arguing about who won. My count was higher—but only because Dad started talking to people instead of simply smiling at them.

After getting comfortable with acknowledging people, you can **add a greeting**, such as a simple "Hello." (Mom suggests: "Beautiful day today," or a compliment.) If you're worried about how people will react, you'll find it encouraging to hear about mindset coach Matt Callanan's experiment. He smiled and greeted sixty people on his morning run and noted how they responded. All but two people acknowledged him in return, either with a greeting, or simply a smile or thumbs up.[22] (The two who didn't respond had headphones on, so it's possible they didn't hear his greeting.)

There's one more thing you can do to prepare for talking to a stranger: You can **imagine having a conversation**. Think of what you could say to start the conversation and imagine the person responding positively. Think of a conversational launch pad topic that you could switch to when it's time to move past the introductory topic. Think of what follow-up questions you could ask. (Mike Yeomans, who has done research on follow-up questions, suggests the fun idea of practicing coming up with follow-up questions whenever you watch a video on social media or hear someone on a podcast).[23] The more often you mentally rehearse having a conversation, the more comfortable you'll feel when you take the final step and actually **start a conversation**.

You're ready! Sid might tell you that you're not, that you should spend more time perfecting every step, or read more books about conversation (I've provided some in the resources). You can do both: start talking *and* keep learning. We learn by doing, after all.

## What if: something goes wrong during a conversation

When people had finished playing my talking to strangers scavenger hunt game, I asked them what had been the worst aspect of taking part in the study. There were 1,336 conversations, so, of course, there were a few that didn't go well (though only twenty-three conversations were not enjoyed at all). For some people, the worst thing had been an awkward or boring conversation, or someone who had been rude, ignored them, or rejected them (all of which were infrequent—see chapter 1). For quite a few people, the worst thing had been their own feelings—of anxiety, self-consciousness, and awkwardness—rather than something that a conversation partner said or did. More than a third of the people who answered the question said that nothing bad had happened, including one who expressed some surprise about this: "There wasn't a worst thing that happened, which was very unexpected." My second favorite answer was that the worst thing had been: "I missed a bus from talking to someone too long." My favorite was: "The study ended."

I've talked to hundreds and hundreds of strangers now, and I've had very few negative experiences. There have been a few times when the other person hasn't wanted to talk, or I've experienced a moment of awkwardness (e.g., when I jokingly invited myself to the French lady's party and she didn't understand me). Occasionally, I've been stuck in a boring conversation or experienced an awkward silence. Once, I lost track of time and was almost late to a dentist appointment. Another time, I was happily chatting with some fellow walkers when I realized that, because I'd followed them, I'd taken the wrong trail, and I had to backtrack. I wouldn't trade away these mildly negative experiences if it meant missing out on all the fun and transformational ones.

Dad was predictably unhelpful on this topic. He said he couldn't remember a single negative conversation. Then he told me about a recent visit to a coffee shop, when he'd sat with someone who started talking about a topic he knew nothing about. The conversation ended only because he had to leave. He also told me about a recent medical appointment, when he chatted with a woman who was waiting with her two kids. He said, sympathetically: "It must be tough to bring your kids to the hospital." The woman opened up, telling him about some of the many hardships in her life. Finally, he told me about a recent trip to the grocery store during which he had attempted to help a woman put her groceries on the belt at the checkout, but she had asked him not to, in a rather abrupt way. Clearly Dad sometimes feels disengaged, ends up listening to some heavy disclosures, and even gets rejected—he just doesn't remember when these things happen. And although you or I might see these as at least a bit negative, Dad doesn't mind that these things happened. He thought maybe it had helped the woman at the hospital to use him as a sounding board. She came out of her appointment and gave him a big hug. She thanked him for listening and told him he'd been kind. That's what he remembered: that this had been a special conversation, and maybe he made a difference that day.

I find it easier to confront the possibility of a negative outcome if I have a plan. What are you most worried about? That you'll be bored or will run out of things to say? That the other person won't want to talk to you, or will misinterpret your intentions (e.g., think you're hitting on them)? That your conversation partner will upset you, will make you feel uncomfortable, or will be argumentative?

First, remember that none of these things are likely to happen. And remember that, by choosing certain types of conversation partners in certain types of contexts, you can reduce the already low odds. Next, think of what you could do if the worst happened. Over the years, I've asked attendees at my How to Talk to Strangers workshops to prethink their responses to various unpleasant outcomes. Whatever the worry, they have suggested **changing the topic** (which is also one of Dad's suggestions), **changing the context**, or **pulling another person into the conversation**. If those tactics fail, you can **end the conversation and walk away** (which is the natural way that most conversations with strangers end anyway).

## Making it a habit to talk to strangers

When I've given talks about my research or done interviews with journalists, I've regularly been asked whether I think that talking to strangers continues to provide benefits, even after you've done it for a while. I do, and that's why I've made a *habit* of talking to strangers. Every conversation helps us feel connected to our fellow humans. Because of our need to belong, I don't think these little boosts lose their potency over time—especially since every person is unique and every conversation is unique. (Or, as Dad likes to say: "Everyone has a story.") We do tend to adjust to things—the twenty-seventh bite of a delicious piece of chocolate fudge cake doesn't taste as good as the first few bites—but more so when things are constant, unchanging. Ironically, then, we're more likely to take for granted the stable feelings of belonging that we get from our close relationships. The variety that's inherent in talking to strangers, on the other hand, allows the little boosts of belonging to retain their potency.

Once you've started talking to strangers, I hope you'll keep doing it. Changing a habit is hard, even when we're highly motivated. You can make it easier for yourself if you:

- establish routines that allow you to regularly cross paths with new people;
- come up with a plan, such as a list of missions (the ones from our scavenger hunt study are on my website[24]) or a weekly target;
- set reminders;
- reward yourself after meeting milestones;
- involve other people who can provide support and accountability; and
- log your conversations and reflect on how they went, to track your progress and help you spot patterns.

When you're in the habit formation stage, try not to make exceptions. Don't pass up an opportunity because you're in a bad mood or just don't feel like it. In my experience, those are the days when you can benefit the most. (I find it can help to set more modest goals on those days: I'll tell myself that I just need to talk to one person and only for a couple of minutes.) But if you do miss a day or an opportunity, practice a little self-kindness. Relapses are inevitable, and research suggests that, in the long-term, one missed opportunity makes little difference to habit formation.[25] Instead, you could read through your log or reflect on a recent conversation—and start talking again the next day.

**You've got this!**

I've given you lots of ideas to help you start talking to strangers. (Hopefully they don't make talking to strangers sound more complicated than it is.) Now you need to experiment, to find what works for you. Watch out for the "not yet" trap (or the "I'm not ready yet" trap). You don't need to wait for the perfect conversation partner or the perfect situation (if they even exist). At some point you just need to go for it. As Dad said when I interviewed him: "Just give it a shot. What's the worst thing that's gonna happen?" Easy for him to say—he's either completely banished or tamed Sid. But that gives me hope that one day, with practice, the rest of us might find it as easy as he does to talk to strangers—and brush off the less-than-perfect conversations.

It's time for you to uncover your own *once upon a stranger* stories. . . .

# Notes

## Introduction

1. Office for National Statistics (2024). The nature of violent crime in England and Wales: Year ending March 2024. Centre for Crime and Justice. https://www.ons.gov.uk/peoplepopulationandcommunity/crimeandjustice/articles/thenatureofviolentcrimeinenglandandwales/yearendingmarch2024

## Chapter 1: Why Talking to Strangers Is Hard

1. Boothby, E. J., Cooney, G., Sandstrom, G. M., & Clark, M. S. (2018). The liking gap in conversations: Do people like us more than we think? *Psychological Science*, 29(11), 1742–1756.
2. Mastroianni, A. M., Cooney, G., Boothby, E. J., & Reece, A. G. (2021). The liking gap in groups and teams. *Organizational Behavior and Human Decision Processes*, 162, 109–122.
3. Wolf, W., Nafe, A., & Tomasello, M. (2021). The development of the liking gap: Children older than 5 years think that partners evaluate them less positively than they evaluate their partners. *Psychological Science*, 32(5), 789–798.
4. Today [@TODAYshow]. (2018, December 12). Have you ever walked away from a conversation with a new person and questioned "I wonder if they like me?". [Video attached] [Post]. X. https://x.com/TODAYshow/status/1072858453339791361
5. Maslow, A. H. (1958). A dynamic theory of human motivation. In C. L. Stacey &

M. DeMartino (Eds.), *Understanding human motivation* (pp. 26–47). Cleveland, OH: Howard Allen Publishers.

6. Baumeister, R. F., & Leary, M. R. (1995). The need to belong. *Psychological Bulletin*, 117(3), 497–529.
7. Sprecher, S., Miller, R., Fehr, B., Kanter, J. B., Perlman, D., & Felmlee, D. (2023). Enhanced mood after a getting-acquainted interaction with a stranger: Do shy people benefit too? *Journal of Social and Personal Relationships*, 40(7), 2110–2126.
8. You're more likely to suffer from social anxiety disorder in a particular year if you're a woman (8 percent vs. 6.1 percent for men) and if you're younger (9.1 percent for 18 to 29 year olds vs. 3.1 percent for people who are sixty or older). These statistics come from data in 2001 to 2003, which is notably before the Covid-19 pandemic; National Institute of Mental Health (n.d.). Social anxiety disorder. https://www.nimh.nih.gov/health/statistics/social-anxiety-disorder
9. Goodman, F. (2023, May 10). How to overcome social anxiety. *Psyche*. https://psyche.co/guides/how-to-overcome-feeling-anxious-about-social-occasions. There are resources listed at the bottom of the article, including links to the Anxiety and Depression Association of America (https://adaa.org/) and the US-based National Social Anxiety Center (https://nationalsocialanxietycenter.com/).
10. Hall, J. A. (2019). How many hours does it take to make a friend? *Journal of Social and Personal Relationships*, 36(4), 1278–1296.
11. Hall, J. A., Holmstrom, A. J., Pennington, N., Perrault, E. K., & Totzkay, D. (2023). Quality conversation can increase daily well-being. *Communication Research*, 52(3), 291–315.
12. Small, M. L. (2013). Weak ties and the core discussion network: Why people regularly discuss important matters with unimportant alters. *Social Networks*, 35(3), 470–483.
13. Kardas, M., Kumar, A., & Epley, N. (2022). Overly shallow?: Miscalibrated expectations create a barrier to deeper conversation. *Journal of Personality and Social Psychology*, 122(3), 367–398.
14. Templeton, E. M., Chang, L. J., Reynolds, E. A., Cone LeBeaumont, M. D., & Wheatley, T. (2022). Fast response times signal social connection in conversation. *Proceedings of the National Academy of Sciences*, 119(4), e2116915119.
15. Stivers, T., Enfield, N. J., Brown, P., Englert, C., Hayashi, M., Heinemann, T., Hoymann, G., Rossano, F., de Ruiter, J. P., Yoon, K.-E., & Levinson, S. C. (2009). Universals and cultural variation in turn-taking in conversation. *Proceedings of the National Academy of Sciences*, 106(26), 10587–10592.
16. Templeton, E. M., Chang, L. J., Reynolds, E. A., Cone LeBeaumont, M. D., & Wheatley, T. (2023). Long gaps between turns are awkward for strangers but not for friends. *Philosophical Transactions of the Royal Society B*, 378(1875), 20210471.
17. Templeton, E. M., & Wheatley, T. (2023). Listening fast and slow. *Current Opinion in Psychology*, 53, 101658.

18. Kardas, M., Schroeder, J., & O'Brien, E. (2022). Keep talking: (Mis)understanding the hedonic trajectory of conversation. *Journal of Personality and Social Psychology*, 123(4), 717–740.
19. Sandstrom, G. M., Boothby, E. J., & Cooney, G. (2020). [Predictions about and experiences of talking to a stranger online during Covid lockdowns] [Unpublished raw data]. Department of Psychology, University of Essex.
20. Welker, C., Walker, J., Boothby, E., & Gilovich, T. (2023). Pessimistic assessments of ability in informal conversation. *Journal of Applied Social Psychology*, 53(7), 555–569.
21. Zell, E., Strickhouser, J. E., Sedikides, C., & Alicke, M. D. (2020). The better-than-average effect in comparative self-evaluation: A comprehensive review and meta-analysis. *Psychological Bulletin*, 146(2), 118–149.
22. YouGov (2023, Jan 2). How confident are you that you could safely land a passenger airplane in an emergency situation, relying only on the assistance of air traffic control? [Data set]. https://today.yougov.com/topics/politics/survey-results/daily/2023/01/02/fd798/3
23. Carim, G., Jr., Campbell, C., Marques, E., Ike, N. & Ryley, T. (2023, Dec 6). Almost half the men surveyed think they could land a passenger plane. Experts disagree. *CNN Travel*. https://edition.cnn.com/travel/how-easy-is-it-to-land-a-passenger-plane/index.html
24. Sandstrom, G. M., & Boothby, E. J. (2021). Why do people avoid talking to strangers? A mini meta-analysis of predicted fears and actual experiences talking to a stranger. *Self and Identity*, 20(1), 47–71.
25. Lieberman, M. D., & Rosenthal, R. (2001). Why introverts can't always tell who likes them: Multitasking and nonverbal decoding. *Journal of Personality and Social Psychology*, 80(2), 294–310.
26. Little, B. (2016, Feb). Who are you, really? The puzzle of personality [Video]. TED Conferences. https://www.ted.com/talks/brian_little_who_are_you_really_the_puzzle_of_personality
27. Zelenski, J. M., Sobocko, K., & Whelan, A. D. C. (2013). Introversion, solitude, and subjective well being. In R. J. Coplan & J. C. Bowker (Eds.), *Handbook of Solitude* (pp. 184–201). Hoboken, NJ: Wiley and Sons.
28. Fleeson, W., Malanos, A. B., & Achille, N. M. (2002). An intraindividual process approach to the relationship between extraversion and positive affect: Is acting extraverted as "good" as being extraverted? *Journal of Personality and Social Psychology*, 83(6), 1409–1422.
29. Margolis, S., & Lyubomirsky, S. (2020). Experimental manipulation of extraverted and introverted behavior and its effects on well-being. *Journal of Experimental Psychology: General*, 149(4), 719–731.
30. Zelenski, J. M., Santoro, M. S., & Whelan, D. C. (2012). Would introverts be better

off if they acted more like extraverts? Exploring emotional and cognitive consequences of counterdispositional behavior. *Emotion*, 12(2), 290–303.
31. Zelenski, J. M., Sobocko, K., & Whelan, A. D. C. (2013). Introversion, solitude, and subjective well being. In R. J. Coplan & J. C. Bowker (Eds.), *Handbook of Solitude* (pp. 184–201). Hoboken, NJ: Wiley and Sons.
32. Welker, C., Walker, J., Boothby, E., & Gilovich, T. (2023). Pessimistic assessments of ability in informal conversation. *Journal of Applied Social Psychology*, 53(7), 555–569.
33. Epley, N., & Schroeder, J. (2014). Mistakenly seeking solitude. *Journal of Experimental Psychology: General*, 143(5), 1980–1999.
34. Sandstrom, G. M., Boothby, E. J., & Cooney, G. (2022). Talking to strangers: A weeklong intervention reduces psychological barriers to social connection. *Journal of Experimental Social Psychology*, 102, 104356.
35. Baumeister, R. F., Bratslavsky, E., Finkenauer, C., & Vohs, K. D. (2001). Bad is stronger than good. *Review of General Psychology*, 5(4), 323–370.
36. Gilbert, D. T., Pinel, E. C., Wilson, T. D., Blumberg, S. J., & Wheatley, T. P. (1998). Immune neglect: A source of durability bias in affective forecasting. *Journal of Personality and Social Psychology*, 75(3), 617–638.
37. Sandstrom, G. M. (2025). [Predictions about and reactions to being rejected when approaching a stranger for a chat] [Unpublished raw data]. School of Psychology, University of Sussex.
38. Montoya, R. M., Kershaw, C., & Prosser, J. L. (2018). A meta-analytic investigation of the relation between interpersonal attraction and enacted behavior. *Psychological Bulletin*, 144(7), 673–709.
39. Hall, J. A., Xing, C., & Brooks, S. (2015). Accurately detecting flirting: Error management theory, the traditional sexual script, and flirting base rate. *Communication Research*, 42(7), 939–958.
40. Shotland, R. L., & Craig, J. M. (1988). Can men and women differentiate between friendly and sexually interested behavior? *Social Psychology Quarterly*, 51(1), 66–73.
41. [deleted account]. (2022). Has anyone had a random conversation on the Tube with a stranger and it not been weird/creepy/awkward/an attempted pick-up? [Online forum post]. Reddit. https://www.reddit.com/r/london/comments/yyfoxc/has_anyone_had_a_random_conversation_on_the_tube/
42. Grierson, J. (2016, Sept 29). "Tube chat" campaign provokes horror among London commuters. *The Guardian*. https://www.theguardian.com/uk-news/2016/sep/29/tube-chat-campaign-provokes-horror-among-london-commuters
43. Sandstrom, G. M., & Boothby, E. J. (2021). Why do people avoid talking to strangers? A mini meta-analysis of predicted fears and actual experiences talking to a stranger. *Self and Identity*, 20(1), 47–71.

## Chapter 2: No Strings Attached

1. Jessica Wilkinson | Family Travel[@ourmicroadventures]. (2025, Jun 21). *Who is your next Gipfelschmaus going to be with?!* [Reel]. Instagram. https://www.instagram.com/reel/DLK5S8CtHdP/
2. Tamir, D. I., & Mitchell, J. P. (2012). Disclosing information about the self is intrinsically rewarding. *Proceedings of the National Academy of Sciences*, 109(21), 8038–8043.
3. Park, J., Ayduk, Ö., & Kross, E. (2016). Stepping back to move forward: Expressive writing promotes self-distancing. *Emotion*, 16(3), 349–364.
4. Greene, K., Derlega, V. J., & Mathews, A. (2006). Self-disclosure in personal relationships. In: A. L. Vangelisti & D. Perlman (Eds.), *The Cambridge Handbook of Personal Relationships* (pp.409–427). New York, NY: Cambridge University Press.
5. Collins, N. L., & Miller, L. C. (1994). Self-disclosure and liking: A meta-analytic review. *Psychological Bulletin*, 116(3), 457–475.
6. Sprecher, S., Treger, S., Wondra, J. D., Hilaire, N., & Wallpe, K. (2013). Taking turns: Reciprocal self-disclosure promotes liking in initial interactions. *Journal of Experimental Social Psychology*, 49(5), 860–866.
7. Bruk, A., Scholl, S. G., & Bless, H. (2018). Beautiful mess effect: Self–other differences in evaluation of showing vulnerability. *Journal of Personality and Social Psychology*, 115(2), 192–205.
8. Kardas, M., Kumar, A., & Epley, N. (2023). Let it go: How exaggerating the reputational costs of revealing negative information encourages secrecy in relationships. *Journal of Personality and Social Psychology*, 126(6), 1052–1083.
9. Kim, S., Liu, P. J., & Min, K. E. (2021). Reminder avoidance: Why people hesitate to disclose their insecurities to friends. *Journal of Personality and Social Psychology*, 121(1), 59–75.
10. Spata, C. (2021, May 24). It's St. Petersburg's bench, but Al owns it. *Tampa Bay Times*. https://www.tampabay.com/life-culture/2021/05/24/its-st-petersburgs-bench-but-al-owns-it/
11. Liberman, N., & Trope, Y. (2008). The psychology of transcending the here and now. *Science*, 322(5905), 1201–1205.
12. Grossmann, I., & Kross, E. (2014). Exploring Solomon's paradox: Self-distancing eliminates the self-other asymmetry in wise reasoning about close relationships in younger and older adults. *Psychological Science*, 25(8), 1571–1580.
13. Grossmann, I., Dorfman, A., Oakes, H., Santos, H. C., Vohs, K. D., & Scholer, A. A. (2021). Training for wisdom: The distanced-self-reflection diary method. *Psychological Science*, 32(3), 381–394.
14. Danziger, S., Montal, R., & Barkan, R. (2012). Idealistic advice and pragmatic choice: A psychological distance account. *Journal of Personality and Social Psychology*, 102(6), 1105–1117.
15. Howell, J. L., Sweeny, K., & Shepperd, J. A. (2014). Psychological distance and the

discrepancy between recommendations and actions. *Basic and Applied Social Psychology, 36*(6), 502–514.

16. Lyubomirsky, S., King, L., & Diener, E. (2005). The benefits of frequent positive affect: Does happiness lead to success? *Psychological Bulletin, 131*(6), 803–855.
17. Small, M. L. (2013). Weak ties and the core discussion network: Why people regularly discuss important matters with unimportant alters. *Social Networks, 35*(3), 470–483.
18. Zhao, X., & Epley, N. (2022). Surprisingly happy to have helped: Underestimating prosociality creates a misplaced barrier to asking for help. *Psychological Science, 33*(10), 1708–1731.
19. Aknin, L. B., Dunn, E. W., Whillans, A. V., Grant, A. M., & Norton, M. I. (2013). Making a difference matters: Impact unlocks the emotional benefits of prosocial spending. *Journal of Economic Behavior & Organization, 88*, 90–95.
20. Aron, A., Melinat, E., Aron, E. N., Vallone, R. D., & Bator, R. J. (1997). The experimental generation of interpersonal closeness: A procedure and some preliminary findings. *Personality and Social Psychology Bulletin, 23*(4), 363–377.
21. Kardas, M., Kumar, A., & Epley, N. (2022). Overly shallow?: Miscalibrated expectations create a barrier to deeper conversation. *Journal of Personality and Social Psychology, 122*(3), 367–398.
22. Hart, E., VanEpps, E. M., & Schweitzer, M. E. (2021). The (better than expected) consequences of asking sensitive questions. *Organizational Behavior and Human Decision Processes, 162*, 136–154.
23. Langston, C. A. (1994). Capitalizing on and coping with daily-life events: Expressive responses to positive events. *Journal of Personality and Social Psychology, 67*(6), 1112–1125.
24. Gable, S. L., & Reis, H. T. (2010). Good news! Capitalizing on positive events in an interpersonal context. In *Advances in Experimental Social Psychology* (Vol. 42, pp. 195–257). Academic Press.
25. Gable, S. L., Reis, H. T., Impett, E. A., & Asher, E. R. (2004). What do you do when things go right? The intrapersonal and interpersonal benefits of sharing positive events. *Journal of Personality and Social Psychology, 87*(2), 228–245.
26. Sim, L., Ip, K. I., Ascigil, E., Edelstein, R. S., & Lee, F. (2024). Cross-cultural differences in supportive responses to positive event disclosure. *The Journal of Positive Psychology, 19*(2), 277–290.
27. Gable, S. L., & Reis, H. T. (2010). Good news! Capitalizing on positive events in an interpersonal context. In *Advances in Experimental Social Psychology* (Vol. 42, pp. 195–257). Academic Press.

## Chapter 3: Puzzle Pieces

1. Kashdan, T. B., Stiksma, M. C., Disabato, D. J., McKnight, P. E., Bekier, J., Kaji, J., & Lazarus, R. (2018). The five-dimensional curiosity scale: Capturing the bandwidth

of curiosity and identifying four unique subgroups of curious people. *Journal of Research in Personality*, 73, 130–149; the five dimensions are: Joyous Exploration, Deprivation Sensitivity, Stress Tolerance, Social Curiosity, and Thrill Seeking.
2. Sandstrom, G.M. (2024). [Perceptions, predictors, and outcomes of people-watching] [Unpublished raw data]. School of Psychology, University of Sussex.
3. Renner, B. (2006). Curiosity about people: The development of a social curiosity measure in adults. *Journal of Personality Assessment*, 87(3), 305–316.
4. Hsee, C. K., & Ruan, B. (2016). The Pandora effect: The power and peril of curiosity. *Psychological Science*, 27(5), 659–666.
5. Tijou, S. (2017, Mar 2). There's now a word for nails on a blackboard—but it's not in English. *BBC News*. https://www.bbc.co.uk/news/newsbeat-39141780
6. chickidychow. (2014). Reddit, what is your equivalent to "nails on a chalkboard"? [Online forum post]. Reddit. https://www.reddit.com/r/AskReddit/comments/2rbjv4/reddit_what_is_your_equivalent_to_nails_on_a/
7. Peterson, C., & Seligman, M. E. (2004). *Character strengths and virtues: A handbook and classification* (Vol. 1). Oxford University Press.
8. Gallagher, M. W., & Lopez, S. J. (2007). Curiosity and well-being. *The Journal of Positive Psychology*, 2(4), 236–248.
9. Schroeder, J., Lyons, D., & Epley, N. (2022). Hello, stranger? Pleasant conversations are preceded by concerns about starting one. *Journal of Experimental Psychology: General*, 151(5), 1141–1153.
10. Atir, S., Wald, K. A., & Epley, N. (2022). Talking with strangers is surprisingly informative. *Proceedings of the National Academy of Sciences*, 119(34), e2206992119.
11. Sandstrom, G.M. (2023). [Attitudes towards talking to strangers while travelling vs. at home] [Unpublished raw data]. School of Psychology, University of Sussex.
12. Nguyen, H. (2023, Mar 29). *Five factors motivating Brits to travel in 2023*. YouGov. https://business.yougov.com/content/46401-travel-motivators-great-britain-poll-2023
13. hmio213. (2022). Why do you travel? [Online forum post]. Reddit. https://www.reddit.com/r/travel/comments/wgba83/why_do_you_travel/
14. Sandstrom, G. M., & Dunn, E. W. (2014). Social interactions and well-being: The surprising power of weak ties. *Personality and Social Psychology Bulletin*, 40(7), 910–922.
15. Sun, J., Harris, K., & Vazire, S. (2020). Is well-being associated with the quantity and quality of social interactions? *Journal of Personality and Social Psychology*, 119(6), 1478–1496.
16. Collins, H. K., Hagerty, S. F., Quoidbach, J., Norton, M. I., & Brooks, A. W. (2022). Relational diversity in social portfolios predicts well-being. *Proceedings of the National Academy of Sciences*, 119(43), e2120668119.
17. Sandstrom, G. M., & Boothby, E. J. (2021). Why do people avoid talking to strangers?

A mini meta-analysis of predicted fears and actual experiences talking to a stranger. *Self and Identity*, 20(1), 47–71.
18. Kushlev, K., Proulx, J. D., & Dunn, E. W. (2017). Digitally connected, socially disconnected: The effects of relying on technology rather than other people. *Computers in Human Behavior*, 76, 68–74.
19. Flynn, F. J., & Lake, V. K. (2008). If you need help, just ask: Underestimating compliance with direct requests for help. *Journal of Personality and Social Psychology*, 95(1), 128–143.
20. Eggleston, C. M., Wilson, T. D., Lee, M., & Gilbert, D. T. (2015). Predicting what we will like: Asking a stranger can be as good as asking a friend. *Organizational Behavior and Human Decision Processes*, 128, 1–10.
21. Gilbert, D. T., Killingsworth, M. A., Eyre, R. N., & Wilson, T. D. (2009). The surprising power of neighborly advice. *Science*, 323(5921), 1617–1619.
22. Rusbridger, A. (2014). *Play it again*. Penguin.
23. My husband hiked up Half Dome in Yosemite National Park. After hours and hours of climbing, including a section at the top that involved clipping himself onto a cable to cross a sheer rock face, he finally made it to the top. At the summit, he saw a man with a whole watermelon strapped to his backpack. I'm sure that watermelon tasted amazing (assuming you like watermelon, which I don't), but the fact that someone doing such a strenuous hike chose to burden himself by lugging an entire watermelon blows my mind!
24. Sandstrom, G. M., Boothby, E. J., & Cooney, G. (2019). [Talking to strangers scavenger hunt] [Unpublished raw data]. Department of Psychology, University of Essex.
25. Hartung, F. M., & Renner, B. (2013). Social curiosity and gossip: Related but different drives of social functioning. *PLoS One*, 8(7), e69996.
26. Granovetter, M. S. (1973). The strength of weak ties. *American Journal of Sociology*, 78(6), 1360–1380.
27. Baer, M. (2010). The strength-of-weak-ties perspective on creativity: A comprehensive examination and extension. *Journal of Applied Psychology*, 95(3), 592–601.
28. Perry-Smith, J. E. (2006). Social yet creative: The role of social relationships in facilitating individual creativity. *Academy of Management Journal*, 49(1), 85–101.
29. Zhou, J., Shin, S. J., Brass, D. J., Choi, J., & Zhang, Z. X. (2009). Social networks, personal values, and creativity: Evidence for curvilinear and interaction effects. *Journal of Applied Psychology*, 94(6), 1544–1552.
30. Perry-Smith, J. E. (2014). Social network ties beyond nonredundancy: An experimental investigation of the effect of knowledge content and tie strength on creativity. *Journal of Applied Psychology*, 99(5), 831–846.
31. Atir, S., Wald, K. A., & Epley, N. (2022). Talking with strangers is surprisingly informative. *Proceedings of the National Academy of Sciences*, 119(34), e2206992119.
32. Mannucci, P. V., & Perry-Smith, J. E. (2022). "Who are you going to call?" Network

activation in creative idea generation and elaboration. *Academy of Management Journal*, 65(4), 1192–1217.
33. De Montjoye, Y. A., Hidalgo, C. A., Verleysen, M., & Blondel, V. D. (2013). Unique in the crowd: The privacy bounds of human mobility. *Scientific Reports*, 3(1), 1–5.
34. Deci, E. L., & Ryan, R. M. (2000). The "what" and "why" of goal pursuits: Human needs and the self-determination of behavior. *Psychological Inquiry*, 11(4), 227–268.
35. Bagheri, L., & Milyavskaya, M. (2020). Novelty-variety as a candidate basic psychological need: New evidence across three studies. *Motivation and Emotion*, 44(1), 32–53.
36. Oishi, S., & Westgate, E. C. (2022). A psychologically rich life: Beyond happiness and meaning. *Psychological Review*, 129(4), 790–811.
37. Zeeb, V., & Joffe, H. (2021). Connecting with strangers in the city: A mattering approach. *British Journal of Social Psychology*, 60(2), 524–547.
38. Foulkes, L. (2024, Oct 28). How to have more meaningful conversations. *Psyche*. https://psyche.co/guides/how-to-have-more-meaningful-conversations
39. Atir, S., Wald, K. A., & Epley, N. (2022). Talking with strangers is surprisingly informative. *Proceedings of the National Academy of Sciences*, 119(34), e2206992119.
40. Kashdan, T. B., McKnight, P. E., Fincham, F. D., & Rose, P. (2011). When curiosity breeds intimacy: Taking advantage of intimacy opportunities and transforming boring conversations. *Journal of Personality*, 79(6), 1369–1402.

## Chapter 4: Sowing Seeds

1. Lyubomirsky, S., King, L., & Diener, E. (2005). The benefits of frequent positive affect: Does happiness lead to success? *Psychological Bulletin*, 131(6), 803–855.
2. Diener, E., Seligman, M. E., Choi, H., & Oishi, S. (2018). Happiest people revisited. *Perspectives on Psychological Science*, 13(2), 176–184.
3. Bonn, G., & Tafarodi, R. W. (2013). Visualizing the good life: A cross-cultural analysis. *Journal of Happiness Studies*, 14, 1839–1856.
4. Antonucci, T. C. (1986). Measuring social support networks: Hierarchical mapping technique. *Generations: Journal of the American Society on Aging*, 10(4), 10–12.
5. Fingerman, K. L., Hay, E. L., & Birditt, K. S. (2004). The best of ties, the worst of ties: Close, problematic, and ambivalent social relationships. *Journal of Marriage and Family*, 66(3), 792–808.
6. Granovetter, M. S. (1973). The strength of weak ties. *American Journal of Sociology*, 78(6), 1360–1380.
7. Moreland, R. L., & Beach, S. R. (1992). Exposure effects in the classroom: The development of affinity among students. *Journal of Experimental Social Psychology*, 28(3), 255–276.
8. Hall, J. A. (2019). How many hours does it take to make a friend? *Journal of Social and Personal Relationships*, 36(4), 1278–1296.

9. Giurge, L. M., Whillans, A. V., & West, C. (2020). Why time poverty matters for individuals, organisations and nations. *Nature Human Behaviour*, 4(10), 993–1003.
10. Sandstrom, G. M., & Dunn, E. W. (2014). Social interactions and well-being: The surprising power of weak ties. *Personality and Social Psychology Bulletin*, 40(7), 910–922.
11. Kushlev, K., Heintzelman, S. J., Oishi, S., & Diener, E. (2018). The declining marginal utility of social time for subjective well-being. *Journal of Research in Personality*, 74, 124–140.
12. Hill, C. A. (1987). Affiliation motivation: People who need people . . . but in different ways. *Journal of Personality and Social Psychology*, 52(5), 1008–1018.
13. Collins, H. K., Hagerty, S. F., Quoidbach, J., Norton, M. I., & Brooks, A. W. (2022). Relational diversity in social portfolios predicts well-being. *Proceedings of the National Academy of Sciences*, 119(43), e2120668119.
14. Tsang, S., Barrentine, K., Chadha, S., Oishi, S., & Wood, A. (2024). Social exploration: How and why people seek new connections. *Psychological Review*, 132(3), 656–679.
15. Holt-Lunstad, J., Smith, T. B., & Layton, J. B. (2010). Social relationships and mortality risk: A meta-analytic review. *PLoS Medicine*, 7(7), e1000316.
16. Helliwell, J. F., Layard, R., Sachs, J. D., De Neve, J.-E., Aknin, L. B., & Wang, S. (Eds.). (2022). *World Happiness Report 2022*. New York: Sustainable Development Solutions Network.
17. Mull, A. (2021, Jan 27). The pandemic has erased entire categories of friendship. *The Atlantic*. https://www.theatlantic.com/health/archive/2021/01/pandemic-goodbye-casual-friends/617839/
18. Sandstrom, G. M., & Dunn, E. W. (2014). Social interactions and well-being: The surprising power of weak ties. *Personality and Social Psychology Bulletin*, 40(7), 910–922.
19. Sandstrom, G. M., & Dunn, E. W. (2014). Is efficiency overrated? Minimal social interactions lead to belonging and positive affect. *Social Psychological and Personality Science*, 5(4), 437–442.
20. Poerio, G. L., Totterdell, P., Emerson, L. M., & Miles, E. (2016). Helping the heart grow fonder during absence: Daydreaming about significant others replenishes connectedness after induced loneliness. *Cognition and Emotion*, 30(6), 1197–1207.
21. Paravati, E., Naidu, E., & Gabriel, S. (2021). From "love actually" to love, actually: The sociometer takes every kind of fuel. *Self and Identity*, 20(1), 6–24.
22. Hirsch, J. L., & Clark, M. S. (2019). Multiple paths to belonging that we should study together. *Perspectives on Psychological Science*, 14(2), 238–255.
23. Paravati, E., Naidu, E., & Gabriel, S. (2021). From "love actually" to love, actually: The sociometer takes every kind of fuel. *Self and Identity*, 20(1), 6–24.
24. Kuwabara, K., Zou, X., Aven, B., Hildebrand, C., & Iyengar, S. (2020). Lay theories of networking ability: Beliefs that inhibit instrumental networking. *Social Networks*, 62, 1–11.
25. Porter, C. M., Woo, S. E., Alonso, N., & Snyder, G. (2023). Why do people network?

Professional networking motives and their implications for networking behaviors and career success. *Journal of Vocational Behavior, 142,* 103856.

26. Hill, C. A. (1987). Affiliation motivation: People who need people . . . but in different ways. *Journal of Personality and Social Psychology, 52*(5), 1008–1018.
27. Yeomans, M., Schweitzer, M. E., & Brooks, A. W. (2022). The Conversational Circumplex: Identifying, prioritizing, and pursuing informational and relational motives in conversation. *Current Opinion in Psychology, 44,* 293–302.
28. Rossignac-Milon, M., Pillemer, J., Bailey, E. R., Horton Jr, C. B., & Iyengar, S. S. (2024). Just be real with me: Perceived partner authenticity promotes relationship initiation via shared reality. *Organizational Behavior and Human Decision Processes, 180,* 104306.
29. Fleck, A. (2022, Nov 22). What do you want to be when you grow up? *Statista.* https://www.statista.com/chart/28802/childhood-aspirations-in-china-us-uk/
30. Morgenroth, T., Ryan, M. K., & Peters, K. (2015). The motivational theory of role modeling: How role models influence role aspirants' goals. *Review of General Psychology, 19*(4), 465–483.
31. Stout, J. G., Dasgupta, N., Hunsinger, M., & McManus, M. A. (2011). STEMing the tide: Using ingroup experts to inoculate women's self-concept in science, technology, engineering, and mathematics (STEM). *Journal of Personality and Social Psychology, 100*(2), 255–270.
32. Roberts, B. W., & Mroczek, D. (2008). Personality trait change in adulthood. *Current Directions in Psychological Science, 17*(1), 31–35.
33. Quoidbach, J., Gilbert, D. T., & Wilson, T. D. (2013). The end of history illusion. *Science, 339*(6115), 96–98.
34. Eveleigh, R. (2024, Jan 29). "This too shall pass." World-first study proves the power of mental health recovery stories. *Positive News.* https://www.positive.news/society/study-proves-power-mental-health-recovery-stories/
35. Slade, M., Rennick-Egglestone, S., Llewellyn-Beardsley, J., Yeo, C., Roe, J., Bailey, S., . . . & Ng, F. (2021). Recorded mental health recovery narratives as a resource for people affected by mental health problems: Development of the Narrative Experiences Online (NEON) intervention. *JMIR Formative Research, 5*(5), e24417.
36. Tait, M. (2024, May 16). When you stand side by side at the dog park, you can reveal your true selves—but not your names. *The Guardian.* https://www.theguardian.com/commentisfree/article/2024/may/17/when-you-stand-side-by-side-at-the-dog-park-you-can-reveal-your-true-selves-but-not-your-names
37. King, L. A. (2001). The health benefits of writing about life goals. *Personality and Social Psychology Bulletin, 27*(7), 798–807.
38. Heekerens, J. B., & Eid, M. (2021). Inducing positive affect and positive future expectations using the best-possible-self intervention: A systematic review and meta-analysis. *The Journal of Positive Psychology, 16*(3), 322–347.

## Chapter 5: Feeling Seen and Seeing Together

1. Granovetter, M. S. (1973). The strength of weak ties. *American Journal of Sociology*, 78(6), 1360–1380.
2. Would I just hang out at a coffee shop, wait until I spotted a regular, and then ask them how happy they were? If I compared regulars to nonregulars, and regulars turned out to be happier, I wouldn't know if it was because being a regular makes people happier or because happier people are the ones who tend to become regulars. Ideally, I would randomly assign some people to be regulars and some people to be nonregulars. That way, even though some people are just naturally happier than others, the already-happy people should be fairly equally distributed between the two groups: Approximately half would be assigned to be regulars and the other half nonregulars. With random assignment, if I found that these two groups differed in happiness, I could be pretty sure it was because they were a regular or not rather than preexisting differences. But I didn't have a magic wand that could turn people into regulars.
3. Sandstrom, G. M., & Dunn, E. W. (2014). Is efficiency overrated? Minimal social interactions lead to belonging and positive affect. *Social Psychological and Personality Science*, 5(4), 437–442.
4. Roddick, C. M., Christie, C. D., Madden, K. M., & Chen, F. S. (2021). Social integration after moving to a new city predicts lower systolic blood pressure. *Psychophysiology*, 58(12), e13924.
5. Milgram, S. (1967). The small world problem. *Psychology Today*, 2(1), 60–67.
6. Dodds, P. S., Muhamad, R., & Watts, D. J. (2003). An experimental study of search in global social networks. *Science*, 301(5634), 827–829.
7. Reynolds, P. (n.d.). *The Oracle of Bacon*. https://oracleofbacon.org/center.php
8. Brotheridge, C. M., & Lee, R. T. (2003). Development and validation of the emotional labour scale. *Journal of Occupational and Organizational Psychology*, 76(3), 365–379.
9. Sandstrom, G. M., O'Dwyer, G. M., Freeman, M. C., Bowkett, E. J. (n.d.). Talking in transit: A reminder-based intervention increases passenger interactions with bus drivers. [Manuscript in preparation]. School of Psychology, University of Sussex.
10. Gunaydin, G., Oztekin, H., Karabulut, D. H., & Salman-Engin, S. (2021). Minimal social interactions with strangers predict greater subjective well-being. *Journal of Happiness Studies*, 22, 1839–1853.
11. Ascigil, E., Gunaydin, G., Selcuk, E., Sandstrom, G. M., & Aydin, E. (2025). Minimal social interactions and life satisfaction: The role of greeting, thanking, and conversing. *Social Psychological and Personality Science*, 16(2), 202–213.
12. Ishiguro, I. (2023). Minimal social interactions and subjective well-being in the Japanese context: Examination of mediation processes using a national representative sample. *Social Sciences & Humanities Open*, 8(1), 100713.

13. mryosupman. (2024). Weirdest/most specific coffee order you've served? [Online forum post].Reddit.https://www.reddit.com/r/barista/comments/18mjshy/weirdest most_specific_coffee_order_youve_served/
14. Gruenfeld, D. H., Inesi, M. E., Magee, J. C., & Galinsky, A. D. (2008). Power and the objectification of social targets. *Journal of Personality and Social Psychology*, 95(1), 111–127.
15. Gruenfeld, D. H., Inesi, M. E., Magee, J. C., & Galinsky, A. D. (2008). Power and the objectification of social targets. *Journal of Personality and Social Psychology*, 95(1), 111–127.
16. Neel, R., & Lassetter, B. (2019). The stigma of perceived irrelevance: An affordance-management theory of interpersonal invisibility. *Psychological Review*, 126(5), 634–659.
17. Wesselmann, E. D., Cardoso, F. D., Slater, S., & Williams, K. D. (2012). To be looked at as though air: Civil attention matters. *Psychological Science*, 23(2), 166–168.
18. For support related to suicide: In the US, you can call or text the National Suicide Prevention Lifeline on 988, chat on 988lifeline.org, or text HOME to 741741 to connect with a crisis counselor. In the UK and Ireland, Samaritans can be contacted on freephone 116 123, or email jo@samaritans.org or jo@samaritans.ie. In Australia, the crisis support service Lifeline is 13 11 14. Other international helplines can be found at befrienders.org.
19. Samaritans. (n.d.). Small talk saves lives. https://www.samaritans.org/support-us/campaign/small-talk-saves-lives/
20. Samaritans. (n.d.). Small talk saves lives. https://www.samaritans.org/support-us/campaign/small-talk-saves-lives/
21. Lezra, B. (2023, Nov 19). A stranger asked me to take her photograph. It saved my life. *The Washington Post*. https://www.washingtonpost.com/lifestyle/2023/11/19/billy-lezra-suicide-prevention-photograph
22. Arminen, I. A., & Heino, A. S. (2023). Civil inattention—On the sources of relational segregation. *Frontiers in Sociology*, 8, 1212090.
23. Arminen, I. A., & Heino, A. S. (2023). Civil inattention—On the sources of relational segregation. *Frontiers in Sociology*, 8, 1212090.
24. TEDx Talks. (2024, July 13). Is the cure for loneliness hiding in your closet? | Mollie Kaye | TEDxSurrey [Video]. YouTube. https://www.youtube.com/watch?v=mcYPiQGyZbM
25. Higgins, E. T., & Pittman, T. S. (2008). Motives of the human animal: Comprehending, managing, and sharing inner states. *Annual Review of Psychology*, 59(1), 361–385.
26. Boothby, E. J., Clark, M. S., & Bargh, J. A. (2014). Shared experiences are amplified. *Psychological Science*, 25(12), 2209–2216.
27. Higgins, E. T., Rossignac-Milon, M., & Echterhoff, G. (2021). Shared reality: From sharing-is-believing to merging minds. *Current Directions in Psychological Science*, 30(2), 103–110.

28. Rossignac-Milon, M., Bolger, N., Zee, K. S., Boothby, E. J., & Higgins, E. T. (2021). Merged minds: Generalized shared reality in dyadic relationships. *Journal of Personality and Social Psychology*, 120(4), 882–911.
29. Shteynberg, G. (2015). Shared attention. *Perspectives on Psychological Science*, 10(5), 579–590.
30. Wiener, H. J., Flaherty, K., & Wiener, J. (2023). Starting conversations with new customers: A research note on the moderating effect of experience on responses to small talk. *Journal of Personal Selling & Sales Management*, 43(3), 195–206.
31. Smith, R. (2025, Jan 21). Starling murmuration guide: Why and when they happen and best places to see one in the UK. *BBC Countryfile*. https://www.countryfile.com/wildlife/birds/what-is-a-murmuration-and-where-are-the-best-places-in-britain-to-see-one

## Chapter 6: Skeleton Key

1. NHS England (2023). 95% of ex-smokers see positive changes soon after quitting. Department of Health and Social Care, Neil O'Brien MP. https://www.gov.uk/government/news/95-of-ex-smokers-see-positive-changes-soon-after-quitting
2. Sandstrom, G. M., & Boothby, E. J. (2021). Why do people avoid talking to strangers? A mini meta-analysis of predicted fears and actual experiences talking to a stranger. *Self and Identity*, 20(1), 47–71.
3. Welker, C., Walker, J., Boothby, E., & Gilovich, T. (2023). Pessimistic assessments of ability in informal conversation. *Journal of Applied Social Psychology*, 53(7), 555–569.
4. Sandstrom, G. M., Boothby, E. J., & Cooney, G. (2022). Talking to strangers: A weeklong intervention reduces psychological barriers to social connection. *Journal of Experimental Social Psychology*, 102, 104356.
5. By this, I mean they rated their enjoyment at or above the midpoint of the scale.
6. Dweck, C. S., & Yeager, D. S. (2019). Mindsets: A view from two eras. *Perspectives on Psychological Science*, 14(3), 481–496.
7. Beer, J. S. (2002). Implicit self-theories of shyness. *Journal of Personality and Social Psychology*, 83(4), 1009–1024.
8. Ciarrochi, J., Heaven, P. C., & Davies, F. (2007). The impact of hope, self-esteem, and attributional style on adolescents' school grades and emotional well-being: A longitudinal study. *Journal of Research in Personality*, 41(6), 1161–1178.
9. Sweeney, P. D., Anderson, K., & Bailey, S. (1986). Attributional style in depression: A meta-analytic review. *Journal of Personality and Social Psychology*, 50(5), 974–991.
10. Butler, A. C., Chapman, J. E., Forman, E. M., & Beck, A. T. (2006). The empirical status of cognitive-behavioral therapy: A review of meta-analyses. *Clinical Psychology Review*, 26(1), 17–31.

11. Jiang, J. (n.d.) 100 days of rejection therapy. Rejection Therapy with Jia Jiang. https://www.rejectiontherapy.com/100-days-of-rejection-therapy
12. Jiang, J. (2012, Nov 18). Rejection therapy day 3—Ask for Olympic symbol doughnuts. Jackie at Krispy Kreme delivers! [Video]. YouTube. https://www.youtube.com/watch?v=7Ax2CsVbrX0
13. Jiang, J. (2015, May). What I learned from 100 days of rejection [Video]. TED Conferences. https://www.ted.com/talks/jia_jiang_what_i_learned_from_100_days_of_rejection
14. Sawhney, V. (2020, Oct 12). Why your brain dwells on unfinished tasks. *Harvard Business Review*. https://hbr.org/2020/10/why-your-brain-dwells-on-unfinished-tasks
15. Wilson, T. D., Centerbar, D. B., Kermer, D. A., & Gilbert, D. T. (2005). The pleasures of uncertainty: Prolonging positive moods in ways people do not anticipate. *Journal of Personality and Social Psychology*, 88(1), 5–21.
16. Carter, A. J., Croft, A., Lukas, D., & Sandstrom, G. M. (2018). Women's visibility in academic seminars: Women ask fewer questions than men. *PloS One*, 13(9), e0202743.
17. Sandstrom, G. M., Croft, A., Gibson, H., & Carter, A. J. (2022). Both men and women expect and receive negative judgment for impolite questions at academic talks, and receive positive judgment for polite questions. [Manuscript in preparation]. School of Psychology, University of Sussex.
18. Gilovich, T., Medvec, V. H., & Savitsky, K. (2000). The spotlight effect in social judgment: An egocentric bias in estimates of the salience of one's own actions and appearance. *Journal of Personality and Social Psychology*, 78(2), 211–222.
19. Savitsky, K., Epley, N., & Gilovich, T. (2001). Do others judge us as harshly as we think? Overestimating the impact of our failures, shortcomings, and mishaps. *Journal of Personality and Social Psychology*, 81(1), 44–56.
20. Wiseman, R. (2003, Jan 9). Be lucky—it's an easy skill to learn. *The Telegraph*. https://www.telegraph.co.uk/technology/3304496/Be-lucky-its-an-easy-skill-to-learn.html
21. Gregory, A. L., Quoidbach, J., Haase, C. M., & Piff, P. K. (2023). Be here now: Perceptions of uncertainty enhance savoring. *Emotion*, 23(1), 30–40.
22. There are, of course, dangerous strangers, but 90 percent of harm toward children comes from people they know. Acknowledging this, children are now being taught that there are "tricky people" that they need to be careful of. They're also being taught that if they're worried that someone might be "tricky," there are strangers that they can turn to for help (e.g., store clerks, police officers, or, in a pinch, parents with children). Williams, K., & See, E. (2022, Nov 9). Stranger danger: It's time to end the rhyme and talk to strangers. Child Advocacy Center. https://www.cacfaync.org/who-we-are/news-events/blog-posts.html/article/2022/11/09/stranger-danger-it-s-time-to-end-the-rhyme-and-talk-to-strangers
23. Janoff-Bulman, R. (1989). Assumptive worlds and the stress of traumatic events: Applications of the schema construct. *Social Cognition*, 7(2), 113–136.

24. Poulin, M., & Cohen Silver, R. (2008). World benevolence beliefs and well-being across the life span. *Psychology and Aging, 23*(1), 13–23.
25. Poulin, M., & Cohen Silver, R. (2008). World benevolence beliefs and well-being across the life span. *Psychology and Aging, 23*(1), 13–23.
26. Sandstrom, G. M., Boothby, E. J., & Cooney, G. (2020). [Predictions about and experiences of talking to a stranger online during Covid lockdowns] [Unpublished raw data]. Department of Psychology, University of Essex.
27. West, T. N., Berman, C. J., Payne, B. K., Muscatell, K. A., & Fredrickson, B. L. (2025). Trust a stranger? Investigating community trust and economic inequality as barriers to positive interactions among strangers. *Journal of Happiness Studies, 26*(6).
28. Sandstrom, G. (n.d.). Gillian M. Sandstrom. https://gilliansandstrom.com/wp-content/uploads/2021/04/scavenger-hunt-missions.pdf

## Chapter 7: The Kindness of Strangers

1. Zhao, X., & Epley, N. (2022). Surprisingly happy to have helped: Underestimating prosociality creates a misplaced barrier to asking for help. *Psychological Science, 33*(10), 1708–1731.
2. Banerjee, R., Hammond, C., et al. (2025). Kindness and well-being: The Unique contributions of receiving, performing, and witnessing acts of kindness. [Manuscript in preparation]. School of Psychology, University of Sussex.
3. Hammond, C. (2022). *The keys to kindness: How to be kinder to yourself, others and the world*. Canongate Books.
4. Hanel, P. H., Wolfradt, U., Wolf, L. J., Coelho, G. L. D. H., & Maio, G. R. (2020). Well-being as a function of person-country fit in human values. *Nature Communications, 11*(1), 5150.
5. Schwartz, S. H., & Bardi, A. (2001). Value hierarchies across cultures: Taking a similarities perspective. *Journal of Cross-Cultural Psychology, 32*(3), 268–290.
6. Curry, O. S., Rowland, L. A., Van Lissa, C. J., Zlotowitz, S., McAlaney, J., & Whitehouse, H. (2018). Happy to help? A systematic review and meta-analysis of the effects of performing acts of kindness on the well-being of the actor. *Journal of Experimental Social Psychology, 76*, 320–329.
7. Bialobrzeska, O., Baba, J., Bedynska, S., Cichocka, A., Cislak, A., Formanowicz, M., Goclowska, M. A., Jakubik, Z., & Kozakiewicz, K. (2023). Keep nice and carry on: Effect of niceness on well-being. *Basic and Applied Social Psychology, 45*(5), 138–156.
8. Aknin, L. B., Barrington-Leigh, C. P., Dunn, E. W., Helliwell, J. F., Burns, J., Biswas-Diener, R., Kemeza, I., Nyende, P., Ashton-James, C., & Norton, M. I. (2013). Prosocial spending and well-being: Cross-cultural evidence for a psychological universal. *Journal of Personality and Social Psychology, 104*(4), 635–652.

9. Aknin, L. B., Hamlin, J. K., & Dunn, E. W. (2012). Giving leads to happiness in young children. *PLoS One*, 7(6), e39211.
10. O'Brien, E., & Kassirer, S. (2019). People are slow to adapt to the warm glow of giving. *Psychological Science*, 30(2), 193–204.
11. Dungan, J. A., Munguia Gomez, D. M., & Epley, N. (2022). Too reluctant to reach out: Receiving social support is more positive than expressers expect. *Psychological Science*, 33(8), 1300–1312.
12. Zhao, X., & Epley, N. (2021). Insufficiently complimentary?: Underestimating the positive impact of compliments creates a barrier to expressing them. *Journal of Personality and Social Psychology*, 121(2), 239–256.
13. Epley, N., Kardas, M., Zhao, X., Atir, S., & Schroeder, J. (2022). Undersociality: Miscalibrated social cognition can inhibit social connection. *Trends in Cognitive Sciences*, 26(5), 406–418.
14. Kumar, A., & Epley, N. (2023). A little good goes an unexpectedly long way: Underestimating the positive impact of kindness on recipients. *Journal of Experimental Psychology: General*, 152(1), 236–252.
15. Echelbarger, M., & Epley, N. (2023). Undervaluing the positive impact of kindness starts early. *Journal of Experimental Psychology: General*, 152(10), 2989–2994.
16. Dungan, J. A., Munguia Gomez, D. M., & Epley, N. (2022). Too reluctant to reach out: Receiving social support is more positive than expressers expect. *Psychological Science*, 33(8), 1300–1312.
17. Moreton, J., Kelly, C. S., & Sandstrom, G. M. (2023). Social support from weak ties: Insight from the literature on minimal social interactions. *Social and Personality Psychology Compass*, 17(3), e12729.
18. Aoun, S. M., Breen, L. J., White, I., Rumbold, B., & Kellehear, A. (2018). What sources of bereavement support are perceived helpful by bereaved people and why? Empirical evidence for the compassionate communities approach. *Palliative Medicine*, 32(8), 1378–1388.
19. Dakof, G. A., & Taylor, S. E. (1990). Victims' perceptions of social support: What is helpful from whom? *Journal of Personality and Social Psychology*, 58(1), 80–89.
20. Dunn, J. (2023, Apr 7). When someone you love is upset, ask this one question. *The New York Times*. https://www.nytimes.com/2023/04/07/well/emotions-support-relationships.html
21. Weinstein, N., Itzchakov, G., & Legate, N. (2022). The motivational value of listening during intimate and difficult conversations. *Social and Personality Psychology Compass*, 16(2), e12651.
22. Collins, H. K. (2022). When listening is spoken. *Current Opinion in Psychology*, 47, 101402.
23. Huang, K., Yeomans, M., Brooks, A. W., Minson, J., & Gino, F. (2017). It doesn't hurt

to ask: Question-asking increases liking. *Journal of Personality and Social Psychology, 113*(3), 430–452.

24. Kluger, A. N., & Itzchakov, G. (2022). The power of listening at work. *Annual Review of Organizational Psychology and Organizational Behavior, 9*(1), 121–146.
25. Abi-Esber, N., Abel, J. E., Schroeder, J., & Gino, F. (2022). "Just letting you know..." Underestimating others' desire for constructive feedback. *Journal of Personality and Social Psychology, 123*(6), 1362–1385.
26. Zhao, X., & Epley, N. (2021). Insufficiently complimentary?: Underestimating the positive impact of compliments creates a barrier to expressing them. *Journal of Personality and Social Psychology, 121*(2), 239–256.
27. Boothby, E. J., & Bohns, V. K. (2021). Why a simple act of kindness is not as simple as it seems: Underestimating the positive impact of our compliments on others. *Personality and Social Psychology Bulletin, 47*(5), 826–840.
28. Wiwad, D., & Aknin, L. B. (2017). Motives matter: The emotional consequences of recalled self- and other-focused prosocial acts. *Motivation and Emotion, 41*, 730–740.
29. Cutler, J., & Campbell-Meiklejohn, D. (2019). A comparative fMRI meta-analysis of altruistic and strategic decisions to give. *NeuroImage, 184*, 227–241.
30. Brady, M., West, T. N., & Sandstrom, G. M. (n.d.). The distinctive moral beauty of kindness to strangers. [Manuscript in preparation]. School of Psychology, University of Sussex.
31. Sandstrom, G. M., Schmader, T., Croft, A., & Kwok, N. (2019). A social identity threat perspective on being the target of generosity from a higher status other. *Journal of Experimental Social Psychology, 82*, 98–114.
32. Harari, D., Parke, M. R., & Marr, J. C. (2022). When helping hurts helpers: Anticipatory versus reactive helping, helper's relative status, and recipient self-threat. *Academy of Management Journal, 65*(6), 1954–1983.
33. Fisher, J. D., Nadler, A., & Whitcher-Alagna, S. (1982). Recipient reactions to aid. *Psychological Bulletin, 91*(1), 27–54.
34. Archer Lee, Y., Guo, Y., Li, G., & Chen, F. S. (2024). Prosocial behavior as an antidote to social disconnection: The effects of an acts of kindness intervention on daily social contact and loneliness. *Journal of Happiness Studies, 25*(4), 39.
35. Aknin, L. B., Dunn, E. W., & Norton, M. I. (2012). Happiness runs in a circular motion: Evidence for a positive feedback loop between prosocial spending and happiness. *Journal of Happiness Studies, 13*, 347–355.
36. Haidt, J. (2003). Elevation and the positive psychology of morality. In C. L. M. Keyes & J. Haidt (Eds.), *Flourishing: Positive psychology and the life well-lived* (pp. 275–289). Washington, DC: American Psychological Association.
37. Silvers, J. A., & Haidt, J. (2008). Moral elevation can induce nursing. *Emotion, 8*(2), 291–295.

38. Schnall, S., Roper, J., & Fessler, D. M. (2010). Elevation leads to altruistic behavior. *Psychological Science*, 21(3), 315–320.

## Conclusion

1. Gurley, G. (2023, Jan 26). Future Cringe. *The New York Times*. https://www.nytimes.com/interactive/2023/01/26/style/culture-regret-crocs-social-media-cringe.html
2. Quercia, D. (2014, Nov). Happy maps [Video]. TED Conferences. https://www.ted.com/talks/daniele_quercia_happy_maps?subtitle=en
3. Maese, E. (2023, Oct 24). Almost a quarter of the world feels lonely. *Gallup News*. https://news.gallup.com/opinion/gallup/512618/almost-quarter-world-feels-lonely.aspx
4. Cacioppo, J. T., & Hawkley, L. C. (2009). Perceived social isolation and cognition. *Trends in Cognitive Sciences*, 13(10), 447–454.
5. Hammond, C. (n.d.). Nine ways to feel less lonely. BBC Radio 4. All in the Mind. https://www.bbc.co.uk/programmes/articles/3nDZXgD7Fz7lBGc3YSQV9jr/nine-ways-to-feel-less-lonely
6. Aknin, L. B., & Sandstrom, G. M. (2024). People are surprisingly hesitant to reach out to old friends. *Communications Psychology*, 2(1), 34.
7. Sandstrom, G. M., & Kelly, C. S. (2020). [Between- and within-person fears about talking to strangers] [Unpublished raw data]. Department of Psychology, University of Essex.

## Appendix: How to Talk to Strangers

1. McNicholas, J., & Collis, G. M. (2000). Dogs as catalysts for social interactions: Robustness of the effect. *British Journal of Psychology*, 91(1), 61–70.
2. Sandstrom, G. M., Ebert, J. E. J., Boothby, E. J., Cooney, G., & Moreton, J. (2022). [Cross-generational conversations: Predictions and experiences] [Unpublished raw data]. School of Psychology, University of Sussex.
3. Hill, C. A. (1987). Affiliation motivation: People who need people . . . but in different ways. *Journal of Personality and Social Psychology*, 52(5), 1008.
4. Locking, A. (n.d.). Andrew's Walks. https://www.andrewswalks.co.uk/
5. Wiener, H. J., Bettman, J. R., & Luce, M. F. (2024). Product facilitated conversations: When does starting a conversation by mentioning a product lead to better conversational outcomes? *Journal of Consumer Psychology*, 34(2), 334–342.
6. Jenkins, R. (2018, Aug 17). British people will spend over four months of their lives talking about the weather, study says. *Independent*. https://www.independent.co.uk/extras/lifestyle/british-people-time-spent-talking-weather-conversation-topic-heatwave-a8496166.html

7. Kushlev, K., Hunter, J. F., Proulx, J., Pressman, S. D., & Dunn, E. (2019). Smartphones reduce smiles between strangers. *Computers in Human Behavior, 91*, 12–16.
8. Kardas, M., Schroeder, J., & O'Brien, E. (2022). Keep talking: (Mis)understanding the hedonic trajectory of conversation. *Journal of Personality and Social Psychology, 123*(4), 717–740.
9. Collins, H. K. (2022). When listening is spoken. *Current Opinion in Psychology, 47*, 101402.
10. Huang, K., Yeomans, M., Brooks, A. W., Minson, J., & Gino, F. (2017). It doesn't hurt to ask: Question-asking increases liking. *Journal of Personality and Social Psychology, 113*(3), 430–452.
11. Yeomans, M. (2025, Jun 25). How to chat with almost anyone. *Psyche*. https://psyche.co/guides/how-to-get-better-at-striking-up-more-rewarding-conversations
12. Kashdan, T. B., McKnight, P. E., Fincham, F. D., & Rose, P. (2011). When curiosity breeds intimacy: Taking advantage of intimacy opportunities and transforming boring conversations. *Journal of Personality, 79*(6), 1369–1402.
13. Templeton, E., Chang, L., & Wheatley, T. (2024). Conversational launch pads: Strangers start their conversations with topics that lead to many other topics. In *Proceedings of the Annual Meeting of the Cognitive Science Society* (Vol. 46).
14. Yuko, E. (2024, Jan 17). Use the 'FORD' method to master small talk. *LifeHacker*. https://lifehacker.com/health/master-small-talk-ford-method
15. Yuko, E. (2024, Jan 27). Use the 'HEFE' method to strike up a conversation. *LifeHacker*. https://lifehacker.com/health/use-the-hefe-method-to-get-better-at-small-talk
16. Kardas, M., Kumar, A., & Epley, N. (2022). Overly shallow?: Miscalibrated expectations create a barrier to deeper conversation. *Journal of Personality and Social Psychology, 122*(3), 367–398.
17. Hart, E., VanEpps, E. M., & Schweitzer, M. E. (2021). The (better than expected) consequences of asking sensitive questions. *Organizational Behavior and Human Decision Processes, 162*, 136–154.
18. American Psychological Association (2017). What is exposure therapy? Clinical practice guideline for the treatment of posttraumatic stress disorder (PTSD) in adults. https://www.apa.org/ptsd-guideline/patients-and-families/exposure-therapy
19. As someone who doesn't love snakes (but has touched a python), I was fascinated to watch this video showing babies (who haven't yet learned to fear snakes) touching, pinching, and even biting massive pythons—or completely ignoring them—as they played with their toys: ABC Science (2024, Nov 2). The surprising reason babies are not afraid of snakes: Secret science [Video]. YouTube. https://www.youtube.com/watch?v=3L4lxusff1c&pp=0gcJCDgAo7VqN5tD
20. Sandstrom, G. M., Boothby, E. J., & Cooney, G. (2022). Talking to strangers: A week-long intervention reduces psychological barriers to social connection. *Journal of Experimental Social Psychology, 102*, 104356.

21. Wood, A., & Niedenthal, P. (2018). Developing a social functional account of laughter. *Social and Personality Psychology Compass*, 12(4), e12383.
22. MATT CALLANAN [@CoachCallanan]. (2022, February 4). I did an experiment. This morning I smiled & said 'Good morning' to 60 people on my #run round. [Image attached] [Post]. X. https://x.com/CoachCallanan/status/1489585483940306952
23. Yeomans, M. (2025, Jun 25). How to chat with almost anyone. *Psyche*. https://psyche.co/guides/how-to-get-better-at-striking-up-more-rewarding-conversations
24. Sandstrom, G. (n.d.). Gillian M. Sandstrom. https://gilliansandstrom.com/wp-content/uploads/2021/04/scavenger-hunt-missions.pdf
25. Lally, P., Van Jaarsveld, C. H., Potts, H. W., & Wardle, J. (2010). How are habits formed: Modelling habit formation in the real world. *European Journal of Social Psychology*, 40(6), 998–1009.

# Resources

If you're interested in learning more, I've compiled a list of books and other resources about talking to strangers, conversation more generally, and the importance of social connection. This list will keep changing as new books get published and new resources come to my attention. Please visit my website (gilliansandstrom.com) for an up-to-date list.

### Talking to strangers: Books

Buckingham, Will (2021). *Hello, Stranger: How We Find Connection in a Disconnected World.*
Esteves, Tony (2021). *Talk2MorePeople: Change Your Life by Meeting People.*
Keohane, Joe (2021). *The Power of Strangers: The Benefits of Connecting in a Suspicious World.*
Stark, Kio (2016). *When Strangers Meet: How People You Don't Know Can Transform You.*

### Talking to strangers: TED Talks

Byk, Camilla (2018). "You Already Know How to Change the World—What's Stopping You?" https://www.ted.com/talks/camilla_byk_you_already_know_how_to_change_the_world_what_s_stopping_you.

Cheng, Cynthia (2022). "The Surprising Power of Talking to Strangers." https://www.youtube.com/watch?v=qSbBUru3Dfo

Esteves, Tony (2025). "How meeting strangers saved my life." https://www.youtube.com/watch?v=HZjvk7xaM7s

Headlee, Celeste (2015). "Ten Ways to Have a Better Conversation." https://www.ted.com/talks/celeste_headlee_10_ways_to_have_a_better_conversation

Kaye, Mollie (2024). "Is the Cure for Loneliness Hiding in Your Closet?" https://www.youtube.com/watch?v=mcYPiQGyZbM

Nightingall, Georgie (2018). "Talking to Strangers: How to Have a Meaningful Conversation." https://www.ted.com/talks/georgie_nightingall_talking_to_strangers_how_to_have_a_meaningful_conversation

Smith, Matt (2022). "Waffling Can Teach Us to Be Better Listeners." https://www.youtube.com/watch?v=UwNyT5aGZko

Stark, Kio (2016). "Why You Should Talk to Strangers." https://www.ted.com/talks/kio_stark_why_you_should_talk_to_strangers

## Talking to strangers: Podcasts

*Strangers on a Bench*, Tom Rosenthal

*Strangers on a Train*, Alexei Sayle, BBC

## Conversation/sociality

Arthanayake, Nihal (2022). *Let's Talk: How to Have Better Conversations.*

Brooks, Alison Wood (2025). *Talk: The Science of Conversation and the Art of Being Ourselves.*

Epley, Nick (forthcoming in 2026). [*A Little More Social: How Small Habits Can Make Us Happier, Healthier, and Better Connected*].

Fine, Debra (2006). *The Fine Art of Small Talk: How to Start a Conversation in Any Situation.*

Fleming, Carol (2018). *The Serious Business of Small Talk: Becoming Fluent, Comfortable, and Charming.*

Headlee, Celeste (2017). *We Need to Talk: How to Have Conversations That Matter.*

Turkle, Sherry (2016). *Reclaiming Conversation: The Power of Talk in a Digital Age.*

## Introversion/shyness/solitude

Cain, Susan (2012). *Quiet: The Power of Introverts in a World That Can't Stop Talking.*

Pan, Jessica (2019). *Sorry I'm Late, I Didn't Want to Come: An Introvert's Year of Living Dangerously.*

Weinstein, Netta, Hansen, Heather, & Nguyen, Thuy-vy (2024). *Solitude: The Science and Power of Being Alone.*

## Friendship

Denworth, Lydia (2020). *Friendship: The Evolution, Biology, and Extraordinary Power of Life's Fundamental Bond.*
Dunbar, Robin (2021). *Friends: Understanding the Power of Our Most Important Relationships.*
Franco, Marisa (2022). *Platonic: How the Science of Attachment Can Help You Make—and Keep—Friends.*
Poswolsky, Adam Smiley (2021). *Friendship in the Age of Loneliness: An Optimist's Guide to Connection.*

## The importance of social connection

Blau, Melinda, & Fingerman, Karen (2009). *Consequential Strangers: Turning Everyday Encounters Into Life-Changing Moments.*
Hertz, Noreena (2020). *The Lonely Century: A Call to Reconnect.*
Kerr, Natalie, & Kurtz, Jaime (2025). *Our New Social Life: Science-Backed Strategies for Creating Meaningful Connection.*
Killam, Kasley (2024). *The Art and Science of Connection: Why Social Health Is the Missing Key to Living Longer, Healthier, and Happier.*
King, Marissa (2021). *Social Chemistry: Decoding the Patterns of Human Connection.*
Merolla, Andy J., & Hall, Jeffrey A. (2025). *The Social Biome: How Everyday Communication Connects and Shapes Us.*
Murthy, Vivek (2020). *Together: The Healing Power of Human Connection in a Sometimes Lonely World.*
Pinker, Susan (2014). *The Village Effect: How Face-to-Face Contact Can Make Us Healthier, Happier, and Smarter.*
Pugh, Allison (2024). *The Last Human Job: The Work of Connecting in a Disconnected World.*
Putnam, Robert (2000). *Bowling Alone: The Collapse and Revival of the American Community.*
Robson, David (2024). *The Laws of Connection: 13 Social Strategies That Will Transform Your Life.*
Sanders, Michael, & Hume, Susannah (2019). *Social Butterflies: Reclaiming the Positive Power of Social Networks.*
Small, Mario (2017). *Someone To Talk To: How Networks Matter in Practice.*
Turkle, Sherry (2011). *Alone Together: Why We Expect More from Technology and Less from Each Other.*

Yates, Jon (2021). *Fractured: Why Our Societies Are Coming Apart and How We Put Them Back Together Again.*

## Kindness and the little things

Hammond, Claudia (2022). *The Keys to Kindness: How to Be Kinder to Yourself, Others and the World.*
Keeling, Miranda (2022). *The Year I Stopped to Notice.*
Keeling, Miranda (2025). *The Place I'm In: What I See When I Stop to Notice.*
Zaki, Jamil (2019). *The War for Kindness: Building Empathy in a Fractured World.*

## About the Author

**Gillian Sandstrom** is an associate professor of psychology at the University of Sussex, where she conducts research on minimal social interactions between strangers and teaches a class called Social Connection and Disconnection. Her research interests also include kindness and well-being, and she is the director of the Sussex Centre for Research on Kindness. Gillian holds a PhD in psychology from the University of British Columbia, an MA in psychology from Ryerson (now Toronto Metropolitan) University, and a BMath in computer science from the University of Waterloo. Her writing has appeared in *Harvard Business Review* and *Scientific American*, and her research has been featured in major media outlets in the US (e.g., *The New York Times*, *The Washington Post*, and *The Wall Street Journal*), the UK (e.g., *The Guardian* and BBC News), and around the world.